Europe's Other: European Law Between Modernity and Postmodernity

Europe's Other: European Law Between Modernity and Postmodernity

Edited by
PETER FITZPATRICK
Professor of Law
Queen Mary and Westfield College
University of London

and

JAMES HENRY BERGERON
Lecturer in Law
University College Dublin

Routledge
Taylor & Francis Group
LONDON AND NEW YORK

First published 1998 by Ashgate Publishing

Reissued 2018 by Routledge
2 Park Square, Milton Park, Abingdon, Oxon, OX14 4RN
711 Third Avenue, New York, NY 10017, USA

Routledge is an imprint of the Taylor & Francis Group, an informa business

A Library of Congress record exists under LC control number: 97039113

Typeset by Manton Typesetters, 5-7 Eastfield Road, Louth, Lincolnshire, LN11 7AJ, UK.

ISBN 13: 978-0-367-00145-2 (hbk)
ISBN 13: 978-0-429-44426-5 (ebk)

Contents

List of Contributors

James Henry Bergeron is a lecturer in the Law Faculty at University College Dublin. He researches in the area of European Community Law and Social Theory, and is currently working on the ontologies of identity in EC Law, the relationship of public and private legal space, and the philosophical foundations of antitrust law. His articles have appeared in *Social and Legal Studies* and the *Dublin University Law Journal*.

Sionaidh Douglas-Scott is a lecturer at King's College, University of London. Her special interests are legal philosophy and EU public law and she has published in both of these areas. She has been a visiting lecturer at American and European universities, including visiting Jean Monnet Professor at the University of Bonn and visiting Professor at the Salzburg forum for international studies.

Peter Fitzpatrick is Professor of Law at Queen Mary and Westfield College, University of London, and has taught at universities in Europe, North America and Papua New Guinea. He has published numerous works on law and social theory, law and racism, and imperialism, including *The Mythology of Modern Law*.

Carole Lyons is Jean Monnet Lecturer in European Integration in the Faculty of Law at the University of Leicester, England. She specializes in the study of constitutional law and rights-related issues in the European Union, in particular questions of citizenship and immigration.

Valsamis Mitsilegas is a Research Fellow in the Faculty of Law, University of Edinburgh. He read law at the Aristotle University in Greece and at the Robert Schuman University in France, before pursuing his postgraduate studies at the University of Kent in England. His research interests focus on issues of culture and identity in the European Union and on the regulation of its financial system.

Krisztina Morvai teaches and researches at the Law School of the ELTE University in Budapest.

Kathleen M. Moore is assistant Professor in the Department of Political Science at the University of Connecticut. Her research interests include religion, law, migration and the construction of identities. She is author of *Al-Mughtaribun: American Law and the Transformation of Muslim Life in the United States* (1995), and is currently writing a book on the emergence of a unique 'minoritarian' legal culture among Muslims living in 'diaspora'.

Inger-Johanne Sand is Lecturer in Law at the Institute of Public and International Law and senior researcher at ARENA (Centre for Advanced Research on the Europeanization of the Nation-state), University of Oslo, Norway. She works in the fields of constitutional and administrative law as well as legal theory, state theory and the sociology of law. She has recently published *Styring av kompleksitet* (Governing Complexity), Bergen, Norway, 1996, on the reorganization of the welfare state and on the consequences for the welfare state and risk societies of recent developments in public law.

Harm Schepel holds degrees from the University of Amsterdam and the International Institute for the Sociology of Law in Oñati, Spain. He is currently a researcher at the European University Institute in Florence, completing his PhD thesis on European Union regulatory law.

Thomas Spijkerboer worked at the Rechtswinkel (Law Shop) Amsterdam from 1982 to 1986. From 1986 to 1992 he worked as a lawyer at the Advokatenkollektief (Lawyers' Collective) Zaanstreek. Since 1993 he has been Lecturer in Migration Law at the Centre for Migration Law of the University of Nijmegen in the Netherlands.

Sarah van Walsum graduated in Law from the University of Amsterdam in 1987. Since then she has worked at the Dutch Centre for Foreigners (Nederlands Centrum Buitenlanders) and the Clara Wichmann Instituut, an academic institute for women and the law. Presently she is working at the Erasmus University of Rotterdam on a legal-anthropological thesis about the impact of Dutch family reunification policies on a specific group of migrants, the Javanese from Surinam.

Acknowledgements

Anne Griffiths and her colleagues provided the convivial occasion and initial impetus behind this volume with the 1996 gathering of the Critical Legal Conference which they organized at the University of Edinburgh. The papers collected here have since undergone considerable revision, often at the behest of bullying editors and we are grateful to the authors for their generous and sustained commitment. Working with Ashgate Publishing was a consistent pleasure and always encouraging and we are particularly grateful to Sonia Hubbard and John Irwin in this. An special thanks to Sarah Kyambi for an excellent index – one prepared with alacrity and care.

Peter Fitzpatrick
James Henry Bergeron

Introduction

Not since the decline of Western Christendom has there existed a body of law which claimed for itself an autonomy from the trammels of nation, a purchase on eternal salvation (for which today read economic progress) and legal supremacy over such a vast and vague entity as that called 'Europe'. The making of such claims for the legal order of the European Union at a time when so many ruling assumptions about law and progress were under challenge might well be expected to have provoked a wide-ranging critique of EU law. Yet until the recent emergence of a few critical voices such as those of Shaw (1995) and Ward (1996), this has not happened. The 'glossators' of EU law view their subject through a narrow legal and technocratic lens, focusing in a 'black letter' mode on issues of rights, remedies and judicial interpretation. With these perceptions, EU law is usually taken to embody an unstoppable dynamic of integration and progress. Such approaches are rooted firmly in modernist assumptions which avoid the impact of current critical, poststructural and postmodern thought.

A somewhat standard account of the EU and its law has by now seemingly settled. With this account, the process of European integration involves a gradual transfer of sovereign power from nation-states to the EU. Theoretical perspectives on the dynamic of this process seldom range beyond functionalist support for a depoliticized economic rationality or a neofunctionalist emphasis on competition and cooperation between rival national elites. In both these contributions to theory, the nation is seen as an entity different from, and in fundamental conflict with, the developing Union. And that opposition typifies not only the claims of those who argue that the Union represents a singular and unstoppable dynamic of state development, but also the claims of those who view it as a frustrated and fractured form of state formation, a Europe of 'bits and pieces'. The goals of European integration themselves are rarely doubted. These are usually rendered as a simple recitation of the aims of the Treaties or as a generalized public good, 'an ever-closer union', and always there is 'a certain idea of Europe' involved. This encompassing 'idea of Europe' inhabits EU law and its claims to a supreme, unified and transcendent legal order under the Treaties. It motivates judicial activism by the Court of Justice. It provides the legal subject of EU law with an expansive unity and a universalist orientation. These, then, are the themes which predominate in the literature on EU law: the theme of an inevitable European dynamic contested by nation, the theme of integration based on unified legal order, and the theme of the integral European subject of that order. And these are themes which preoccupy much of this collection.

It may at first seem strange that a new area of law, and one of such great influence, should be so comparatively conservative in its academic orientation. But the failure to consider the area from critical, poststructural and postmodern perspectives can perhaps be explained by the self-justifications indulged in by its academic proponents. These tend to take the encompassing view that the acceptant study of something so intrinsically dynamic, progressive and just plain good is its own complete justification. It may also be that the sheer size and complexity of the corpus of EC law puts serious roadblocks in the path of analysis and critique. But we sense that there is more to it, and the engagement with conservative complacency is a large impetus for this book.

An immodest aim of this collection, then, is the orientating of EU law in directions where it has not much ventured. It hopes to make a distinctive contribution by engaging with EU law from a theoretical range which is innovatively broad but which nonetheless finds common ground in the critique of modernity. It is surely time that EU law was subjected to that sceptical and critical gaze long since turned on law in general. Although accommodating the critical approaches recently advanced by Shaw, Ward and others, our primary focus is with identity and alterity in relation to the constituting of 'Europe' and its law. Our cohering concern is with the 'Other' that 'Europe' rejects or disowns, yet against which it also assumes its identity. The form of this alterity which mostly concerns us is the 'nation' which the EU claims to transcend but which provides not only the particularity against which a generalized European identity is created, but also the fragmented contrary against which a unified EU law is constituted. We especially criticize the consensus sustaining EU law as an integral endeavour in practical and academic terms – either as an achieved whole or as one that deserves to be and is in the process of becoming so. The Other of Europe also extends to that diversity of peoples marginalized by the dominating confines of the law. This suppression of 'other voices', of heterogeneity and diversity, and indeed of other intellectual traditions, within a hegemonic Euro-thrall is something the collection is particularly set against.

Our cohering concern with the Other of Europe and of Europe's law must, however, extend beyond the formal borders of EU law and recognize further designs of European law and of what it is for law to be 'European'.

European-ness is a quality that dubiously sustains not only EU law but also the European Convention on Human Rights and the particular claims of nations to this quality in their relation to the non-European. The idea of being European, and its ontological presupposition of European Being, have rarely been examined in relation to law. The collection then, while focusing considerably on EU law and its grand elevation, accommodates important and related instances of specifically 'European' claims to law.

The volume is divided into three parts. The first four chapters, two by Bergeron, and the others by Fitzpatrick and by Schepel, examine the claims of EU law to transcend nation and its connected claims to a coherent and autonomous European identity. At the heart of these claims is the question of the EU's 'postmodernism' and all three contributors address this. The second part of the collection contains contributions by Mitsilegas, Douglas-Scott, Sand and Lyons, and it shifts the focus to the negative construction of European identity in EU law through acts of institutional policy aimed at excluding the defining Other. The last part, with contributions by van Walsum, Spijkerboer, Moore and Morvai, moves beyond the borders of EU law to explore the similarly self-constituting claims made for national laws and for human rights in terms of their European-ness.

Jim Bergeron begins the engagement with EU law by exploring the ontological suppositions underlying the case-law of the European Court of Justice. For Bergeron, the modernity of EU law hides a complex mythical vision of the European individual of Enlightenment teleology. This is the same 'individual' who inhabited modernity during the heyday of the nation-state and who makes similar claims to transcendence and a universal orientation once achieved through a negation of the primitive Other.

By creating directly effective and supreme rights for its legal subjects, the Court of Justice colonizes this myth of modernity for EC law. The claim of the nation-state to a singular relationship with the individual is linked in EC law to quasi-national assertions of progress and universality. The Court's stigmatizing of national sentiments as retrograde, its adoption of a teleological mode of judicial interpretation, and its rejection of national rules protecting symbols of national culture are all viewed by Bergeron as part of EU law's encompassing claim to progress beyond and transcend nation, which now becomes the Other that Europe is not, but from which Europe assumes its identity. So, the myth of modernity in the form of an heroic European jurisprudence now exists in an even more abstract and 'whitened' state.

Peter Fitzpatrick's concern is also with how the myth of European identity sustains the EU as an exemplary community and sustains nationalism as the pivot of the European legal order. For Fitzpatrick, the nation exists in between the universal and the particular and this contradictory condition is mediated in a myth of progress operatively involving the exclusion of others from the project of nation. This still leaves a permanent irresolution within national identity. And it is law which comes to 'deal with' the irresolution.

The configuration of law, myth and nation serves to construct Europe and its law. Drawing on the story of Europa, a frequent starting-point for accounts of European history and identity, Fitzpatrick instances the irresolution of that identity in its integral reliance on an Asia as that which Europe definitively is not but once was. Europe joins the nation-state in its contradictory claims to the universal and to a particularism of blood and soil – a contradiction 'resolved' in the negative formation of identity against certain excluded others. This exclusion is manifested in the establishment of the EU's external boundaries and in the confining of European citizenship to nationals of member states only, thus focusing the rights of EU nationals into a distinct and privileged identity over and against non-nationals.

These similarities between the EU and nation do create a tension, Fitzpatrick concludes, since both are occupying the same terrain, whether in legal terms or in terms of the identification and commitment of their citizens. The tension is more one between competing nationalisms than between nation and supra-nation. The division between these nationalisms is muted through law, however. The European-ness of law, subsisting at EU and national levels, provides a singular place and a universal orientation which can accommodate the duplexity and plural location of nationalism in the EU. Fitzpatrick sees all this as a modernist project. He rejects claims which would see in the EU a postmodern institution. While he agrees with Schepel that legal pluralism infuses the EU legal order, this does not for him alter the modernist orientation of EU law within which pluralism is a spur to unification. Further, the EU does not engage with its eternally challenging Others through a postmodern ethic of regard for difference and specificity but, rather, constitutes and comprehensively subordinates the Other in terms of its own project.

Like Bergeron and Fitzpatrick, Harm Schepel in his contribution is concerned with legalist assertions of unity and supremacy sustained by the integrationist vision of a 'linear progress towards essentially uncontested objectives'. But whereas the previous contributions tend to focus on temporal aspects of the mythology of EU law, Schepel employs a spatial analysis exploring the interaction of EU law with other normative orders. Drawing on recent work on legal pluralism, Schepel argues against the view of state law as the only actor in the normative ordering of society, and puts special emphasis on the mutual dependence, yet antagonism, between law and administration. He sees law depending on the disciplinary mechanism of administration and prepared to deliver on its claims to equality and autonomy only within administration's normalizing bounds.

The operation of law in the EU demonstrates its plural nature, and gives the lie to the totalizing claims made by the Court of Justice. The Court has had to engage the courts of the Member States in order to enforce EU law's claims to 'supremacy'. A similar ambivalence exists in the interaction of the Commission with non-EU agencies, such as bodies which establish harmonized technical standards – agencies which create EU legal norms on the basis of their own institutional dynamics. Should subsidiarity become an effective principle in European governance, the pluralist trend towards conjoint processes of 'law' creation seems set to continue. This 'postmodernism' subsists in the co-existence of multiple legal sites for social interaction and struggle at the local, national and international levels. For Schepel, this amounts to a postmodernism which, if not welcome, at least presents a more accurate explanation of European governance than the totalizing myth of EU law. In this sense, EU law engages in a postmodern legal universe, despite, and to some extent because of, its own modernist claims.

Schepel's postmodern view of the legal environment of the EU is challenged in Bergeron's second contribution. This views the operation of the EU internal market as a defence of modernity in an increasingly postmodernist global political economy. For Bergeron, it is not so much the legal environment as contemporary culture and economy which constitute the 'postmodern condition' within which the EU functions, and which the EU tries to subsume in an attempt to create a new modernity. This condition is founded in the essentially symbolic nature of the economy. Permeating this symbolic economy is the sign of nation. Bergeron turns the usual argument for the internal market on its head. Instead of creating an economic sphere free of the trammels of nationality, the legal structure and subject matter of the internal market deeply inscribes a reference to nation as the Other which that market rejects yet relies on for its motive force. But this is an ever more abstract and rarefied 'nation', one made friendly to the demands of market mobility through the breaking of any necessary link with the original national territory.

The role of law in this postmodern condition, Bergeron argues, is to stabilize the symbol which is not the prime market commodity, a stabilization ever more under threat from the forces of globalization and cultural hybridity. The operation of the internal market and of its law seeks to reconstitute this postmodern condition as the result of rational planning and political will, rather than the result of globalization run wild. Once again, 'Europe' finds a way to depict external force as the result of internal will, and cultural change as constitutional design. It is only the Other, the inhabitants of non-Europe, for whom globalization acts as an overwhelming force of nature.

The second section of the collection involves the formation of European identity as a goal of institutional policy. Where the preceding contributions attempted to draw out an identity which was implicit in the law and structure of the EU, Sand, Mitsilegas, Douglas-Scott and Lyons describe and analyse the explicit attempt to create Europe, the European and the Other through acts of policy. For Johanne-Inger Sand, the very possibility of a coherent EU 'policy' presents problems. Sand argues for a vision of the EU, not as a unified entity based on singular discourses of integration, but as a complex interaction of different discourses. Because they serve different functions, legal, political, economic, and administrative, discourses communicate only indirectly with each other. The message of each is read within the discursive frameworks of the others. As a result, competing rationalities and unintended results of policy are inscribed into the very structure of the EU. Although the same treaties, texts and processes are referred to in these discourses, the way in which these texts are severally used creates systematic gaps and incoherence. In particular, the codes of language in which EU 'political' decisions are taken are, of necessity, transformed into legislative texts which become subject to the differing rationalities of law and administration. By enclosing the language of political compromise and pious aspiration in a discourse of effective, unified and supreme law, the EU legal order serves to mask the underlying incoherence of the policy process.

As with Schepel's analysis, Sand's is spatial, focusing as it does on competing discourses of governance within the EU. Although these competing systems exist in all political institutions, the problems for legitimacy and policy coherence are greater in the EU where standard national norms of integrative and democratic decision-making are less fully realized. There is a lack of fit between the primarily liberal goals of the Treaties and understandings of political legitimacy which emphasize common backgrounds, histories and language traditions. Without this cultural consensus, Sand argues, the EU policy process fails to cohere.

Valsamis Mitsilegas shifts the discussion from conjoint national cultures to the possibility of European culture, pondering the inclusion of 'culture' as an enumerated Community competence in the Maastricht Treaty, and considering the implications of a legal mobilization of culture for the project of creating a European identity. For Mitsilegas, culture is inextricably bound up with processes of differentiation and the creation of identity through the exclusion of others. In this sense, culture is a code which serves to identity the Other while highlighting the attributes which constitute an 'Us'.

The EU's explicit engagement with culture begins with the Court of Justice's acceptance of cultural justifications for national restraints on the free movement of goods, something very seldom allowed in fact. For Mitsilegas, all this entails the classic partition between culture and economy, with the cultural values of the nation-state – involving its cinema, bans on Sunday shopping, the national language and such – usually being subordinated to the economic rationality inherent in the legal concepts of non-discrimination and proportionality employed by EU law. But with Maastricht, culture takes on a new and positive role. The new articles which insert 'culture' into the Treaty attempt to recognize and support 'the flowering of the cultures of the Member States' while 'bringing their common cultural heritage to the fore'. This vision of unitary national cultures, allowing at most for regional diversity within nations, offers little or nothing to cultural, ethnic or racial minorities existing inside those borders. Equally difficult is the notion of a 'common cultural heritage'. Just conceivably this could import the cultural heterogeneity of modern Europe, but it resonates more with the stereotypical attributes of a White Christian Europe. 'Culture' so far lacks clarity or effectiveness as a legislative competence. Its role in the EU Treaty remains primarily symbolic. The key question for Mitsilegas is whether this 'culture' will be defined in terms of European Citizenship and its privileging of the European national over the non-European Other, or whether it could engage with the wide diversity of peoples and traditions.

The place of the non-European as Other also concerns Carole Lyons. The creation of a European identity, with its inherent exclusion of others from that identity, involves the EU adopting the symbols of an 'EU nationhood' in such modes as flags, anthems and cultural policy. But a less overt manner of creating this sense of European uniqueness involves the establishment of a sense of superiority or specialness. The inculcation of this privileged identity takes effective form in EU policies on immigration, asylum and policy cooperation. These policies, Lyons argues, contribute to inaccurate perceptions of resident, non-EU nationals as non-white, impoverished and therefore threatening in some manner to the 'stability' of Europe. Such a policy, in short, creates a simple and distinct image of those 'others' who serve as a basis for the formation of European identity. Lyons sees EU law as enhancing this policy of exclusion and identity formation. EU legislation and the jurisprudence of the European Court grant rights of free movement only to nationals of the EU Member States. Non-Europeans enjoy such rights only where derived from family ties to the 'European'. The expansion of these EU rights in terms of 'European citizenship' increases this sense of European-ness and renders 'others' as second-class European residents.

Sionaidh Douglas-Scott takes the analysis of European identity through a telling instance in the creation of a 'European' Common Foreign and Security Policy. As Douglas-Scott points out, adopting the myths and symbols of security and defence is an ultimate act of European definition and this establishes a world of 'others' who are seen as political and military threats. The competencies of the EU institutions in this area remain rudimentary, however, with the symbolic effect of the Common Foreign and Security Policy far outweighing its institutional and political force.

This Policy quite explicitly involves the assertion of identity. Douglas-Scott sees in this a shift from the EU imagined in terms of 'civilian power' to a more ambitious and aggressive stance, an extraversion of the nation of 'blood and soil' as against the cold impersonality of a trading community. But the policy is continually undermined by an institutional weakness and fragmentation resulting from the unwillingness of Member States to cede to 'Europe' the high-politics of security and defence.

The last section extends the analysis of identity beyond the borders of EU law proper to include alterity within the claims of European-ness made by national law and within the contradictory idea of 'European' human rights. Laws on immigration, asylum, blasphemy and the protection of human rights are powerful definers of just what the European nation is prepared to allow, in some ultimate sense, into itself. The contributions by van Walsum, Spijkerboer, Moore and Morvai explore the defining inscription of an exclusionary sexuality, race, religion and class into the lofty inclusiveness of systems of European Law.

Sarah van Walsum explores the implications of recent changes in Dutch immigration law dramatically extending the power of the state into the intimate spheres of marriage and birth. This was done in an apparent attempt to control illegal residence. The indeterminate nature of this illegality, the increasing focus on sexuality, and the broad network of control involved in extensive identity checks all create an immigration regime which parallels the regulation of sexuality in the nineteenth century.

Ostensibly, the definition and legal exclusion of the 'illegal alien' affects the non-European but, as van Walsum emphasizes, this definition and exclusion also generate a realignment within the whole Dutch population. This realignment has racist implications and is to an increasing extent gendered. It accords well with a growing demand for cheap, casual and unpaid labour, disproportionately composed of women, in the context of international competition to attract highly mobile capital. It also accompanies cut-backs in social spending which have increased the gap between rich and poor. The need to exert control over those most strongly affected by the resulting insecurity – women and members of ethnic minorities – has grown accordingly. With the help of new information technology and building on the constructed identity of the 'illegal alien', the Dutch state is transforming welfare institutions apparently designed to protect the 'worthy poor' against the powerful into an elaborate and pervasive network of control.

Thomas Spijkerboer questions the notion of unambiguous sexuality which enters into the 'European' self-conception of the nation and the resulting determination of what is, and is not, of the 'political'. Using a Dutch court decision on a gay asylum-seeker from Russia as an example, and Fassbinder's film *Querelle* as an illuminating parallel scene, Spijkerboer develops the thesis that to recognize certain gays and lesbians as members of a persecuted social group qualifying as refugees makes a presumption of clear and univocal sexuality. This presumption is at the core of heterosexuality as a normative system and enters into even the most 'progressive' of national laws on asylum. It finds expression in the judicial voice which construes the position of the asylum-seeker in terms of a rigid homosexual-heterosexual dichotomy, ignoring or presuming factors in the decision on asylum which might otherwise be more thoroughly considered.

Drawing on Fassbinder's radical critique of sexual orientations, Spijkerboer suggests that sexual orientation in refugee law should not be conceived of in terms of social group, but in terms of political opinion. In this way, refugee law can resist reproducing rigid sexual orientations and leave some space for people who, in Fassbinder's words, react a little differently to reality.

Employing a similar critique of dualist reductions, Kathleen Moore engages with the complex forces forming Muslim identities in Britain. For Moore, the restrictive duality of West and East, Europe versus Islam, and so on, hides both the reality of a highly differentiated and heterogeneous British Muslim population and the dynamism of the processes through which these communities define themselves. These processes can, intriguingly, include Islamic claims to abstract and universal authority in circumstances where Europe becomes Islam's Other.

Moore argues from the vantage-point of a constitutive understanding of law. In this perspective, law infuses and alters subject communities, just as these communities alter law. The employment of British blasphemy laws against *The Satanic Verses*, for example, demonstrates how Muslims in diaspora constitute themselves around the legal concepts and rights of the dominant community. These acts of legal self-identification and resistance alter ways of thinking within Muslim communities and structure social action and expectations.

Concluding the collection, Christina Morvai provides a compelling narrative of her experience at the centre of European human rights law, especially of how class serves to constitute what is operatively 'European' in this endeavour. She reveals how in practice rights secured in the European Convention on Human Rights take on their very European-ness through an exclusionary and elitist quality. The European Commission of Human Rights, despite its high calling, is a bureaucracy deeply involved with its own composition, internal hierarchy and efficiency. Reflecting this ethos, 'humanity' gives way to almost unbridled administrative discretion in the early and crucial stages of a human rights complaint. Little concern is shown for poor or disadvantaged people who make applications alleging human rights abuses in the language of real life, rather than the language of law. They become the Other of European human rights as a legal enterprise.

The spectre of the Other haunts Europe then, as it haunts modernity generally. Whether based on grounds of nation, race, gender, sexual orientation, religion or material disadvantage, 'Europe' differentiates and identifies itself and its law through the exclusion of others outside its formal boundaries and through rejection of the Other within. The implicit orientation of this collection is towards a more inclusive and diverse Europe, a Europe more responsive to difference and less concerned with 'reasserting its rightful role in the world'. And that orientation inevitably opposes the claims to encompassing unity, transcendence and progress which have for so long characterized the modernist discourse of European integration and European law.

REFERENCES

Shaw, J. (ed.) (1995), *New Legal Dynamics of European Integration*, London: Oxford University Press.

Ward, I. (1996), *A Critical Introduction to European Law*, London: Butterworths.

PART I
BETWEEN MODERNITY AND POSTMODERNITY

1 An Ever Whiter Myth: The Colonization of Modernity in European Community Law

James Henry Bergeron

Metaphysics – the white mythology which reassembles and reflects the culture of the West ... has erased within itself the fabulous scene that has produced it, the scene that nevertheless remains active and stirring, inscribed in white ink, an invisible design covered over in the palimpsest.
(Jacques Derrida, *Margins of Philosophy*)

The nearer your destination, the more you're slip-sliding away.
Paul Simon, 'Slip-Sliding Away'

INTRODUCTION

This first chapter examines the ontological structures underlying EC law and the legal scholarship by which it is transmitted. It is a commonplace of EC legal studies that the Court of Justice has traditionally employed a purposive approach to the interpretation of EC law when weighing the scales of justice in cases before it. That approach has been variously described and evaluated in terms of integration (Easson, 1988), teleological jurisprudence (Louis, 1979), and the legal expression of *une certaine idée de l'Europe* (Pescatore, 1983), yet the meaning of integration, the nature of its teleological legal subject, and the substance of that *certaine idée* seldom extends beyond the surface level of description or analysis.[1] Indeed, the scholarship of Community law is conspicuous for the relative absence of critical voices, a more common criticism of judicial activism being that the Court has not gone far enough.[2] It is proposed that this tradition of critical restraint and general support for the Court's role stems from values deeply embedded in the discourse structure of EC law; values which the Court and the European legal community see as essential elements of European identity. The triumph of the European legal order consists precisely in this – that EC law has captured and colonized the Enlightenment concept of progress in a way which makes the concept inseparable from the Community institutions, and most especially from the Court. The result is not so much a *l'Europe des juges* as the legal community acting as a kind of 'vanguard party', redefining the essential elements of modernity – individuality, universalism and primitive negation – in European terms. It is in the chorus of scholarly approval of this discourse that the unity of the European legal order rests.

At the heart of the discourse of EC law is myth. Not myth as a child's fable, but as a transforming signifier capable of re-ordering the 'radical imaginary' of the European polity. The successful 'constitutionalization' of the EC Treaties, and the consequential relative autonomy of the Community, owes much to the incorporation into European Community law of the mythical structures of modernity which imbue national political culture and, increasingly, the political culture of a globalized West.[3] The social contractarian justifications for the primacy of Community law; the implication of a primitive 'other' in the form of the old 'nation' state; the establishment of Community law and its sovereign legal subject as a transcendent entity; and their usurpation of the myth of progression collectively constitute a colonization of the mythical structure of national law and the representation of that structure as an external and autonomous, yet transcendent and supreme entity – a sovereign European law only tenuously connected to state, nation or community. This mythical reconciliation of contradictions results in a further 'whitening' of law and Western society.

MYTH AND THE STRUCTURE OF MODERNITY

Recent critical work on the nature of modern law has emphasized the mythical elements inherent in its structure (see Carty, 1990, 1991; Derrida, 1990, Goodrich, 1990). As Fitzpatrick points out,

> The mythic composition of law can be made out in its contradictory attributes. Law is autonomous yet socially contingent. It is identified with order yet it changes and is historically responsive. Law is a sovereign imperative yet the expression of a popular spirit (Fitzpatrick, 1992, p. x)

In an attempt to understand how modern law maintains its apparent unity in spite of those contradictions, Derrida, Fitzpatrick and others have focused attention on the ways in which Occidental being takes its identity in negation of certain primitive 'others'. In this act of negation, Occidental being rejects external sources of meaning and value, and endows itself with deific properties of transcendence, universal being and infinite progression. In doing so, a mythology of the Enlightened Individual is evoked which serves much the same social functions as myth in 'pre-modern' societies.

Myth serves essential social functions. Far from being a mere superstition or fable, myth defines reality. It endows a society with sacred origins, identity and purpose. As Eliade notes,

> Myth narrates a sacred history; it relates an event that took place in primordial time, the fabled time of the 'beginnings'. In other words, myth tells how, through the deeds of Supernatural Beings, a reality came into existence ... Myth, then, is always an account of a 'creation'; it relates how something was produced, began to be. (Eliade, 1963, pp. 5–6)

Myth also distinguishes between order and chaos, and between nature and culture; it establishes the power and symbolism of the 'centre'; myth avoids the 'terror of history' by allowing a 'return to origins'. Above all, myth mediates the contradictions of human existence. It transcends the divide between the particular and the universal, the profane mortal world and the sacred, eternal cosmos (see Adorno and Horkheimer, 1979; Eliade, 1965; Lévi-Strauss, 1963, 1986; Fitzpatrick, 1992). To accomplish this, archaic myth allows for human existence in separate and internally harmonious mythical realms. History is reversible: the profane can be purified, and environmental or social catastrophe remedied, in an 'eternal return' to the time of beginnings (Eliade, 1965).

The analysis of mythic structures undertaken below corresponds largely to that pioneered by Lévi-Strauss (see Lévi-Strauss, 1963, pp. 206–12). This model comprises the following elements: (1) that the meaning of myth resides not in any one element, but in the combination of those elements; (2) that myth exhibits specific and more complex properties than mere 'language', i.e. beyond ordinary phonemes, morphemes and sememes; (3) that these elements, or mythemes, are primarily concerned with a relation between functions (or symbols) and subjects; and (4) that the true mytheme constitutes a bundle of relations which are simultaneously diachronic and synchronic, *langue* and *parole*, existing in both reversible time and irreversible time. It explains not only the past, but the present and future. For the sake of example, Lévi-Strauss's famous deconstruction of the Oedipus myth is reproduced in Figure 1.1 (see Lévi-Strauss, 1963, pp. 13–218). The story is broken into four columns representing discrete types of relations.

Cadmos seeks his sister Europa, ravished by Zeus			
		Cadmos kills the Dragon	
	The Spartoi kill one another		
			Labdacos (Laios' father) = lame (?)
	Oedipus kills his father, Laios		Laios (Oedipus' father = left sided (?)
		Oedipus kills the Sphinx	Oedipus = swollen-foot (?)
Oedipus marries his mother, Jocasta			
	Eteocles kills his brother, Polynices		
Antigone buries her brother, Polynices, despite prohibition			

Figure 1.1 Lévi Strauss's deconstruction of the Oedipus myth

By disregarding one-half of the diachronic dimension of the Oedipus myth (left to right), and focusing only on the columns as a unit, the myth's inherent meaning is made explicit: the first column relates to events which overrate the blood-tie; the second to its under-rating. Third column events relate to monsters being slain by men. In Greek mythology, monsters were seen as creatures whose death was a condition precedent to the emergence of humanity – a humanity born directly from the Earth itself (and not originally from the union of man and woman, thus autochthonous). This struggle is implicit in the battles with the Dragon and Sphinx, yet their contemporary existence is an implicit denial of the autochthonous nature of man. Conversely, the fourth column deals with elements of the myth which relate to lameness or difficulty walking. A common trait of world mythologies relating to the autochthonous nature of mankind is the newly arisen beings' inability to walk, or to walk only clumsily. Thus the fourth column is linked by the affirmation of the autochthonous nature of mankind. Column four is to column three as column one is to column two. The self-contradiction of both pairings is overcome by recognition of the structural similarity of their contradictory attributes.

> By a correlation of this type, the overrating of blood relations is to the underrating of blood relations as the attempt to escape autochthonomy is to the impossibility to succeed in it. Although experience contradicts theory, social life validates cosmology by its similarity of structure. Hence cosmology is true. (Lévi-Strauss, 1963, p. 216)

This form of reasoning, although logical (and indeed highly sophisticated) in its own terms, was anathema to Baconian and Newtonian models of scientific reason, which purported to supplant myth and superstition with scientific truth based on Cartesian principles of 'rational' mind. The supernatural gives way to the natural; religion to science and history; and society to the individual. Yet the structures of Enlightened thought betray a strong fellowship to archaic myth. By creating itself in historical time, rather than in sacred time, the sovereign individual of Enlightenment internalizes the 'terror of history' which it sought to avoid; internalizes it as part of its essential self (see Adorno and Horkheimer, 1979, pp. 27–30; Eliade, 1965, pp. 150–60; Fitzpatrick, 1992, p. 28). In doing so, the subject of Enlightenment (and ultimately of liberalism) becomes the self-reflective and unitary source of meaning and value. The subject itself transcends the contradictions between the general and the particular, fate and fortune, the profane and the sacred, by the mere fact of its existence, eternal progression and universal becoming. The tremendous contradictions inherent in such a claim, particularly in a society committed to scientific understanding, 'rational' enquiry etc., a society which 'dared to know', is resolved by defining itself not in terms of what it is, but in terms of what it is not.[4] Derrida, writing of the impossibility of escaping metaphor in Western metaphysics, describes the phenomenon as the creation of 'white mythology' (Derrida, 1982, p. 213).

Thus 'denigrated myth becomes the obverse of a Western world', a world which 'now took identity as the culmination yet negation of all that preceded it' (Fitzpatrick, 1992, pp. 29–30). This identity is defined and opposed to certain primitive and myth-ridden 'others', in which Occidental being recognizes its own origins and away from which it advances in a constant progression. So constituted, the outstanding characteristic of modernity is raw human will, the 'will to power' as Nietzsche recognized.

The Enlightenment rejection (and implicit absorption) of myth is reflected in the structure of Western law and in the claims of unity, universality and progression made on behalf of its legal subject. Thus the 'Sovereignty of the People' is reflected in the power of positive law, yet the potential absolutism of that power is tempered by judge-made law which derives from other sources – reason, general principles etc. The inherent irreversibility of statute (and thus the reality of history and the contingency of life) is juxtaposed to the reversibility of the 'good old' common law (or Roman/ Civil law) representing eternal reason. And within the latter, the subject-matter of the law inherently defines its legal subject. Such claims, of course, can themselves only be mythical. Thus the rejection of mythology in modern law is part of the mythology of modern law (Fitzpatrick, 1992, p. ix). Given the loss of a transcendent divine or natural law as the source of authority to substantiate its extensive claims, modern law and its legal subject takes identity from what it is not. And what it is not is the primitive, the particular and the myth-ridden.

> Thus modern law emerges, in a negative exaltation, as universal in opposition to the particular, as unified in opposition to the diverse, as omnicompetent in contrast to the incompetent, and as controlling of what has to be controlled. (Fitzpatrick, 1992, p. 10)

THE MYTHICAL STRUCTURE OF EUROPEAN COMMUNITY LAW

From the legal perspective, the European Community has often been characterized as a 'rolling back of the state', a charter of free movement and economic liberty based on the restraint of national law in favour of the individual. Such a view ignores the lesson of Western history that the rise of the 'individual' is co-terminus with, and in fact indispensable to, the development of the modern state. In the Community experience, the rise of the individual in EC Law is strongly linked to the jurisprudence of the Court of Justice, particularly the doctrines of direct effect and supremacy of Community law. By thus elevating the individual as a sovereign subject of the Treaties, in competition with the nation-state, the European Court of Justice broke the monopoly of the nation-state over its defining characteristic – its claim of sovereignty – and developed in its jurisprudence a tradition of discourse which has been remarkably successful in claiming the autonomy and supremacy of the Community legal order. In doing so, the Court of Justice, in a consistent development of case-law supported by a plethora of Community legal scholars, has colonized the mythical structures of modernity which characterize national law. Taking as its clay an ambitious international treaty, the Court creates the European legal order and its sovereign legal subject as transcendent being, endowed with those familiar qualities of universality and progression. And in so doing, constructs the legal subject of the Treaties as an extroversion of the nation itself.

ESTABLISHING TRANSCENDENCE: THE DIRECT EFFECT AND SUPREMACY OF EC LAW

The 1957 Treaties of Rome were negotiated and ratified as international treaties, in accordance with the rules of public international law. As such, they were an agreement between states. Nowhere in the EEC Treaty are individuals mentioned. This is important, because, with very few exceptions, international law does not recognize the existence of individuals. The universe of international law is conceived of as populated only by nation-states, reflecting the dominant role of the 'Great Powers' in defining this 'international' law. That is to say, the individual is not the transcendent source of being in international law, as it is in the law of liberal-democratic nation-states. This lack of a role for the legal individual of international law paralleled the lack of state structures existing on the international level. Put another way, the concept of transcendent being implies not one mythical entity but two: the sovereign subject and that which gives the subject form and substance; the state, mediated by law. The referent of the sovereign subject of nineteenth and twentieth-century liberal society was the nation-state. The myth of the nation-state was that its essential attributes – autonomy from the global collective, cultural values of universal validly, and the negation of primitivism in its self-congratulatory claim to uniquely 'civilized' society – simply paralleled those same qualities assumed to exist at the level of the individual. And the God of the nation-state was a jealous God, conserving this transcendent, yet polar, relationship with the individual to itself.

In its landmark judgement in Case 26/62 *N.V. Algemene Transport – en Expeditie Onderneming Van Gend en Loos* v. *Nederlandse administratie der Belastingen* [1963] ECR 1, the Court of Justice began the construction of an ontologically primary individual as sovereign subject of the Treaties. In rejecting arguments that the determination of individual rights remained in the realm of national constitutional law, and thus lay outside the European Court's jurisdiction, it held that the EEC Treaty

> constitutes a *new legal order* in international law, for whose benefit the States have limited their sovereign rights, albeit within limited fields, and the *subjects* of which comprise not only the member-States but also their nationals. Community law, therefore, apart from legislation by the member-States, not only imposes obligations on *individuals but also confers on them legal rights*. [1963] ECR 1, 12 [my emphasis].

These rights were to be 'directly effective' in the judicial system of the Member States. In other words, the national judiciary was expected to uphold the directly effective Community rights of individuals over contrary national law, as part of the Community legal system which has been 'integrated' into the national legal systems.[5]

But the doctrine of direct effect was only a prelude to the greater claim, in Case 6/64 *Flaminio Costa* v. *ENEL* [1964] ECR 585, that Community law must hold primacy over national law in all cases. Community law could not be overridden by a conflicting national law since, according to the Court, the Member States, by 'creating a Community of unlimited duration ... have limited their sovereign rights, albeit within limited fields'. Community law, 'an independent source of law' cannot 'because of its special and original nature' be overridden by national law 'without being deprived of its character as Community law and without the legal basis of the Community itself being called into question'. Thus, as the Court stated in Case 106/77 *Amministrazione delle finanze dello stato* v. *Simmenthal SpA* [1978] ECR 629, the Treaty represents 'a permanent limitation of their sovereign rights', based on 'obligations undertaken unconditionally and irrevocably', the violation of which would 'imperil the very foundations of the Community'.

It is important to consider the development of direct effect and supremacy as part of a single strategy. In *Van Gend en Loos*, the Court established the individual as a subject of the Treaty. The direct effect of Article 12 EC converted a state-level prohibition against imposition of national customs duties into an individual right against that imposition. Future cases expand these rights to most of the economic guarantees of the EEC Treaty. Being so endowed, the individual of the Treaties slowly takes definition as the *homo economos* we are familiar with in national law, inhabiting a 'private' realm of the 'economy' at the level of a European 'civil society'. But with this important difference: the individual of the Treaties is constituted in negation of the nation. The rights which define its existence as a legal subject operate untrammelled by the bounds or limitations of national society and its law, and explicitly protect that subject against national transgression of its 'rights'.

The centrality of the individual to the Community project is widely recognized in the academic literature. Easson, applauding the creation of direct effect and the problems which would have been caused by leaving the Community process in the hands of national governments, observes, 'All this changes as a consequence of direct effect. Individuals have an immediate remedy, in their own national courts, against the defaulting state' (Easson, 1988, pp. 104–5). Mitchell agrees: approving the Article 177 reference procedure, through which direct effect was created, expanded and enforced, he asserts that 'the picture of past development indicates how much is still to be gained by continued deepening of that co-operation, and gained by individuals for whom ultimately the Communities exist' (Mitchell, 1979, p. 4). Judge Lenz adds his support, the Community legal system being an essential basis for the further development of Community law 'and for it to be applied so as to extend to the legal position of the individual citizen' (Lenz, 1988, p. 9). But perhaps the clearest expression of this ontological elevation comes from Judge Lecourt, who sets out with boldness the options facing the Community:

> Either the Community, for individuals, is a fascinating but distant abstraction, of concern only to governments, which apply its rules at their discretion; or else it is *an effective reality* for them and therefore a creator of legal rights and duties. (Lecourt, 1976, p. 248) [My emphasis]

In parallel with the development of direct effect, the Court's claim of supremacy transforms the legal subject of the Treaties into a sovereign subject. The Court thus creates the European legal subject – the individual – as the centre-piece of the Treaty, reversing its original structure. And by making the individual ontologically superior and prior, the Community itself becomes so. The myth of transcendence, as operative political concept, brings into existence not one, but two entities: the 'sovereign subject' itself, and the 'state' which defines and empowers it. It was through this process of transcendent individuation that the nation-state marginalized the multiple sources of identity and power in medieval society, replacing them with a bi-polar relationship between the state and the individual mediated through law and the concept of sovereignty. By creating and defining the sovereign legal subject of Europe, the Court gives rise to its necessary parallel, the 'European state', thus colonizing the structure of law in modernity, and 'hoisting the nation-state on its own petard'. The law of this European 'state' empowers and vindicates its Supranational Being against the limitations imposed by national legal orders. And in doing so the Community takes on those qualities of autonomy, progression and negation which it recognizes in the nation-state's relationship with its legal subject.

In constructing its sovereign subject and itself, the Court's jurisprudence teems with mythic creativity. The autonomy of Community law is expressed in the 'state-like' claim made for it as an 'independent', 'autonomous' and 'superior' source of law, yet the need for national implementation and enforcement calls forth contradictory claims for its contingency, as an 'integral' source of law, a source capable of acting on lower legal orders, but resistant, by virtue of its 'autonomy', to influences from below. The essential claim for Community law, that it constitutes a 'new legal *order*', belies the experience of the Community and its law as the harbinger of *change*, often radical and socially destabilizing change.

To establish its claims, the Court returns to the founding act of the Communities – the establishment of the Treaty – as a return to sacred origins. This sacred act of creation endows the Treaty with the enduring and propelling force of reality. 'For only the sacred is in an absolute fashion, acts effectively, creates things and makes them endure' (Eliade, 1965, p. 11). Thus the 'founders' of the Treaty establish history by 'creating a Community of unlimited duration' through 'a permanent limitation of their sovereign rights', based on 'obligations undertaken unconditionally and irrevocably'. And like Hobbes's social contract, this is a once-for-all event. The nation-states of the Great Time of the Beginnings (1957) are endowed with a capacity to reflect and act in their own interests which is denied their post-Treaty incarnation. The source of the Community's authority is now the Treaties, the creation of Member States now 'subject' to the system they created: like the God of universal order, they become trapped in their own creation (Fitzpatrick, 1992, pp. 52–3). The positive ontology of virtue (or at least positive necessity) which motivates the founding act of the Treaties is replaced by a general distrust, particularism, short-sightedness and narrow-mindedness ascribed to the Member States, often effectively considered to be 'in-and-against' the Community concept.

The myth of EC law can be well described in structural terms. Graphing the diachronic discourse of the judgements in *Van Gend en Loos*, *Costa* and *Simmenthal*, the synchronic structure, shown in Figure 1.2, emerges.

Member States create EC as an international treaty	EC constitutes a new legal order	National law creates individual rights	Community law creates individual rights
National courts must enforce Community law			
EC law is integral to national law	EC law is an independent source of law		
Enforcement under Art. 169&170 EC may be ineffective	Enforcement under Article 177 EC is effective		
EC is based on a self-limitation of national sovereignty	EC is based on a permanent and irrevocable transfer of sovereignty		

Figure 1.2 The myth of EC law

The elements of the first column have as their common feature the power and sovereignty of the nation-state. The second column expresses its inversion, the supremacy of Community law. The third column associates the historical link between the nation-state and the individual (another mythical triad) mediated by the concept of rights, with the Community's claim to a similar relationship. The basic contradiction facing the Court was thus to reconcile: (1) the Community as a product of treaty without the political, economic or military means to oppose the collective will of the Member States, and thus a creature of national sovereignty; and (2) a need for the supremacy of Community law over national law. This is achieved by mythical association with the internal contradiction of the sovereign individual of Enlightenment, whose finite and limited nature is mediated by its internalization of history and invocation of self-determined progress. In semiological terms, one might say that the individual is not yet already perfected. That which it will be is foreshadowed, and in mythical time precedes, that which it now is. The individual is thus to its contradictions as Community law is to the nation-state, and the double-contradiction is validated by recognition of the similarity of structure. Specifically, both are mediated by association with the concepts of autonomy, progress and negation, an association bound together by the establishment of an order of individual rights at Community level. As in archaic myth, the alchemic qualities of the individual–nation-state relationship are assimilated by the Community in its parallel association with the individual.

So empowered, the Community order represents its identity (as does the individual) in terms of its essential nature. Indeed, one of the Court's strongest and most typical justifications for the direct effect and sovereignty of the Community legal order is the mere fact of its existence as a *legal* order. As Jean-Victor Louis urges, in one of the most esteemed texts on European law, 'It is the Treaty which is the real source of primacy and not the provisions of the national constitutions ... Because of its special and original nature Community law must be accorded primacy' (Louis, 1979, p. 95). This circularity of argument is repeated in the case-law. National law cannot trump Community law, so the Court has it, without its 'being deprived of its character as Community law and without the legal basis of the Community itself being called into question'. For Judge Pescatore, common sense dictates that all legal rules are implemented so as to be effective. To be effective implies individual rights and duties. It logically follows that 'direct effect is nothing but the ordinary state of law' (Pescatore, 1983, p. 177). Pescatore's implicit point is that Community law *is* law as defined in the national sense of the term, in other words in terms of the sovereign individual and the sovereign state. Once Community 'law' is accepted in those terms, he is quite right that direct effect and supremacy follows as a matter of course.

Created in negation of the chaos of European national rivalry and competition, the Community law evokes 'a unity capable of transcending its diverse and contradictory elements, thus making coherent legal order possible' (Fitzpatrick, 1992, p. 86). But the myth works because it is based on what it is not. In the next sections, I will explore the Court's development of the dynamic and universal sovereign subject of the Treaties and the primitive and static realm of the national that constitutes its origin and 'other'.

ESTABLISHING A PROJECT: THE MYTH OF PROGRESSION IN EC LAW

The contradictions inherent in placing the liberal individual at the centre of transcendent being is mediated through the myth of progression. As Fitzpatrick points out,

> In modernity, Man's finitude becomes reconciled with the infinite and eternal, in terms of progression ... [as] an interim apotheosis, one which rejects the preceding being but which also contains that being and prefigures all the object is yet to become. (Fitzpatrick, 1992, p. 40)

By predicting its supremacy on the transcendence of its legal subject, Progression becomes an essential element in the mythical structure of the Community legal order. Community law cannot 'compete' with the law of nation-state as a source of order or transcendent being in terms of what it is. It can only attempt to do so in terms of what it is not, and in terms of what it will be. This is so because that law is established and contained in a treaty, the language and provisions of which pose limits on the jurisdiction of the Community and of its Court, although these have been substantially extended through creative interpretation, as we shall see in the next section. The Treaty of Rome established a European *Economic* Community. The supremacy of Community law is justified by a transfer of sovereignty 'albeit within limited fields'.

Yet this incapacity has become a major source of strength for the Community in mythical terms, as the Court and its commentators adopt neo-functionalist theory as Community jurisprudence. EC law and its literature stress that the European legal order is an incomplete project, in a state of progression. Thus, for Louis, the objectives of the Community are to be achieved 'on the principle of progressive realisation, which is central to the system' (Louis, 1979, p. 19). This theme is echoed by Bieber, who notes that the Treaties do not establish 'a static legal order complete from the outset' but 'a legislative process' reflecting the nature of the Community as a 'gradually evolving legal system' (Bieber, 1988, pp. 148–9), the progressive realization of which 'entails the progressive surrender of rights by the States' (Louis, 1979, p. 35).

The jurisprudence of the European Court constantly invokes this myth of progression, especially when the Court is faced with a crisis in its claim for transcendence or universality of the European legal order. The Treaty remits to the Council (in other words, the Member States) the creation of most positive law. Regulatory structures must therefore be established as Council regulations or directives. Should the Council prove recalcitrant (as is often the case) the Court is faced with a 'reality-gap' between the Community's claims and its ability to act. To mediate the crisis, recourse is had to the myth of progression. Member States are allowed to regulate areas where the Court has claimed a basic competence for the Community only 'in the present state of Community law' or 'pending the adoption of Community rules'. The mythical supremacy of Community law is maintained in the presence of a resistant reality.

These limitations often do not seriously undermine the ontological dimensions of the Court's legal subject. Indeed, these complex and compromise-ridden rules would compromise the mythic purity of the subject which its orientation on the directly effective basic rules of the 'four freedoms' gives it. The Court has, however, used the slowness or unwillingness of the Council to enact legislation as a pretext for expanding the directly effective rights of the Treaty. To the extent that it can, the Court makes progression happen. This action is justified on the obverse of the progression myth: that inactivity on behalf of the Member States or the Council, which slows or reverses progression, threatens to bring the entire European project tumbling down. Thus, 'To abandon this design', Louis urges, 'would not bring about the stabilisation of the Community achievement at the level reached so far, but a more or less rapid process of disintegration' (Louis, 1979, pp. 128–9). Easson makes that case even more forcefully. Faced with non-observance of the Treaty, which brings 'into disrepute the entire fabric of Community law' he considers that 'usurpation is to be preferred to disintegration' (Easson, 1988, p. 119)

This 'ruin' argument is supported by another myth in the same 'mythical field': that since the Treaty is a *traité cadre* or open text, the Court has acted quite properly and in a non-ideological way in 'filling in the gaps'. Although based on a common mode of interpretation in Civil Law systems, the credibility of the *traité cadre* approach is strained in its application by constitutional courts, a concept unknown during the genesis and maturation of the Civil Law. By starting from the assumption that the Treaty does not mean what it says, but only foreshadows what it is destined to become, judicial activism cloaks itself in the mythical certainty of teleological reasoning. The two myths are complementary, since the incomplete nature of the Community, as an entity in progression, justifies judicial activism, and opposition to judicial activism becomes opposition to the 'European idea' (see Cappelletti, 1989, pp. 390–1).

The theme of Community progression thus 'enfolds the transcendent within the temporal – mundane reality is sustained in the prospect of perfectibility' (Fitzpatrick, 1992, p. 51). But as Fitzpatrick points out 'progress does not just go somewhere, it comes from somewhere', i.e. progress invokes origins (ibid.). To those origins and their negation in the legal constitution of European being we now turn our attention.

ESTABLISHING UNIVERSALITY: THE NEGATION OF THE NATIONAL

The novelty of the Community legal order lies in that it is the realm of 'politics', and 'state' at the level of the 'nation' that Community law *takes its identity in opposition to and in progression away from.* Representing the universal as opposed to the particular, the transcendence of its sovereign subject is secured only to the extent that it can subordinate the national realm when the two collide. Consequently, the Community legal order cannot be content with a transfer of sovereignty 'albeit within limited fields', but must, in accordance with the imperatives of progress, expand those fields to universal proportions. Even if such a claim is 'temporarily' insupportable, the claim of transcendence requires that it is the Court which makes the determination. As with national legal 'orders', there cannot be 'gaps' in the law. The Court itself must decide where the Community does and does not have competence, thus claiming a universal jurisdictional competence, or *competenz-competenz* denied to the institution of which it is part.

This process of universalization and its negation of the national can be demonstrated in a number of areas of Community law. One of the strongest examples, the Court's development of the 'free movement of goods', will be discussed here. Article 30 EC provides that 'quantitative restrictions on imports and all measures having equivalent effect shall ... be prohibited between Member States'. Quantitative restrictions, commonly called 'quotas', traditionally referred to protectionist customs rules by which states would limit the import of goods to a certain number, or would ban importation altogether. Through direct effect, the international law prohibition against the imposition of quotas became an individual right against that imposition.

The Court began its universalization of the free movement of goods in the *Italian Art Treasures* case. In that case, the Court rejected an Italian claim that art treasures did not constitute goods within the meaning of the EEC Treaty, holding that

> Under article 9 of the Treaty the Community is based on a customs union 'which shall cover all trade in goods'. By goods, within the meaning of that provision, there must be understood products which can be valued in money and which are capable, as such, of forming the subject of commercial transactions. The articles covered by the Italian law, *whatever may be the characteristics which distinguish them from other types of merchandise, nevertheless resemble the latter, inasmuch as they can be valued in money and so be the subject of commercial transactions*
> Case. 7/68 *Commission* v. *Italy* [1968] ECR 423, 428–9 [my emphasis]

All 'goods' capable of commercial value thus fall within the jurisdiction of Community law. By reducing all aspects of material life to its 'economic' aspect, to commodities, the Court again expands its jurisdiction, and the ontological domain of its subject.

The Court's next opportunity to expand the scope of Article 30 EC, and thus its own jurisdiction and the ontological dimensions of its legal subject, came in Case 8/74 *Procureur du Roi* v. *Benoit and Gustave Dassonville* [1974] ECR 837. A Belgian decree required that imports of spirits be accompanied by certificates of origin issued by the exporting state, as evidence of authenticity. A Belgian importer of Scotch whiskey which was in 'free circulation' in France was made subject to criminal proceedings for not being in possession of such certification. In answer to a preliminary reference on the validity of such a rule, the Court stated that

> All trading rules enacted by member States which are capable of hindering, *directly or indirectly, actually or potentially*, intra-Community trade are to be considered as measures having an effect equivalent to quantitative restrictions. [1974] ECR 837, 852 [my emphasis]

By interpreting the nature of laws reductively in terms of their effects on trade, the Court greatly expanded the scope of 'quantitative restrictions'. But the very scope of the claim created an immense contradiction, since the Community had no equivalent rules in place, and yet 'consumer protection' is a value capable of being encompassed within the dimensions of its legal subject. The limits of the Community order are resolved through recourse to the myth of progression: the Court 'in the absence of a Community system' allows the Member State to regulate unfair trading practices. But this return is now a delegation. And the entire plenitude of power is not returned: henceforth the Member State must act 'reasonably', must not 'act as a hindrance to trade' and, above all, must not create policy based on national considerations.

The doctrine of *Dassonville* is exceptionally broad, but the case itself dealt with an administrative regulation which could, indeed, be considered a 'trading rule', by virtue of its orientation towards imported goods. In Case 120/78 *Rewe-Zentral AG* v. *Bundesmonopolverwaltung fuer Branntwein* [1979] ECR 649, (*Cassis de Dijon*), the Court moved further towards the universalization of Article 30 in fact, in the sense that all national laws, regardless of their spirit, purpose or intent, were to be assessed, allowed or prohibited on the basis of their economic effects. German law prohibited the manufacture or sale of fruit liquors with an alcohol content of less than 25 per cent. The French liquor Cassis de Dijon has an alcohol content of 15–20 per cent. In a preliminary reference resulting from an action contesting the refusal of the *Bundesmonopolverwaltung* to allow the import of Cassis de Dijon into Germany, the Court refined its doctrine, requiring the 'mutual recognition' of goods 'lawfully produced and marketed' in other Member States. Again, citing the myth of progression, the Court limited the scope of its rule pending the completion of the Community. But the scope was limited only to 'mandatory requirements' of fiscal supervision, public health, fair trading and consumer protection, concerns which did not seriously impact the ontological dimensions of its sovereign subject. And it would be the Court which would determine whether those rules were justified or proportional in each case.

The first and most obvious corollary of this doctrine is that the nation-state can no longer directly regulate trade in support of its 'national' interests. A good example is provided by the *Sheepmeat* cases.[6] Before the Court, the French government attempted to justify its restriction of British mutton and lamb imports on, among other things, the serious economic and social consequences for disadvantaged regions in France dependent on sheep-rearing. This argument was rejected out of hand. Such concerns, while legitimate, could only be remedied by Community action. But the effect goes much further than this. Areas of national policy which are not directly related to, but have an effect on, inter-Community trade are also impacted by Community law. National pricing policies have become extremely limited by Article 30. Maximum prices and price-fixing, used usually as welfare or anti-inflationary measures, are limited by the requirement that they are not fixed 'at such a level that the sale of the imported product becomes, if not impossible, more difficult than that of domestic products'.[7] In other words, one element in the establishment of maximum prices is the need for any potential importer to make a profit. Minimum prices, used to provide price support for ailing markets, are limited by the need to ensure that a potential importer's lower cost prices are fully reflected in the retail selling price.[8] International trade policy must therefore be an essential consideration in what were previously mostly domestic concerns. The extent to which

Member State governments are expected to uphold the European legal order, even as it creates such havoc, is reflected in the *Leclerc* cases. The French automobile garage chain Leclerc adopted a policy of selling petrol below French minimum retail prices. Responding to the French government's assertion that such restrictions were justified under Article 36 EC on the basis of public policy and public security, in view of an anticipated threat of social unrest and violence following the immediate removal of price controls, Advocate General VerLoren Van Themaat responded that

> The acceptance of civil disturbances as justification for encroachment upon the free movement of goods would ... have unacceptably drastic consequences. If roadblocks and other effective weapons of interest groups ... were accepted as justification, the existence of the four fundamental freedoms of the Treaty could no longer be relied on ... In such cases, the concept of public policy requires, rather, effective action on the part of the authorities to deal with such disturbances. Case 231/83 *Cullet* v. *Leclerc* [1985] ECR 305.

And so, in a rather startling reprise of nineteenth-century 'Luddite' logic, the problem is defined as the threat to the economic and legal *order* of the Treaties, and the rights of its sovereign subject, caused by the violence of the ignorant or short-sighted, rather than as violence caused by social *change* demanded by the European legal *order*.

The second, less obvious corollary of the Court's universalization of Article 30 is that the nation-state is not only prohibited from directly intervening, except through the Community or with its approval (via approved state aids etc.), but is also prevented from taking sides, on the nation's behalf. Thus an Irish government-sponsored advertising programme to encourage consumers to 'buy Irish' and to emphasize the relationship between national purchases and unemployment, French policies intended to improve the reputation of French watches abroad and Dutch measures designed to maintain high-quality standards in the flower bulb market, were all rejected as 'measures having an equivalent effect'.[9]

But the area of case-law which is perhaps most illuminating of the negation of the national is that dealing directly with juridified manifestations of national culture. I shall use as example cases dealing with appellations of origin and identity. In Case 12/74 *Commission* v. *Germany* [1975] ECR 181, a 1971 German law reflecting traditional usage required that the appellation *sekt* could only be used to describe a German quality sparkling wine, and may only be applied to foreign wines where German is an official language throughout the whole of the country of production. Foreign sparkling wines were allowed (and required) to use the appellation *schaumwein*. Similar rules existed for other 'German' wines and spirits.

In an action brought by the Commission opposing these restrictions, the Court held that appellations of origin were permitted only where the area of origin conferred on the product a 'specific quality or specific characteristics', a test not met by definition on the basis of 'national territory or a linguistic criterion'.

The German government argued, using opinion polls, that these terms were traditionally associated in the mind of Germans with 'German' wine, and that therefore to allow their use by wines without the requisite German connection was to distort their meaning. Culture and language might comprise elements which by definition were not friendly to market integration, but the German government saw no reason to alter German language or culture on that account. The Court disagreed:

> ... the defendant puts forward opinion polls in order to show that, at the date referred to above, in the opinion of the German consumer the appellations *sekt* and *weinbrand* referred to the domestic product. As, however, the protection accorded by the indication of origin *is only justifiable* if the product concerned actually possesses characteristics which are capable of distinguishing it from the point of view of its geographical origin, in the absence of such a condition. *This protection cannot be justified on the basis of the opinion of consumers* such as may result from polls carried out on the basis of statistical criteria. [1975] ECR 181, 197 [my emphasis]

I have dwelt at length on the *Sekt* case to demonstrate how the national is negated in this large area of case-law. The Court reasons that appellations of origin can only relate to the physical qualities of commodities. Evidence that Germans might in fact disagree, and be reticent enough to link these products with German origin, as cultural goods, is not so much denied as ignored. It is not relevant since the sovereign subject of the Treaties is constituted without such a bias. What matters is not so much what Germans actually think as what they are *justified* in thinking. By redefining the word *sekt* from 'quality German sparkling wine' to simply 'quality sparkling wine', the Court renders the term useful to, and brings it within the ontological dimension of, the sovereign subject of the Treaties.

This outcome has been repeated in a number of cases involving cultural goods. The Italian word for vinegar, *aceto*, which necessarily implied 'wine-vinegar' has been rejuridified as simple 'vinegar' to accommodate the market needs of cider-vinegar producers;[10] Belgian standards defining 'brioche' fell before sub-standard French imports;[11] The term 'pasta' in Italy has been redefined and no longer implies exclusive use of durum wheat;[12] Imported gin can be sold in Holland which would not meet Dutch requirements for 'jenever' but can lay claim to that name.[13] Similar transformations have befallen Edam and Emmanthal cheeses, German sausages, and the traditional *bocksbeutel* shape of Franconia wine bottles.[14]

The most dramatic instance of such conflict occurred in Case 178/84 *Commission* v. *Germany* [1987] ECR 1227. The German *Biersteuergesetz* (Beer Purity Law) carried forward a legal tradition dating back to the Bavarian *Reinheitsgebot* of 1516. Under the provisions of the *Biersteuergesetz*, only beers made from barley, malt, hops, yeast and water (and some sugars in the case of top-fermented beer) may be bottled and sold in Germany or imported into Germany, under the name or representation of 'bier'. These rules exclude beers made from rice, maize or sorghum, which constitute many of the beers produced for the mass market outside Germany.

Before the Court, the German government forcefully argued that maintenance of the *Biersteuergesetz* was essential in order to protect German consumers because, in their minds, the designation 'bier' was inseparably linked to the beverage manufactured solely from the ingredients laid down by the traditional law. The Court rejected this position, holding that consumers' conceptions are 'likely to evolve in the course of time within a member State', indeed 'the establishment of the Common Market is ... one of the factors that may play a major contributory role in that development'. The legislation of a Member State must not 'crystallise given consumer habits so as to consolidate an advantage acquired by national industries concerned to comply with them'.

The Court's reasoning in such cases was starkly demonstrated in the British *Indications of Origin* case. A 1982 British law required that certain goods offered for retail sale, including clothing and textile goods, domestic electrical appliances, footwear and cutlery, be marked with their country of origin. As the rule was equally applicable to domestic and imported goods, the validity of requiring indications of origin *per se* was now firmly at issue. The British government defended its law on the basis of 'consumer protection', arguing that knowledge of national origin was of value to a great majority of their consumers 'since consumers regard the origin of the goods which they buy as an indicator of their quality or true value'. It cited a survey carried out among United Kingdom consumers indicating a link between the national origin of goods and public perceptions of quality. 'They like to know, for example, whether leather shoes have been made in Italy, woollen knitwear in the United Kingdom, fashion-wear in France and domestic electrical appliances in Germany.'

The Court endorsed the view of the Commission and Economic and Social Committee, that knowledge of origin 'did not fill a genuine consumer need', noting that

> ... it has to be recognised that the purpose of indications of origin or origin-making is to enable consumers to distinguish between domestic and imported

> products *and that this enables them to assert any prejudices which they may have against foreign products.*[15]

The paradox of the Court's reasoning is *that it is precisely that connotation of value, linked to nationality, which the would-be importer seeks to exploit.* By 'attaching' the appellation or indication of origin, they benefit from the inseparable connotation, in a phenomenological sense, of 'nationality'. The inherent contradiction of its legal subject, that it exists in a 'natural' material and commercial environment in which nationality is deeply embedded symbolically, and its desire to operate outside of those constraints is made manifest. One of the functions of myth, as Lévi-Strauss demonstrated, is to mediate the contradictions of origins and the obsession with identity, achieved by the transformation of nature into culture. In archaic cultures, the transformation is symbolized by the transformation of raw into cooked food. In a market society, nature becomes culture through the act of exchange. By association with the transcendental will of the subject, an object of exchange becomes 'real' and part of 'civilization'. This process takes a new twist in EC Law: now 'culture' is relegated to 'nature', and transformed back into 'culture' through its re-commodification in more market-friendly forms.

The enlightened being of Community law thus differentiates itself from the national; seen as opposite from what Community law and its sovereign subject is, as well as the Community's pre-creation. Community law assumes the mantle of the 'general good' and becomes the bearer of the 'public interest', whereas national interests and values are reduced to the particular and the quaint. Confronted with national values expressed as cultural goods, these are transformed into cultural commodities. In doing so, Community law denies the 'nation' a cultural project or agenda since no harm is seen in piece-meal tampering or alteration in the name of European market integration.

This denial of a 'national agenda' has a close parallel in colonial 'repugnancy clauses' wherein tribal laws and customs were, condescendingly, allowed to operate except in specific cases where they were considered 'repugnant' to Enlightened morality (Fitzpatrick, 1992, p. 30). To some extent, that technique of colonization is employed in Community law. In the nineteenth century legal form of colonization, an image of modernity and the modern Western man was held up before colonial subjects, and their laws and customs, which were found wanting. Similarly in the Community situation, the new sovereign subject of modernity, which infuses European law and its institutions, is held up to national governments, and laws, and sometimes even the people themselves, who are found wanting.

CONCLUSION

The purpose of this chapter was to consider one aspect of the European Court's *certaine idée de l'Europe*: the colonization of the mythical structure of modernity by Community law and the representation of that structure as a sovereign and transcendent source of law, of universal dimensions and linked to a myth of progression. It hopes to have discharged that task, or at least to have raised questions which will prompt others to give better answers. The approach adopted above allows for at least a speculative explanation as to why this mythical mode of discourse has come about.

Returning to the 'origins' of this paper, we remember that Eliade, Fitzpatrick and others have traced the emergence of myth in society as a response to the otherwise intolerable contradictions of life, an antidote to the 'terror of history'. It is proposed that the Community and its legal order represents a reflexive response to the breakdown of the national 'myth' of sovereignty, omnicompetence and racial superiority, following the rise of the two Superpowers in the 1950s and 1960s, and the subsequent technological ascendancy of Japan. It is a commonplace in the memoirs of the 'founders' of the Community that a key consideration was to regain or reassert Europe's 'rightful place in the world'. On a less imperialistic plane, it is also true that the Common Market and its concomitant assumption of European co-operation was an essential element in consolidating the social-democratic welfare state in Europe. Given the tensions of Cold War rivalry in which Europe became the battle-ground of superpower confrontation, predictions of the cultural and political eclipse of Europe by North America and the Far East and the gradual deterioration of the Keynesian welfare state model in the mid-1960s, the need for continued co-operation at the European level and pooling of national sovereignty would have seemed an attractive, if not essential, response.

But the manner by which this co-operation was achieved at the judicial level indicates something more. Even within the myth of modernity, some myths are better than others, in that some myths may be more successful in mediating contradictions, in avoiding the 'terror of history'. To this extent, EC law hoped to rescue the myth of modernity by colonizing it and placing it in an 'ever whiter' dimension; negating contradictory national elements, raising the law above the ability of 'national' legislatures to compromise, recreating the myth of progression in an even more abstract, and therefore uncontradictable, realm. The result is a 'heroic' jurisprudence. The student of EC law would not gain from the law any indication of the context of relative decline of those years when the Court declared and developed 'a new legal order', only the sense of participating in a progressive enterprise firmly oriented towards a future that was already judicially known.

But the mythical 'necessity' of the Community can also be considered in terms of its complex ongoing relationship to the nation. The Community can be seen as an imperial project which seeks to preserve the nation as a political actor by mediating in mythical terms the contradiction between the nation-state concept and its limits. The Community achieves this by removing from the nation-state control over the global economy, which it could no longer unilaterally determine. In that sense, 'nationalism' is relegated to the realm of the primitive. But the 'nation' acts as a foil to the Community in each case; thus questions of justice are constantly put in terms of 'national' or 'European' jurisdiction, law or policy, to the detriment of other characterizations. The nation (with all of its hierarchical and patriarchal connotations) is thus preserved in its 'mythic purity' as is the Community itself. And in that sense, the EC absolutely relies on the continued existence of the nation-state, which it has superseded, and away from which it progresses. The 'national' is the 'other' which the EC is not, a source of identity formed in negation. An 'ever whiter myth', covered over in the palimpsest of European Community Law.

NOTES

1 Indeed, description often passes for analysis. The argument is commonly made that criticism of the European legal order could be diffused if fundamental principles were properly explained and understood. See, e.g. Mitchell's foreword to Louis (1979, pp. 3–4). Responding to criticisms of the EC that 'the Court goes too fast, and that lawyers play too great a role', Mitchell notes that 'these reactions, understandable as they may be, merely make a detached study, which returns to the essential framework ... more important'. Some of the current criticism 'springs from lack of clarity about fundamentals'.

2 Consider the chorus of disapproval of the Court's unwillingness to extend the direct effect of directives horizontally. See Curtin (1990), Coppel (1994).

3 On the 'constitutionalization' of the Treaties, and the Court's role in it, see Easson (1988, p. 103). 'For a lawyer, and perhaps for a political scientist too, the most striking feature of the European Community and that which distinguishes it most clearly from other international groups or organizations of states, is the essentially federal nature of its legal system. What are in their initial conception multipartite treaties have been transformed into constitutional documents and the Court of Justice has evolved into a constitutional court. That this is so is almost entirely the doing of the Court itself, for the "constitutionalisation" of the treaties rests principally upon the twin concepts which it has developed, of direct effect and supremacy of Community law.'

4 Fitzpatrick (1992, p. 62).

5 See also Case 17/67 *Firma Max Neumann* v. *Hauptzollamt Hof/Saale* [1967] ECR 441.

6 See Case 232/78 *Commission* v. *France* [1979] ECR 2729.

7 Case 65/75 *Tasca* [1976] ECR 291; see also Case 13/77 *GB-Inno-ATAB* [1977] ECR 2115, Cases 16-20/79 *Joseph Danis* [1979] ECR 3327.

8 Case 82/77 *Openbaar* v. *Van Tiggele* [1978] ECR 25.

9 See Case 249/81 *Commission* v. *Ireland* [1982] ECR 4005; Case 53/76 *Procureur de la Republique Besancon* v. *Bouhelier* [1977] ECR 197; Case 94/79 *Pieter Vriend* [1980] ECR 327.
10 Case 193/80 *Commission* v. *Italy* [1981] ECR 3019.
11 Case 130/80 *Fabriek* [1981] ECR 27.
12 Case 407/85 *Drei Gloken GmbH and Kritzinger* v. *USL Centro-Sud and Provincia* [1988] ECR 4233.
13 Case 182/84 *Miro* [1985] ECR 3731.
14 See Case 286/86 *Ministere Public* v. *Gerard Deserbais* [1988] ECR 4907, Case 210/89 *Commission* v. *Italy* [1990] ECR I 3697, Case 274/87 *Commission* v. *Germany* [1989] ECR 229 and Case 16/83 *Karl Prantl* [1984] ECR 1299.
15 Case 207/83 *Commission* v. *United Kingdom* [1985] ECR 1201.

REFERENCES

Adorno, T. and Horkheimer, M. (1979), *Dialectic of Enlightenment*, London: Verso.

Bieber, R. (1988), 'On the Mutual Completion of Overlapping Legal Systems: The Case of the European Communities and the National Legal Orders', *European Law Review*, **13**.

Capelletti, M. (1989), *The Judicial Process in Comparative Perspective*, Oxford: Oxford University Press.

Carty, A. (1990), 'Introduction: Post-Modern Law', in Carty, *Post-Modern Law: Enlightenment Revolution and the Death of Man*, Edinburgh: Edinburgh University Press.

Carty, A. (1991), 'English Constitutional Law from a Postmodernist Perspective' in Fitzpatrick (ed.), *Dangerous Supplements: Resistance and Renewal in Jurisprudence*, London: Pluto Press.

Coppel, J. (1994), 'Rights, Duties and the End of Marshall', *Modern Law Review*, **57**.

Curtin, D. (1990), 'The Province of Government: Delimiting the Direct Effect of Directives in the Common Law Context', *European Law Review*, **15**.

Derrida, J. (1982), *Margins of Philosophy*, Chicago: University of Chicago Press.

Derrida, J. (1990), 'Force of Law: The "Mystical Foundations of Authority"', *Cardozo Law Review*, **11**.

Easson, A. (1988), 'Legal Approaches to European Integration: The Role of the Court and Legislator in the Completion of the European Common Market', *Legal Issues in European Integration*, **2**.

Eliade, M. (1963), *Myth and Reality*, New York: Harper & Row.

Eliade, M. (1965), *The Myth of the Eternal Return or, Cosmos and History*, Princeton: Princeton University Press.

Fitzpatrick, P. (1992), *The Mythology of Modern Law*, London: Routledge.

Goodrich, P. (1990), *Languages of Law: From Logics of Memory to Nomadic Masks*, London: Weidenfeld & Nicolson.

Lecourt, R. (1976), *l'Europe des Juges*, Brussels.

Lenz, C.O. (1988), 'The Court of Justice of the European Communities', *Legal Issues in European Integration*, **2** (1).
Lévi-Strauss, C. (1963), *Structural Anthropology*, Harmondsworth: Penguin.
Lévi-Strauss, C. (1986), *The Raw and the Cooked: Introduction to a Science of Mythology*, Harmondsworth: Penguin.
Louis, Jean-Victor (1979), *The Community Legal Order*, Luxembourg: Office for Official Publications of the European Communities.
Mitchell, J. (1979), Foreword to Louis, Jean-Victor (1979), *The Community Legal Order*, Luxembourg: Office for Official Publications of the European Communities.
Pescatore, P. (1983), 'The Doctrine of "Direct Effect": An Infantile Disease of Community Law', *European Law Review*, **8**.

2 New Europe and Old Stories: Mythology and Legality in the European Union

Peter Fitzpatrick

INTRODUCTION

Although I will argue that the 'New Europe' of the European Union and its law can be understood in the bad old terms of nation and national law, in arguing like this there is a danger of simply affirming the persistence and solidity of those terms. My argument will, then, be somewhat refined to show that nation and its law are transposed onto the European Union (EU) not so much because they provide some secure template but more because they are insecure or unresolved and, as such, protean and adaptable.

The EU in its self-presentation has transcended nation. Obviously, it does involve giving significant sovereign power to an international body. But the argument will be that the EU achieves something like transcendence, not by becoming different to its member nations, but rather by containing them in a replication of their own forms and dynamic. It is true that the EU does elevate a law made in large part 'directly applicable' without the mediation of the member state. And this law is further elevated to an ultimate ascendency through the expansionist jurisprudence of the European Court of Justice. That jurisprudence and the Maastricht Treaty would transform nationals of the member states into citizens of the EU – into the subjects of its own distinct and complete law. However, in all this the EU takes on and vigorously promotes the attributes of the nation. What is especially ironic here, as Bergeron shows so vividly, is that the EU and its law are formed and exalted as epitomes of the universal and progressive in opposition to the particular and reactionary realms of the nation (Bergeron in this volume,

Chapter 1). In such opposition what is emphasized, of course, is the 'badness' of nations – the atavistic nation of warlike and divisive assertion, the nation of blood and soil. Yet nation, as we shall see, also partakes of the universal and progressive. Nation is an indistinguishable sharing of these contrary characters. What this indicates is not so much a deadly opposition between the nations of the member states and the super-nation of the EU but, rather, a compatability or even similarity between them. We could say that the outcome is not so much a matter of the EU outflanking the nation as one of nation outflanking the EU – or outflanking the standard, supranational version of the EU. Such a conclusion is not, however, without its corrosive consequences for the viability of the national idea, as we shall also see.

The similarity between nation and the EU may suggest that here we have some stable essence of nation which manifests itself in these varying locations. While similarity is there, it does not import stability. Nation exists in-between the universal and the particular. And this 'space' in between can never be settled or resolved. What would putatively secure the identity of nation in that space is a mythology of becoming within the national or (Western) European project, a mythology tied to the exclusion of others from that project. This exclusion has to be somewhat paradoxical. It cannot be fully effective or complete since the excluded – whether in the figure of the immigrant, the refugee, the brooding terrorist, the resurgent ethnic, and so on – must remain proximate and constantly challenging for the identity based on it to be sustained. Because of the necessity of this challenge for identity to subsist, the resolution derived from exclusion is never achieved. Resolution remains tied to irresolution, the stability of identity to its instability. Furthermore, the effectiveness of a mythic resolution can be neither invariant nor eternal. Given the limit of mythic efficacy and the ambivalence of exclusion, there is a persistence of irresolution. Law, then, becomes that which is 'in place of' irresolution and operatively compensates for it.

Those lines of argument account for most of this chapter but first I will set this scene of European identity, myth and law in the limit which confronted an archaic mythology, a limit which can be aptly traced in the genealogy of Europa.

THE ORIGIN MYTH

There is a fondness for starting accounts of Europe with the story of Europa and her abduction by Zeus.[1] In this myth of origin, Europa is usually described as a Greek goddess and thereby endowed with European credentials and a useful transcendence. She was, however, more interestingly mixed, being neither simply Greek nor, apart from some local reputation, a goddess.

So, let us borrow a more precise beginning from Calasso's *The Marriage of Cadmus and Harmony*, an account whose immense popularity lends it a certain telling quality (Calasso, 1994). He begins:

> On a beach in Sidon a bull was aping a lover's coo. It was Zeus. He shuddered, the way he did when a gladfly got him. But this time it was a sweet shuddering. Eros was lifting a girl onto his back: Europa. Then the white beast dived into the sea, his majestic body rising just far enough above the water to keep the girl from getting wet. … Trembling, Europa hung on to one of the bull's long horns. (Calasso, 1994, p. 5)

And so on in much the way one would readily expect.[2]

Thereafter, in a series of explorations around that scene, Calasso incessantly poses the question 'But how did it all begin?' and, respecting the elusiveness of origins, each answer is immediately rendered incomplete by a re-posing of the question – 'But how did it all begin?'. The second search for an answer is set earlier that same day:

> Shortly before dawn, asleep in her room on the first floor of the royal palace, Europa had had a strange dream: she was caught between two women; one was Asia, the other was the land facing her, and she had no name. The two women were fighting over her, violently. Each wanted her for herself. Asia looked like a woman from Europa's own country, whereas the other was a total stranger. And in the end it was the stranger whose powerful hands dragged her off. It was the will of Zeus, she said: Europa was to be an Asian girl carried off by a stranger. (Calasso, 1994, pp. 4–5)

On waking, she walked down to the mouth of the river and the story is much the same as before. But the description of Europa as 'an Asian girl' is soon complicated. In his next posing of the question, 'But how did it all begin?', Calasso focuses immediately on 'a shining gold basket' in the hand of Europa as she walks in Asia towards its shore – and 'what Europa was carrying … was her destiny' (Calasso, 1994, p. 5). The basket, we are told,

> … was the family talisman. On the side, embossed in gold, was a stray heifer apparently swimming in an enamel sea. … And there was a golden Zeus too, his hand just skimming the bronze-coloured animal. In the back-ground, a silver Nile. The heifer was Io, Europa's great-great-grandmother. (Calasso, 1994, p. 5)

This same Io was loved by Zeus. Hera out of jealousy had transformed her into a heifer forced to leave Greece and to roam the world until the intervention of the god – 'the light touch of Zeus's hand' – allowed her to settle in Egypt, Asia's African connection (cf. Hegel, 1956, p. 91).

The exchanges, correspondences, inversions, transformations involved in Io's journey from a putative Europe and the return journey, as it were, of Europa being carried by Zeus to Europe, the exquisitely small linking of all these things in the golden basket, these are what the structural study of myth is made of, but Calasso resists the temptation and resorts finally to a nineteenth-century mode of rendering myth, one which would see myth as an attenuated form of history. So, the last two instances of Calasso's posing the question 'But how did it all being?' reveal, in abrupt summary, the abduction by the Phoenicians of an Io equivalent and the counter-abduction by the Cretans of an Europa-equivalent. 'Out of these events', concludes Calasso, 'history itself was born', since which 'the war between Europe and Asia has never ceased' (Calasso, 1994, pp. 7–8).

Calasso is invoking here the idea of history as impelled by the abduction of women but what he may also have in mind is something taken up in his interpretation of these stories:

> At the time of Europa and Io, the veil of ephiphany was still operating. The bellowing bull, the crazed cow, would once again appear a god and girl. But as generation followed generation, metamorphosis became more difficult, and the fatal nature of reality, its irreversibility, all the more evident. (Calasso, 1994, pp. 11–12)

Metamorphosis comes to a sad and shameful terminus in the monstrous Minotaur, the child of Europa's daughter-in-law, Pasiphaë. Thereafter, Calasso concludes:

> Humans could no longer gain access to other forms and return from them. The veil of epiphany was rent and tattered now. If the power of metamorphosis was to be maintained, there was no alternative but to invent objects and generate monsters. (Calasso, 1994, p. 12)

Extravagant as it may seem, we can see the story of Europa in terms that Zizek once used to describe a certain Freudian myth, see it as something 'that should be presupposed (reconstructed retroactively) if one is to account for the existing social order' (Zizek, 1991, p. 208). The myth becomes much like Europa's talismanic basket in its concentrated accounting for how 'we' came to be where and what we are. So, there is point, and more point than is usually allowed, to the invocation of Europa at the beginning of books on Europe since Europa mythically settles questions of Europe's border and of its 'objectness' – questions of its identity. Well-rehearsed as questions about borders and identity may be in the academic literature, they yet retain an exigent complexity.

To start with the border. Borders divide. They separate distinctly. But if the border were completely effective in this separation, it could not be a border between the separated objects – using 'objects' as I think Calasso does. Objects completely separated would not bear any relation to each other at all. They may, at best, exist in parallel universes, but there would be no call for a border between them. For the border to exist there must be a relation, and thence some commonality, between the objects. Relation, in turn, imports a mutual extension and giving way of one object to another. But obviously the border cannot be purely relational either. In a pure relation, the objects would simply disappear in each other or in some combination different to either, and there could be no border between them. The border, then, exists in-between putative conditions that the existence of the object makes impossible – the condition of complete separation and the condition of complete relation. Europa becomes, then, no longer the standard and simple source of an integral European identity but the figure of inexorable irresolution within that identity.

Europa's claim to be of a distinct European origin is far from comprehensive. Her great-great-grandmother was the Grecian Io. And if she were comprehensively European, she could hardly provide the origin for a Europe that would have to exist already to make her European. She is somewhat more compendiously described as 'an Asian girl' but one who is, in terms of her dream, 'caught between two women'. One of these women is called Asia and she 'looked like a women from Europa's own country'. The other woman 'had no name'. The name 'Europe' could not be acquired until there was an originating connection, a relation, with Asia. This is established in the myth through Europa's being carried off to what can then become Europe. But as we have seen, the object, Europe in this case, cannot simply 'be' in relation. It has to have an identity which precedes the relation and precedes its own origin in the relation. So, Europa has to be already in part European in a descent from Io.

To extract this impossibility of European identity from the myth is, of course, to strip it of its transcendent charge and to deny it the ability to mediate the contradictions of an all too solid world. Within the transports and transformation of Europa's story, there remains no 'alternative but to invent objects and generate monsters' (Calasso, 1994, p. 12). Objects then took identity not through a positive transcendence but in a negative, bellicose rejection of what the object was not. In terms of one of Malraux's musings: 'There is no Europe. There never was one. ... What is understood today by European can only be defined negatively: Europe is what Asia is not' (see Heldring, 1987, p. 93). Such assertions import, as we have seen, an inexorable relation, a recognition of commonality and comparability. Asia is similar as well as different to Europe. A barbarian Asia is constitutively and chasmically different to a civilized Europe. Yet Europe is also the same as Asia and this in two ways. For one, civilized Europe is the product of a universalist progression from a barbarism to which it may at any time revert. For another, barbarian Asia may also respond to the call of the universal and advance in the ranks of human civilization. In this 'logic' of identity, Asia provides both the point of constant difference to Europe yet is also able to become the same as Europe. This impossibly mixed entity is the modern equivalent of Calasso's monster. Out of 'monster's' wide range of meanings, what I am emphasizing here, of course, is the monster as an impossible combination of disparate elements, as with the poor Minotaur. Asia is one of the modern monsters which carries the dissonance, the irresolution of European identity itself.

Modern nation is a neo-mythic reflection of this monsterous combination. Nation is a distinct and specific place. It occupies a particularity of blood and soil which is always close to barbarism. Yet modern nation is also a carrier of the universal. This is not only a matter of nation's now 'universal' or global coverage. It is also a matter of some nations and collections of nations exemplifying universal qualities – qualities of civilization and development, of rationality and an orientation towards the general. Being universal, these qualities should be found everywhere, and where they are merely incipient they can be fomented. So, Europe 'has always given itself the representation or figure of a spiritual heading, at once as project, task, or infinite – that is to say universal – idea' (Derrida, 1992, p. 24). To assert the claim to the universal is to create a fraught relation with all that is thereby set outside of and opposed to the universal. This expansive universal identity must also be turned inwards and particularly located. Hence it also becomes 'the memory of itself that gathers and accumulates itself, capitalizes upon itself, in and for itself' (Derrida, 1992, p. 24). Certain particular nations and collections of nations become exemplary of a virtuous universalism. The world of nations thence becomes classified and organized along a spectrum ranging from the most 'advanced' liberal democracies, to nations still afflicted by an evil and atavistic particularity. 'There is always', says Balibar, 'a "good" and a "bad" nationalism': this is 'the dilemma within the very concept of nationalism itself' (Balibar, 1991, p. 47).

EUROPE AND THE EUROPEAN UNION

Europe shares with nation an intriguing inability to be rendered as anything palpable at all. Either it is a universalized project, or part of one, and thus incapable of assuming any limited identity, or it is given specific characteristics which turn out to be not exclusive to it.[3] There is and has to be a persistent vacuity in efforts to say what Europe is. In a piece plangently, not to say plaintively, titled 'What is Europe, Where is Europe?', Seton-Watson found that:

> The word 'Europe' has been used and misused, interpreted and misinterpreted, in as many different meanings as almost any word of any language. There have been and are many Europes. (Seton-Watson, 1985, p. 9)

He considers several contenders – the bounds of Charlemagne's Empire or the bounds of Christendom, for example – but is convinced by none. Europe's bounds have remained chronically uncertain, especially in their eastern definition. The usual effort at positive definition takes the form of the list. Duroselle's miscellany provides an example:

> ... we have been influenced by ancient Greece, by Judaism, and by Christianity, Megaliths, Roman roads and monuments, local autonomy, Romaneseque art, the cathedrals, the universities, the explorers, the Industrial Revolution, human rights: these and many more elements are of the essence of Europe. (Duroselle, 1990, p. 413)

The lists can be more economical if hardly any less concerted. The following from the Netherlands Ambassador for International Cultural Cooperation is close to standard:

> What determines and characterises European culture? ... Europe is formed by the ... community of nations which are largely characterised by the inherited civilisation whose most important sources are: the Judaeo-Christian religion, the Greek-Hellenistic ideas in the fields of government, philosophy, arts and science, and finally, the Roman views concerning law. (Pieterse, 1991, p. 3)

Faced with the dissipation of positive description, Malraux's resort to a negative coherence – 'there is no Europe. ... Europe is what Asia is not' – seems inevitable. Such an outcome is also the only one that can be consistent with Europe's universalist claims since the universal cannot be positively delimited.

The arrogation of what it is to be 'European' by the EU seems to relieve it of any necessity to identify itself. The main Treaty, although establishing a 'European Economic Community', betrays no interest in the nature of this Europe. And although the preamble to the Maastricht Treaty on European Union is replete with the by now standard invocation of 'liberty, democracy, and respect for human rights and fundamental freedoms and the rule of law', nowhere is the explicit nature of the union confronted. This list is added to variously in different settings. The 'Declaration on the European

Identity', agreed to by the members of the Community in 1973, revealed that they were distinguished by 'the same attitude to life' and a commitment to the 'individual'. To take one more example, the putative preludes to membership of the EU which have now been extended to almost all countries of 'Central and Eastern Europe', while listing most of those qualities, put additional emphasis on the prerequisite ability to protect minorities and to operate a market economy. All of these characteristics are hardly exclusive to the EU and its members. They can even be notoriously absent. Democracy, for instance, is hardly characteristic of the EU itself.

If the EU does not differ from nation in the failure of its effort at positive self-definition, it is no more distinguished in its resort to negative affirmation. This is an affirmation in opposition to what is 'non-European'. And that which is 'non-European' is, as Cris Shore says, 'being defined with increasing precision and thus, as if by default, an "official" definition of Europe is being constructed'; and as he also says, 'the new European order ... is coming to mean a sharper boundary between "European" and "non-European"' (Shore, 1993, pp. 786, 793).

The story of how this boundary came to be put in place has already been told, and well told (e.g. Paliwala, 1995). It is a story of the erection of a 'Fortress Europe' enclosing a distinct European identity. It unfolds in the joining of two momentous effects: the progressive elimination of internal or national boundaries within the EU and the increasingly draconic enunciation of an 'external' boundary around the EU, setting it against certain excluded 'others'. This scene has been consolidated in the Maastricht Treaty and its accompanying proliferation of shadowy but potent EU and peri-EU regimes identified obliquely by place or official numbering – Dublin, Shengen, Trevi, K.4, and so on – all 'harmonizing', refining and heightening the exclusion of the refugee and the would-be immigrant. The Maastricht Treaty itself predisposes 'asylum', 'immigration', and 'nationals of third countries' to distinctly negative connotations by dealing with all these in conjunction with 'combating unauthorised immigration, residence and work ... terrorism, unlawful drug trafficking and other serious forms of international crime' (Art. K.1).

These modes of exclusion do not simply operate at some supposed external border of the EU; the excluded are also within. Maastricht thrusts a thin citizenship on nationals of the EU's member states, and even if this adds little to rights those nationals already had under the original Treaty, it is nonetheless, and as we will see later, a full citizenship based on 'natural' affiliation and not confined to its capacity to participate in a 'common market'. It serves to focus the rights of nationals into a distinct identity which is privileged above the identity of resident non-nationals. These are variously estimated to number between 10 and 15 million – the range presumably being related to the impossibility of calculating the number of 'illegal immigrants'. So, that sense of proximate threat conducive to the negative formation of identity does not simply impinge on some frontier region but can also be intimately invoked as an ominous internal presence. This danger within then requires, of course, greater inter-governmental co-operation between member states of the EU in the cause of more controls, surveillance and gathering of information. Again, there is little that is original in these EU and peri-EU regimes. They adopt and give effect to the same obsessions as those of many member states – the victimization of the refugee being a recent example (see Tuitt, 1996).

THE EUROPEAN UNION AND THE EUROPEAN NATION

In sum, recent realizations of the 'European Union' would seem to incline it definitively towards classic attributes of nation. We can discern this in its assertion of set bounds and in the creation of a citizen-unit to which a central authority can relate, by-passing all 'intermediate' entities. But of course in its self-presentation, and for its apologists, the EU is more, much more:

> The [EU] is typically portrayed as a logical development of the Enlightenment: a force for progress inspired by science, reason, rationality and humanism … . These discourses also tend to portray the European Parliament and Commission as heroic agents of change, on the side of history, leading Europe forward in search of its supposed 'federal destiny'. (Shore, 1996, pp. 102–3)

Even more extravagantly, but still not untypically, Delors would have it that 'the European identity is a sense of the universal, the world started out from *chez nous*' (in Grant, 1994, p. 163).

This surpassing quality of the EU's identity, together with its specifically supranational character, would seem to be confirmed conclusively in the rejection by the EU of a nationalism typified by its member states. Bergeron has located the EU's quality of the universal in its 'negation of the national' (Bergeron, this volume, Chapter 1). This is the nation whose barely suppressed primordial urges constantly attend the precarious achievements of a civilization which is universally oriented. Those who persist in summoning this nationalism against the EU, 'those who awaken phantoms', were for Delors quite beyond the pale (see Grant, 1994, p. 223). More positively, the information booklet issued by the European Commission, *A Citizen's Europe*, sees the EU as 'an attempt to establish between States, the same rules and codes of behaviour that enabled primitive societies to become peaceful and civilized' – the member states, in other words, are the new primitives (see Shore, 1993, p. 793). To illustrate this fundamental attitude, we could take Schepel and Wesseling's close and cogent observation of 'the mindset' of lawyers involved with EU law, whether in legal practice or in the academy (Schepel and Wesseling, 1996). In this mindset, there is a constellation of malign attributes associated with the nation-state and national sovereignty – such as war, decay, nationalism, politics – and these are arraigned against a benign EU intrinsically associated with contrary attributes such as integration, peace, cosmopolitanism, progress and law.[4]

If, however, we move beyond this convenient confinement of nation to a primordial specificity, the EU begins to appear more like than unlike the nation. Nationalism was also a child of Enlightenment. It makes claims, as we saw, to an expansive project and a universal dimension – claims which seem in their content and their history indistinguishable from those associated with the EU. But the same claims had, somewhat paradoxically, to be tied to nation as particular. The achievement of the universal would dissolve all particularity, and hence any situated existence at all. And so universal assertion 'needs its Other; if it could ever actualize itself in the real world as the truly universal, it would in fact destroy itself' (Chatterjee, 1986, p. 17). The EU's formative rejection of the 'badness' of member nations as 'other' is a rejection of qualities which it exhibits in assuming a situated identity. To overcome this 'fracturing' of its identity, there is an extraversion of these rejected qualities. This is affirmed, as we have seen, through regimes marking and supposedly rejecting an other which is 'without'. Those who are without are physically beyond the bounds of the EU or they have only a provisional or illegitimate existence within its territory. In all these combined ways – the assertion of a particular and prerogative claim, the arrogation of the universal and of an expansive project, and the affirmation of elevated being in opposition to an other without – the EU takes on an identity that seems indistinguishable from that of nation. As with the formation of modern nation, the EU now seeks to create or convert citizens who will be allied to the EU and in this alliance all that is particular or local will be overcome. It would be tempting to see this in Marx's terms as tragedy the first time around and farce the second, if the elements of tragedy and farce were not so well-mixed for both. This is not an alliance forged from a perfect pre-existence of contracting parties. It is more a matter of, as d'Azeglio put it in another setting, 'we have made Italy, now we have to make Italians' (see Hobsbawm, 1992, p. 44). The means adopted have usually been as calculating and tawdry as those used by national élites in their creation of traditions, rituals, public symbols and ancestor figures (see Shore, 1993; Shore and Black 1994).[5]

The resulting citizenry is one of a national kind. This may at first seem surprising. The commitment to a 'common market' should involve some affirmation of a universal which goes beyond its confinement in the particularity of a national place. And the huge historical and practical force of the EU's intrinsic assertion of the market operates not just beyond but in opposition to nationally based claims of its member states. But this assertion of the market is not one made in the setting of a purely international treaty which is itself confined only in terms of the market. Assertion takes place in national terms and it occupies the same 'space' of irresolution in between the universal and the particular which characterizes nation. Citizenship itself mediates this irresolution. It combines membership of the particular national community with what is expansively and universally 'civil'. Citizenship of the EU is, in short, a 'true' citizenship, conceived and operative in nationalistic terms. It is neither confined nor extended in terms of market functions – in terms of a 'market-citizenship'.[6] It is also a 'true' citizenship in its potent discrimination against non-citizens.

We could begin to illustrate this argument in the European Court's interpretation of Art. 119 of the EC treaty where it says that:

> Article 119 pursues a double aim. First, in the light of the different states of the development of social legislation in the various member-States, the aim of Article 119 is to avoid a situation in which undertakings established in States which have actually implemented the principle of equal pay suffer a competitive disadvantage in intra-Community competition as compared with undertakings established in States which have not yet eliminated discrimination against women workers as regards pay. Secondly, this provision forms part of the social objectives of the Community, which is not merely an economic union, but is at the same time intended by common action, to ensure social progress and seek the constant improvement of the living and working conditions of their peoples.[7]

There is a somewhat muted dissonance here. In terms of the first aim, all 'women workers' are universally the object of its dispensation. But the second 'social' objective relates ambiguously to 'peoples' of the member states. The ambiguity comes closer to a resolution in other provisions of the Treaty set against discrimination. Art. 48, for example, provides that 'freedom of movement for workers shall be secured within the Community', and this 'shall entail the abolition of any discrimination based on nationality between workers of the Member States as regards employment'. This protection seems to extend to workers universally. But 'workers of the Member States' here means workers who are nationals of those states. In its confined particularity, this restriction is every bit as antithetical to the market as discrimination on the ground of gender would be. In terms of ensuring parity of conditions between member states, the market is just as distorted or just as much undermined by disparity in pay on national grounds – a disparity, say, between a citizen of the EU and a non-citizen – as it would be in the case of discrimination on the ground of gender countered by Article 119.[8] This adoption of a 'natural' affiliation, going beyond 'freedoms' confined to the market, is now explicitly affirmed by the Maastricht Treaty in its creation of a 'Citizenship of the Union' and of political rights such as the right to vote in and stand for election to certain offices; there is also a recognition that 'the political will of the citizens of the Union' needs to be 'expressed' (see Art. 8 and 138a of the EC Treaty).

This creation of a natural affiliation does, however, signal some qualification of my analysis so far. That analysis sought to show that the EC both contains and is contained by nation, and furthermore that it is 'like' nation precisely in that ambivalence. Nation does, however, involve a singularity of attachment, a cleaving to the particularity of a place and of a people. Europe has had its enduring collectivities of nations, the Great Powers and the comity of nations, or Voltaire's 'kind of great republic' that is Europe (see Gong, 1984, p. 46). But these were manifestations of nation's universal orientation. They remained compatible with a singularity of attachment to each member state. Indeed, with the EU itself there is a persistent and plausible line of argument, which would not only affirm the exuberant survival of nations and their law, but would also see the EU as merely an extension of the member nations which retain their predominant force (see especially Milward, 1992). Be that as it may, the EU is now a disturbing scene of conflicting nationalisms. The EU as a nation writ somewhat large and the member nations occupy the same terrain, the same place, not only as a matter of formal legal and constitutional allocation but also in terms of the existential commitment of their citizens.[9] To an extent, this conflict is muted in the universal orientation of nation. One can be both distinctly French and a cosmopolitan European, usually without great discomfort. But the dissonances are there and probably intensifying. The specific challenge of the EU to the nations of the member states consists, moreover, not only in the explicit and trumpeted conflict between them (the little Englander always obliges with instances). Rather, the EU's challenge to its members in their particularity comes also from the similarity which it foments between them. The EU increasingly enters into the particularity of the member states in ways that would absorb them into equivalence. It calls on them to become the same as each other not only by demanding adherence to its uniform prescriptions but also by shaping the commonality, or potential for it, that supposedly exists within each of them.[10] The European Court stands, as ever, ready to hasten the process with its location of Community-wide fundamental rights extracted from national locations, or with its imposition of general requirements for the interpretation of national laws. The overall scene is, however, not one of a supranational or intrinsically anti-national EU set against its antithesis in the nation-state. Both the EU and its members conform to the characters of nation and it is the resulting conflict or duality that is antithetical to a nationalism which must be instanced in singularity.

To an extent, this conflict is mediated by the similar constitution of the EU and the European nation in exclusion and in their exclusion of a broadly similar 'other'. Perhaps we can see now a heightening, and exacerbation of exclusion by both the EU and its member nations so as to make these nationalisms more the same, more indistinguishable – to help them revert, as far as may be, to their primal singularity. But there does remain a disruptive duplexity of nationalisms in Europe, the fragmenting effects which are currently manifest in many member countries.

THE EUROPEAN NATION AND EUROPEAN LAW

The concluding strand of the argument involves an opposition between the duplexity of European nationalism and the quality of law in the EC. In most modernities of a European kind, law has been well positioned to compensate for the ambivalence of nation – for the irresolution in-between its particular and universal orientations. This irresolution has been putatively resolved in a rule of law which combines particular determination and universal comprehension. Law, as the rule of law, bounds and sets limits, yet it also extends to all possibility. Law and nation have thence subsisted in a long, isomorphic relation. It is this positioning of law which enables its resolving quality to encompass the duplexity of nationalism within the EU. I will now outline some obvious characteristics of EU law in a way which, hopefully, supports this contention.

Perhaps it may not be entirely obvious to say that EU law comprises a modern legal system since some of the EU's more indulgent observers would see it otherwise. In the words of one of them, 'the institutional, juridical, and spatial complexes associated with the Community … constitute nothing less than the emergence of the first truly postmodern international political form' (Ruggie, 1993, pp. 140, 169; and cf. Ward, 1996, p. 194). To the contrary, Bergeron sees the European Court of Justice engaging successfully in a modernist mission of state formation (Bergeron, this volume, Chapter 1). Although the European Court is often perceived as being excessively creative in this, the original Treaty was not set against the Court's construction of a modern statist constitution for the EU. As Perry Anderson has indicated, it is hardly necessary to have the panoply of an executive authority, a legislature and a supreme court to run a customs union (Anderson, 1996, p. 14). To this list of the unnecessary, we could add the presence of a singular, modernist legal system of the universally encompassing variety. EU law is not, in its pervasive scale and tentacular reach, confined to some residual role – confined to supplementing or working through other systems and holding them together solely for a specific purpose established in an international treaty. EU law is in large measure 'directly effective' and it increasingly operates in a direct relation to its distinct, individual legal subjects, now recognized as its own citizens. And, as is notorious, the European Court has been pre-eminently successful in fashioning a coherent constitution for the EU based on the judges having 'une certaine idée de l'Europe' as an encompassing totality.

All of which is not to deny that there are other legal systems involved within the EU – including, but certainly not limited to, those of the member states. As Schepel so richly reveals, legal pluralism does well in the EU (Schepel, this volume). Nonetheless, EU law, especially in its elevation by the European Court, is oriented towards a universal consummation. It is to be secured against the dissipated and decadent arena of the particular and local, including, as we saw, the diversity of the member nations. The EU and its legality do not, of course, merely seek to suppress these things. And complete suppression would in any case deny the EU its dynamic of identity and coherence in opposition to them. The EU and its law treat with their proximate and constantly challenging others. They accommodate and incorporate dimensions of them. EU law does this, however, not in a postmodernist responsiveness to and regard for such things in their quivering specificity but in a monadic orientation of them in terms of its own work, its own project.

So, my assertion of the encompassing and universalist quality of EU law is, in a seeming paradox, tied to a necessary recognition of its limits. EU law is confined and incomplete in both its formal range and its actual efficacy, and this not least in its continuing dependence on nation for much of its effect. But this deficit is readily resolved in the mythology of Europeanism where such shortcomings are seen as both an obstacle and a spur to a progress which is overcoming them. Much of the diversity or plurality of law within the EU can be subordinated in a unitary frame by viewing it as something that is being countered in this progress. Again, the parallels with the formation of modern European nations are hardly remote.

Despite these transcendent, universalist dimensions, the law we have been considering is specifically located. It is the law of a member nation of the EU or the specific 'national' law of the EU. Since this division in the location of law is formally set within EU law itself, since there is no sovereign authority overarching the division, the EU does seem to take on a postmodern colour. Furthermore, and as Darian-Smith indicates so graphically, people within the EU seem to engage successfully with a plurality of legal systems, and they do so in ways which do not look to some ultimate and singular resolution

(Darian-Smith, 1995). But just when we seem to have a unitary and modern law on the retreat, it comes into its own. Law can be readily located now in different but overlaid national settings as the law of the EU or the law of a member nation. But in a significant sense, law in both these locations is also the same. This sameness subsists in national terms since nation and a national law are not just of a particular place. They are also, as we saw, universalist extraversions. Where this capacity for extraversion took some operative form, such as in the comity of nations, then the various included nations were seen as having the same quality of law (see e.g. Gong, 1984, p. 46). Even though the legal system of the EU is distinct from the legal system of a member state, they both exhibit a shared quality of law. They are both plenitudinous, 'advanced' legal systems of a modern kind, 'supreme' in the coverage of their respective spheres. This similarity is both illustrated and heightened in those efforts of the European Court which, as we saw earlier, would combine elements of the various member states into something of a common law of the EU. In short, nation gives a place to law, and the similarity of law in different places retroacts on and unites these primal locations of law. This subsuming similarity of law is made palpable in its 'Europeanness'. The universal, whether inhering in law or nation, must be instanciated and 'Europe' has provided a cohering combination of particular place and universal exemplarity. Law in its 'Europeanness', whether the law of the EU or of a member state, provides then an equable and singular place accommodating the duplexity of nationalism in the EU.

If this line of argument were to hold, we would expect law and its 'Europeanness' to be accorded a central part in the EU scheme of things and, *mirable dictu*, such would seem to be the case.[11] The very orientation of law towards the general itself counters diversity between member nations and holds them in a uniform relation to the 'Europeanness' of the EU. More palpably, we find in Schepel and Wesseling's depiction of the mindset of 'European' lawyers that a transcendent and unifying law 'law' is associated integrally with the EU and, in this, it is set against a contrary 'politics' diffusely and definitively located in the member nations. They find that the identification of the EU's legal community with the aspirations and ethos of the Union is close to complete (Schepel and Wesseling, 1996). If we were to focus on the most potent members of that legal community, we would find that 'European integration', the constitutional coherence of the EU, and the pervasion of its dictates and ideas are all causes accorded a distinct and large place in the jurisprudence of the European Court of Justice. Indeed, the project of union has found a more constant support in 'l'Europe des juges' than in the political arena of the EU.

Despite this elevation of law in its relation to 'Europe', the argument that law compensates for the duplexity of nationalism within the EU is not exactly irrecusable. It does, however, attempt to engage with the persistence of nationalism, and of law as national, within the EU in the face of an abundant observation of their terminal decline, yet again. But what this chapter would more confidently claim is that these easy assertions of decline miss a target which is more complex and more elusive than they would allow. Such assertions would confine nation to a particularity of blood and soil and set it against a numinous and universalist 'Europe' of the EU. But, as we have seen, this supposed opposition is within nation itself. So constituted, nation extends its protean range to the EU as well. The contest between the EU and the member states becomes, not a contest between nationalism and something else, but rather one between competing nationalisms, and in the competition nationalism is heightened rather than diminished. That competition revealed a duplexity in nationalism which countered the claim of nation to a singular particularity, to an exclusive territorial attachment. It was law in its 'Europeanness' which, so the argument finally ran, compensated for and, in a way, remedied this now manifestly plural location of nation.

ACKNOWLEDGEMENTS

Original thanks for their generosity and care to Anne Griffiths and the other organizers of the 1995 gathering of the Critical Legal Conference at which an approximation of this chapter emerged as a plenary talk. And thanks to Colin Perrin, yet again, for salutary comments. I am also most grateful to Julie Herd for so effectively processing all of this and to Eve Darian-Smith, Maria Drakopoulou, John Fitzpatrick and Joanne Scott for invaluable references.

NOTES

1 For examples of the ridiculous and the sublime see, respectively, Duroselle (1990) and Hay (1968). Greek origins, if perhaps the most prevalent, are not the only ones bestowed on Europe. As befits the irresolution of origins sketched in this chapter, there is a persistent inability to establish an origin for Europe (cf. Kristiansen, 1996). And, of course, the themes of exclusion and inclusion which I extract from the myth of Europa have been much debated in relation to Europe (see Bernal, 1988).

2 Graves, however, endows Zeus only with 'small, gem-like horns' (1955, p. 194, vol. 1).

3 For the equivalent failure to identify nation see, respectively, Gellner (1983) and Smith (1986). The line of argument in the text does not deny that Europe can be identified in material terms. Barlett (1993), for example, does so identify Europe magnificently. But to recognize such a material limit as definitive would counter a claim to the universal. Furthermore, it is the lack of a set or resolved divide between particular location and

the universal 'in' nation or 'in' Europe which makes nation or Europe possible as the combination of these antithetical elements. This irresolution also enables an illimitable project associated with Europe to be maintained without the constraints of a specific history.

4 It could be telling to observe how apologists for the EU as supranational deal with its rampantly nationalistic assertions. Weiler, for example, would indulgently accommodate them as rhetorical excess and add the uneasy prescription that they 'should' not be there (Weiler, 1996, pp. 253–4).

5 To take a recent example of some advertisements placed by the Commission: 'One of the adverts features a passenger firmly telling an airline steward that if her flight is overbooked, EU regulations entitle her to a seat on the next flight or compensation of at least £130. The background music is Beethoven's Ode to Joy, the EU anthem, and the inescapable message is that the union is a very good thing for the citizen' (*Guardian*, 27 December 1995). Much of this is now done in the name of culture (see generally Shore, 1996). 'Culture', in its modern sense, has become a mediating category which can putatively combine the most general characteristics with an intense particularity. Hence, it makes possible such feats of legerdemain as the post-Maastricht Article 128 of the Treaty where it provides that 'the Community shall contribute to the flowering of the cultures of the Member States, while respecting their national and regional diversity and at the same time bringing the common cultural heritage to the fore'.

6 This could be too broad. There may be confinement in terms of the market of the rights of citizens to freedom of movement under Article 48 of the Treaty (see Kingston, 1996, pp. 152–4).

7 *Defrenne* v. *Sabena (No 2)*[1976] 2 C.M.L.R. 98 at 122.

8 As with gender discrimination, the point would extend also to disparity in any means countering this discrimination on national grounds.

9 Federal systems present an obvious parallel but one that cannot be taken very far because with federated nations a predominant and singular national identity is widely engendered, not least through powers typically concentrated in the central government. These are the kinds of powers currently placed somewhat at a remove from the apparatus of the EU as 'pillars' of distinctly inter-governmental decision-making under the Maastricht Treaty.

10 This may seem to be contradicted by various moves to absorb the EU into national and even more localized scenes – subsidiarity being the most talked of. But these moves to put and keep the power in question 'within' these scenes and the 'European dimension' is always there providing the form and some of the force of any answer.

11 There are other reasons for law's centrality in the EU, but all I am concerned to extract here is some supportive compatibility between this centrality and the argument about the duplexity of nationalism. In a milieu where things are constitutively unresolved, it is obviously difficult to talk of precise connection and of distinct causes and effects.

REFERENCES

Anderson, P. (1996), 'Under the Sign of the Interim', *London Review of Books*, 4 January.

Balibar, E. (1991), 'Racism and Nationalism', in E. Balibar and I. Wallerstein, *Race, Nation, Class: Ambiguous Identities*, London: Verso.

Bartlett, R. (1993), *The Making of Europe: Conquest, Colonization and Cultural Change 950–1350*, London: Penguin.
Bernal, M. (1988), 'Black Athena Denied: The Tyranny of Germany Over Greece and the Rejection of the Afroasiatic Roots of Europe 1780–1980', *Comparative Criticism*, **8**.
Calasso, R. (1994), *The Marriage of Cadmus and Harmony*, London: Vintage.
Chatterjee, P. (1986), *Nationalist Thought and the Colonial World: A Derivative Discourse*?, London: Zed Books.
Darian-Smith, E. (1995), 'Law in Place: Legal Mediations of National Identity and State Territory in Europe', in P. Fitzpatrick (ed.), *Nationalism, Racism and the Rule of Law*, Aldershot: Dartmouth.
Derrida, J. (1992), *The Other Heading: Reflections on Today's Europe*, Bloomington: Indiana University Press.
Duroselle, J.B. (1990), *Europe: A History of Its Peoples*, London: Viking.
Gellner, E. (1983), *Nations and Nationalism*, Oxford: Blackwell.
Gong, G.W. (1984), *The Standard of 'Civilisation' in International Society*, Oxford: Clarendon Press.
Grant, C. (1994), *Inside the House that Jacques Built*, London: Nicholas Brealey.
Graves, R. (1955), *The Greek Myths*, Harmondsworth: Penguin.
Hay, D. (1968), *Europe: The Emergence of an Idea* (2nd edn), Edinburgh: Edinburgh University Press.
Hegel, G.W.F. (1956), *The Philosophy of History*, New York: Dover.
Heldring, J. (1987), 'Perceptions of Europe in the Netherlands', in A. Rijksboran *et al.* (eds), 'Europe from a Cultural Perspective', The Hague: Nijght and Van Ditmar Universitair.
Hobsbawm, E.J. (1992), *Nations and Nationalism since 1780*, Cambridge: Cambridge University Press.
Kingston, J. (1966), 'Citizenship of the European Union', draft paper, London: British Institute of International and Comparative Law.
Kristiansen, J. (1996), 'European Origins – "Civilization" and "Barbarism"', in P. Graves-Brown *et al.* (eds). *Cultural Identity and Archaeology: The Construction of European Communities*, London: Routledge.
Milward, A.S. (1992), *The European Rescue of the Nation-State*, London: Routledge.
Obradovic, D. (1996), 'Policy Legitimacy and the European Union', *Journal of Common Market Studies*, **34** (2).
Paliwala, A. (1995), 'Law and the Constitution of the "Immigrant" in Europe: A UK Policy Perspective', in P. Fitzpatrick (ed.), *Nationalism, Racism and the Rule of Law*, Aldershot: Dartmouth.
Pieterse, J.N. (1991), 'Fictions of Europe', *Race and Class*, **32** (3).
Ruggie, J.G. (1993), 'Territoriality and Beyond: Problematizing Modernity in International Relations', *International Organization*, **4** (1).
Schepel, H. and Wesseling, R. (1996), 'La communità giudici, avvocati, funzionari e *clerks* nella scrittura dell'Europa', *Sociologia del Diritto*, **23** (1).
Seton-Watson, H. (1985), 'What is Europe, Where is Europe?', *Encounter*, **65** (2).

Shore, C. (1993), 'Inventing the "People's Europe"? Critical Approaches to European Community "Cultural Policy"', *Man*, **28** (4).

Shore, C. (1996), 'Imagining the New Europe: Identity and Heritage in European Community Discourse', in P. Graves-Brown *et al.* (eds). *Cultural Identity and Archaeology: The Construction of European Communities*, London: Routledge.

Shore, C. and Black, A. (1994), 'Citizens, Europe and the Construction of European Identity', in V. Goddard *et al.* (eds), *The Anthropology of Europe: Identity and Boundaries in Conflict*, Oxford: Berg.

Smith, A.D. (1986), *The Ethnic Origins of Nations*, Oxford: Blackwell.

Tuitt, P. (1996), *False Images: Law's Construction of the Refugee*, London: Pluto.

Ward, I. (1996), *A Critical Introduction to European Law*, London: Butterworths.

Weiler, J.H.H. (1995), 'Does Europe Need a Constitution? Demos, Telos and the German Maastricht Decisions', *European Law Journal*, **1**.

Zizek, S. (1991), *For They Know Not What They Do: Enjoyment as a Political Factor*, London: Verso.

3 Legal Pluralism in the European Union

Harm Schepel

INTRODUCTION

If it is true that the problem in thinking about the European Union in political terms is 'the limits imposed by the nation-state on our habitual ways of thinking about politics' (Schmitter, 1992, p. 380), the same is true *a fortiori* about the conceptualization of European law. Not so much the clinging on to national sovereignty, though, impedes the elaboration of a useful theory of European law as, perhaps, the all too explicit rejection of it. 'Progressive' thinking about European law rebuilds sovereignty on a European scale and rehearses the constellation of ideas associated with it – politics as public discourse about state intervention in civil society; law as a technical mechanism to focus and enable an interventionist politics; power as a force to be juridically concentrated and allocated; a commitment to the separation of the public and the private (Kennedy, 1994, p. 9). It has no time for fragmentation of social power and pluralization of law-creation. With the Community legal order now blown to 'bits and pieces' (Curtin, 1993), the 'jurists' cosmos' (Höland, 1993, p. 181) of Europe, so tied up with integration as a linear process towards essentially uncontested objectives, so used to an idea of law as a site that lends rational superiority over any conception of Europe that seeks to do without the totems of statehood (Schepel and Wesseling, 1997), finds itself in crisis (Shaw, 1996).

Paradoxically, non-legalistic or 'contextual' approaches to European law (e.g. Reich, 1986; Joerges, 1989; Snyder, 1990, 1993, 1994; Micklitz, 1991; Harding, 1992; Harlow, 1992) often reinforce this constellation of ideas by relentlessly pointing out how European law falls short of the promises contained in these notions. It does so whether it decries the dominance of big business and lack of diffuse interest representation in the production of law, describes the rocky and costly paths towards European litigation or points to divergencies and gaps in the implementation of European law. When Armin Höland describes European law in analogy to the Danube – springing off somewhere, then disappearing into dark muddiness only to reappear a few miles further (Höland, 1993) – he not only describes a research problem for the sociology of European law – how 'European' is that law when it reaches polluted harbours? – but also, if unwittingly, a problem of the sociology of European law. This is a sociology of European law caught in presuppositions of hierarchy, unidirectionality and unity; a sociology of European law desperately seeking a European legal culture (Wieacker, 1990; Gibson and Caldeira, 1996), instead of assuming pluralism, complexity, polycentricity (Arnaud, 1991). It helps sustain the self-styled image of European law as a rational force aiming at the at once inevitable and necessary – 'Europe' – against the dark and murky attractions of national power politics.

My point, at least here, is not to bemoan the politically dubious implication of such research, of 'instrumentalism' or the 'pull of the policy audience' (Sarat and Silbey, 1989; Trubek and Esser, 1989). My aim here is merely to suggest, however tentatively, a socio-legal approach to European integration that is not so much about European law as it is about the way European Union law interacts with other legal and non-legal normative orders. It is based on a concept of legal pluralism, parting from the seemingly innocent observation of 'the simple fact that several legal systems coexist at the same moment' (Van de Kerchove and Ost, 1994, p. 134).[1] In the realm of European integration, the concept is certainly not new. It has been championed by André-Jean Arnaud (1991, 1995), who has reminded us of both the historical contingency of the idea that law cannot have several springs and the practical untenability of that idea in present-day Europe. In its subversion of both the state and universal legal reason, the concept is all too obviously attractive both for a liberal strand of European integration studies that modestly looks to move us 'beyond the sovereign state' (MacCormick, 1993) and a more postmodernly ambitious strand that would even have us step 'beyond the nation-state and beyond modernism' (Ward, 1995, p. 28). In this vein, legal pluralism risks getting caught in the familiar canons of European studies that contrapose the Union to its Member States, supranationalism to intergovernmentalism and integration to decay, canons intimately informed by European law's self-description. In this chapter, I argue that the concept of 'legal pluralism' is promising just because it allows us to break away from law's self-description in terms of hierarchy and identity and urges us to look closer at interrelationships between different interacting systems of normative ordering. This will help to open up space, I hope, to see recursivity rather than linearity, continuity rather than rupture and mutual dependence rather than opposition in the relationship between the Community and its Member States, between state law, non-state 'law' and European law and between politics and civil society.

The argument proceeds in the following somewhat erratic way. The first and most obvious part (supranational legal pluralism) is concerned with issues of hierarchy and unity. It discusses the interrelationships between Community law, the European Convention of Human Rights and national law. The rather modest aim of this part is to complement the rhetoric of self-proclaimed supremacies with the sophisticated mechanisms of co-optation and symbolic appropriation that govern these relationships. The second part (subnational legal pluralism) continues the theme of hierarchy, but now in terms of the relationship between non-official law and official Community law. This is the stuff of the 'new' legal pluralism, a movement whose main ideas will be briefly posited before turning to a case study of annexation and what Bob Cover called 'jurispathos' (Cover, 1983) of the social economy movement. The relationship between law and other social forms is the subject of the third part (integral plurality) which discusses the relation between law and administration before turning to a brief look at the role of non-legal systems in European economic governance. The fourth part (transnational legal pluralism) couples questions of hierarchy with those of identity. It focuses on transnational 'stateless' normative phenomena whose 'legal' status is all but obvious. This is the stuff of post-modern theories of legal pluralism, theories that will be briefly discussed before turning to a case study of the interrelationship between Community law and one such transnational normative phenomenon, technical standards-setting. The themes here are legal disintegration through Europeanization, and Europeanization through organized differentiation. The argument is one of assuring 'centrality by organized decentring', to paraphrase Boa Santos (Sousa Santos, 1992, p. 133). Finally, some conclusions will be drawn as regards the analytical and normative possibilities of the concept of legal pluralism.

SUPRANATIONAL LEGAL PLURALISM

As is proper to legal systems, both Community law and national constitutional laws proclaim themselves supreme. Legal discourse involving the European Community is an ever more refined and sophisticated version of this basic dilemma. It is this situation, that of the 'simultaneous existence – within a single legal order – of different rules of law applying to identical situations', that Arnaud invites us simply to rejoice in rather than despair over (Arnaud, 1991, 1995). This, clearly, is too much to ask of European lawyers and politicians alike. Rather than wholeheartedly embracing this 'polycentricity', this part tries to map the various ways in which the

Community legal order deals with competition of other legal orders. The basic pattern is revealed by a twist on Gurvitch's classic exploration of the relations between his 'social law' and state law (Gurvitch, 1932). A half century before the critics of informal justice (e.g. Abel, 1982) he already described the State's response 'in last resort' to combat competing orders trying to dispossess the state of its pretended legal monopoly as 'l'annexion de certains de ces ordres concurrents pour les transformer en alliés et les faire servir à la cause étatiste' (Gurvitch, 1932, pp. 73–4). Paradoxically perhaps for modern sensibilities, Gurvitch chose public international law as his prime example of 'pure and independent social law', superior to and independent from state law (Gurvitch, 1932, p. 53). To attribute to the European Community, for some still governed by a subspecies of public international law, the tactics of maintaining monopoly Gurvitch ascribed to the state might seem like heresy, yet that is precisely my intention. But then again, European Community law is a far cry from *ius gentium*.

Supremacy

In a rhetoric that preceded George Bush by almost thirty years, the European Court of Justice held in the early classics *Van Gend en Loos*[2] and *Costa- ENEL*[3] that the European Community constituted a 'new legal order of international law'. Amidst incredulous politicians, rebellious national constitutional courts and enthusiastic legal writers, the Court of Justice from there on established and built on the doctrines of supremacy and direct effect in a process the judges themselves are fond of calling the 'constitutionalization' of the Treaty (Mancini, 1989). Conducted in a spirit of hardly concealed hostility towards national legal systems in the early years, the process has recently changed in character, however. Of late, case-law shows a remarkable shift, in that national legal systems are now being enlisted in the cause, especially through the remarkable career of the 'fidelity' clause of Art. 5 EC (Lang, 1990) and the imposition of European law in between national political and judicial spheres. In *Francovich and Bonifaci*,[4] the Court established the principle, albeit of ambiguous import, that Member States are liable in tort for damage caused because of the inadequate transposition of directives. In *Marleasing*[5] it stretched the concept of 'conciliatory interpretation' to its very limits, forcing national judges to 'interpret' national law so as to bring it in line with directives, even if the former is in flagrant aberration of the latter. In Van Empel's jubilant words, the court 'has mobilized the national courts in their role of guardians of Community Law, where need be *against* the other parties in the *trias politica* at their respective national levels' (Van Empel, 1992, pp. 15–16).

A similar cooperative moodswing can be discerned in legal doctrine where a leading legal theorist conceptualizing Community law and Member State law recently coined the expression 'co-ordinately valid legal systems', in that 'each for certain purposes presupposes the validity of the other' (MacCormick, 1996, p. 561). Coordination, however, should not lead to anarchy. Discussing the 'Maastricht' decision of the *Bundesverfassungsgericht*[6] which famously made its obedience conditional to the Union's good behaviour, former ECJ judge Ulrich Everling reminds his fellow countrymen that 'the very existence of the Community depends upon the immediate and unquestioned validity and application of its law in all Member States' (Everling, 1994, p. 12). Moreover, if each constitutional court decided about the application of Community law 'according to its own estimations, traditions, and interests, the unity of the Community's legal order would be threatened' (Everling, 1994, p. 12).

Fundamental rights

And yet the German constitutonal court seems in touch with the times where it offers to guard the respect for fundamental rights in 'cooperation' with the Court of Justice, an offer again refused by Everling (Everling, 1994, p. 13). Even he, though, should admit the precarious position of fundamental rights in the new legal order. The Court of Justice has established a highly complicated relationship of the Community legal order with the European Convention of Human Rights (ECHR) and national constitutional principles. Failing any mention of fundamental rights in the EEC Treaty, it has elaborated a doctrine by which these rights are 'an integral part' of the 'general principles of Community law': in protecting these rights, the Court is, on the one hand, 'inspired' by the Member States' common constitutional principles, and, on the other, supplied with 'guidelines' by international treaties to which the Member States adhere, notably and most significantly among them, the ECHR.[7] The 'inspiration' does not go so far, however, as not to mention that 'the validity of a Community measure or its effect within a Member State cannot be affected by allegations that it runs counter to either fundamental rights as formulated by the constitution of that State or the principles of a national constitutional structure'.[8]

Transfrontier television

The history of European transfrontier television-regulation is a beautiful example of institutional and legal pluralism and symbolic appropriation. In the early 1980s, some Member States, in an effort to protect the carefully guarded state monopoly and/or the pluralism of their media, prevented the reception in their territory of television signals originating abroad. To break the deadlock, the Commission started working on a directive at the same time as the Council of Europe was entertaining plans for a Convention on the same topic. Some Member States emphatically supported the Council of Europe in this rather unedifying contest, considering the sensitive issue of television regulation more appropriately dealt with under the symbolic regime of the European Convention of Human Rights than in the economic logic of the EEC Treaty (Hondius, 1988; Schwartz, 1989). At this point the Commission made its mastermoves of institutional coordination and symbolic appropriation. The institutional competition was solved by coordinating the texts of the different legal instruments so as to exclude conflict. The 1989 Directive[9] is thus perfectly compatible with the Convention, the more so by having drawn in bits and pieces of Art. 10 ECHR. From the beginning, the Commission's efforts to open up the television market was accompanied by a large-scale doctrinal assault on the relationship between the economic logic of the EEC treaty and the symbolism of the ECHR (Commission, 1984; Schwartz, 1986; Schwartz, 1990). According to Schwartz's thesis, reproduced in the preamble of the Directive, Arts 59 and 62 EEC on the freedom to provide services are 'a special manifestation of a more general principle, namely the freedom of expression as enshrined in Art. 10 ECHR'. Consequently, the derogation from Arts 59 and 62 EEC, Art. 56 [1] EEC is 'an expression of' Art. 10 [2] ECHR, which implies that the former may not be interpreted differently, or any more widely, than the 'necessity' clause contained in the latter (Schwartz, 1986, p. 29). That is, the freedom to provide services throughout the internal market can only be curtailed if 'necessary in a democratic society'. The Commission tried to convince the Court of the merits of this construction as early as in the 1985 *Cinénethèque* case.[10] In 1991 the Court was finally persuaded in *ERT*,[11] where the ECHR was invoked to shed light on the limitations on the power of Member States to apply derogations for reason of public order, public health, and public security to Arts 59 and 62 EEC.

We are now then faced with an economic 'freedom' elevated to the status of a fundamental right by appropriation and distortion of the ECHR.

SUBNATIONAL LEGAL PLURALISM

With the 'new' legal pluralism, sociologists of law have carried over concepts and observations from colonial to western societies to study the relationships of normative orderings of communities, social fields and organizations to state law. (Moore, 1973; Galanter, 1981; Sousa Santos, 1985; Belley, 1986; Griffiths, 1986; Macaulay, 1986; Merry, 1988; Selznick, 1992, p. 468ff.) 'The new legal pluralism moves away from questions about the effect of law on society or even the effect of society on law toward conceptualizing a more complex and interactive relationship between official and unofficial forms of ordering' (Merry, 1988, p. 873).

At times, the movement romantically celebrates the strength of communal life in defiance of the 'jurispathos' of the cold monster's machinery.[12] In the words of the late Bob Cover:

> The position that only the state creates law thus confuses the status of interpretation with the status of political domination. It encourages us to think that the interpretive act of the court is privileged in the measure of its political ascendance. Although this position may be good state law – the Constitution proclaims itself supreme – the position is at best ambiguous when viewed as a description of what the various norm-generating communities understand themselves to be doing. Insular communities often have their own, competing, unambiguous rules of recognition. They frequently inhabit a nomos in which their distinct *Grundnorm* is supreme from its own perspective. (Cover, 1983, p. 43)

To the scorn of some commentators (Tamanaha, 1993), the movement thus stubbornly refuses to limit the concept of law to state law. Calling only the normative ordering of the state 'law' would be, so the argument goes, to crumble to 'the ideology of legal centralism' (Griffiths, 1986, p. 3) and to deny that the functions of law can be performed as well by other systems.

Cooperatives

Utopian and anachronistic as they may seem to some, cooperative societies are an important socio-economic phenomenon in the European Union, sheltered from the forces of market competition by a complex patchwork of internal norms of solidarity and, at least in some Member States, protective public law. Cooperatives and other forms of social economy have a strained relationship with the Common Market (de Combrugghe, 1993; Jacobi and Vesterdorf, 1993). Art. 58 EC extends the four freedoms to companies or firms, explicitly including cooperatives. The cooperative movement has since 1975 been arguing for and proposing a European Cooperative Statute (Dabormida, 1989, p. 49ff), along the lines of the 'normal' Societas Europea. The final Commission proposal[13] shows remarkable similarities to the proposal tabled by the Coordinating Committee of Associated Cooperatives,[14] itself a clear compromise of the cooperative principles established by the

International Cooperative Alliance in favour of capitalist modes of organization and financing. However, the ICA's 'pure and independent social law' makes a backdoor entrance into European law: given the legal cooperative void in Denmark, Danish legal entities allowed to set up a SCE had to be defined by the Commission proposal as 'cooperative societies and associations as defined and recognized under the principles formulated by the International Cooperative Alliance'.

However, while the European legislator is thus quite open to the cooperative movement, the Court of First Instance in *Dansk Pelsdyravlerforening* v. *Commission*[15] has declared open hunting season by reiterating, and applying explicitly to cooperatives, its standard jurisprudence that the notion of 'undertaking' in Art. 85 EC includes all entities exercising an economic activity, regardless of their legal form. In the case, the Commission refused an exemption under Art. 85 [3] EC, holding that the clause in the statutes of the cooperative prohibiting the individual members of the cooperative to sell their products through other venues than the cooperative constituted a breach of Art. 85 [1] EC. The Danish government intervened in the case, bringing up the matter of principle concerning the relation between competition law and the principles of the cooperative movement. The cooperative nature of the enterprise implies, so the argument runs, that any action contrary to the economic interests of the cooperative would be contrary to the interests of its members, which goes against the principle of solidarity.[16] The Court disagreed, and sweepingly denied that the conditions of applying competition law to cooperatives are to be any different than those relative to other forms of organization of economic activity.[17] Moreover, the Court allowed itself a completely unfounded statement of suspicion by voicing concern over the fact that enterprises sought to 'escape' national law governing other forms of association only 'in the name of cooperative principles'.

What we have here is supremacy by annexation of cooperatives into the common market on the one hand, and blunt 'jurispathos' on the other.

INTEGRAL PLURALITY

The debate on the boundaries of the 'legal' is not only a matter of conceptual confusion. The debate framed this way keeps law and other forms of social ordering squarely in terms of competition and functional equivalence, thus obscuring more intricate relationships. A huge step forwards has been made by Peter Fitzpatrick's invention of 'integral plurity', based on Foucault's work on relational power. Foucault himself already posited 'sovereignty and disciplinary mechanisms' as 'two absolutely integral constituents of the general mechanism of power in our society' (Foucault, 1980, p. 108). Fitzpatrick has consistently pointed to the fundamental coherence and mutual dependence of law and other social forms, 'integral yet necessarily opposed' (Fitzpatrick, 1992, p. 149; 1984, p. 128; 1995, Henry 1983). Law depends on what is contrary to it, in that it is only prepared to deliver on its mythical promise of equity and self-determination within the boundaries set by the normalizing processes of administration. Significantly for our subject, there is a 'mythical truth of coherence' between the extension of individual legal rights and the elevation of the rule of law on the one hand, and the (legal) elevation of the market as the optimal mechanism of societal exchange on the other: 'The market itself has been vaunted not just as a liberation from state regulation, but as a means of introducing greater discipline, especially self-discipline, including an appreciation of the inevitability of authority and hierarchy' (Fitzpatrick, 1992, p. 148).

Law and expertise in European economic governance

Banalizing Fitzpatrick's thesis, one could see this coherence of seemingly opposed instruments of social ordering repeated in the Maastricht Treaty's two fundamental innovations of European Community law. On the one hand, the Treaty makes a bleak promise of protecting fundamental rights and confers 'citizenship' on hardworking Europeans, a status enhanced with the promise of keeping it a rare commodity by closing off the Union's borders in an obscure conflation of terrorism and immigration. On the other hand, the Treaty endows these newly found citizens with responsibility for their own lives by the inclusion of an excavated adagium of catholic good behaviour turned legal principle, 'subsidiarity'.

Discussed mainly as a vague principle governing the relationship between the territorial administrative levels of the Union (e.g. Toth, 1994; Lenaerts and van Ypersele, 1994), this principle of subsidiarity promises to become a vehicle of decentralization intricately linked to an exercise in dejuridification. In the Communication the Commission issued on the principle, it stated:

> In practical terms, subsidiarity means that, when exercising its powers, the Community must, where various equally effective options are available, choose the form of action or measure which leaves the Member States, individuals or businesses concerned the greatest degree of freedom. Beyond this general rule, though, is the implication that if a binding measure proves necessary, the actual degree of regulation should be kept at a minimum. (Commission, 1992, p. 13)

And thus, 'the main choice where subsidiarity is concerned is between binding and non-binding measures' (Commission, 1992, p. 14).[18]

To sum up with Scharpf, 'apparently, the intention is now to avoid, as far as possible, the detailed establishment of substantive norms in the Council of Ministers which would then have to be converted into national laws and administratively implemented in the Member States. Instead the aim is to take greatest possible advantage of corporatist, quasi-governmental, or subnational processes of norm formation, concretization, and enforcement' (Scharpf, 1994, p. 23).

Read in this key, subsidiarity codifies a dominant story in law and society, according to which there is ever more 'law', but at the same time 'the boundaries of the legal world are becoming blurred and indefinite on every front' (Galanter, 1992, p. 18). In the European Union, Dezalay sees the legal field transformed by 'merchants of law', transnational mega-law firms mediating between legal, political and economic processes (Dezalay, 1992). Committees of thousands of experts and national administrators meet daily in Brussels producing what has been called 'infranational law' of uncertain status, ranging from recommendations and guidelines to product specifications and far-reaching decisions on the legitimacy of banning British beef from the continent. 'Scientific expertise' is becoming a dominant model of denationalized decision-making in the Union, consecrated and sanctioned by the Court of Justice (Joerges, 1997).

European legal discourse reacts to this advancement of expertise and administration with a call for public institutionalization and designs for legal procedures that would ensure accountability. Within the framework of the defining dichotomies of public and private, and law and administration, that indeed is the only thing it can do. In Fitzpatrick's 'integral plurality', these opposing and mutually excluding instruments of governance collapse in mutually reinforcing expressions of one mechanism of exercise of power.

TRANSNATIONAL LEGAL PLURALISM

Whether in the version of differentiated autopoietic communicative subsystems (Luhmann, 1993) or in the more traditional version of the growing strength of formal organizations (Streeck, 1983; Streeck and Schmitter, 1985; Mayntz, 1991, 1993), or somewhere in between (Willke, 1992), modern social theory seems overwhelmingly to point to a diminished governing capacity of the 'state', or even to posit the state as 'one societal actor among others' (Willke, 1986, p. 467) or, worse yet, a 'decentralized netting of public and private collective actors', bargaining and networking their way through life in a 'loosely coupled configuration of cooperation, replacing the hierarchical unity of the traditional state' (Teubner, 1993).

Added to the internal pressure of differentiation are the external ones of internationalization, or globalization. Autonomous functional systems and organizations in their own dynamic logics do not adhere neatly to territorial boundaries. Thus, the State is not only a 'tragic' but also a 'local' hero (Willke, 1992, p. 362ff.) in the face of lateral global systems and the internalization of societal actors (Teubner and Willke, 1984, p. 9; Willke, 1992, p. 362ff.). The objection Streeck has to Cohen and Rogers' project of 'associative democracy' (Cohen and Rogers, 1992) could be extended to several modern projects of governance:

> Associative democracy is about socially responsible self-governance of functional groups. But underlying this idea is an image of 'complete' sets of social functions nested into national states, of coterminous territorial and functional boundaries, and of boundaries that are difficult to cross. There are many indicators that assumptions like these are outdated and that a more adequate imagery would be one of 'variable geometry' of social systems and subsystems – national, international, and supranational – with different functional areas organized at different levels and with a variety of frames of reference between which social actors may freely switch in pursuit of their objectives and interests. (Streeck, 1992, p. 517; Streeck and Schmitter, 1991)

From these basic premises two version of legal pluralism emerge, their differences partly due to their divergent choices of units of analysis.

Boa Santos discerns a new form of plurality of legal orders consisting of

> partial legal fields constituted by relatively unrelated and highly discrepant logics of regulation existing in the same state legal system. As it loses coherence as a unified agent of social regulation, the state becomes a network of microstates, each one managing a partial dimension of sovereignty (or of the loss of it) with a specific regulatory style and logic. (Sousa Santos, 1995, p. 281)

He thus keeps his feet firmly within the state, conceptualized no longer primarily as source of law but as a site of localization of transnational influences.[19]

Gunther Teubner takes off from the state altogether and to do so brushes the dust off Eugen Ehrlich's 'living law' (Ehrlich, 1913) in a globalizing posthumous tribute. Where Ehrlich accepted no frontiers for the norms and customs of his Bukowina, Teubner accepts only world society as bounding off the new global social law of Lex Mercatoria (Teubner, 1997). To sustain his thesis of 'global law without the state', he redefines legal pluralism as 'no longer a set of conflicting social norms in a given social field but as multiplicity of diverse communicative processes (Teubner, 1992, pp. 1450–1). Loyal to his constructivist epistemology of law (Teubner, 1989), he then solves the question of legal identity by holding that law, as discursive practice, produces its own boundaries. His global legal universe does not allow for hierarchical distinctions, replaced with the distinction of centre/periphery. Political lawmaking is thus decentred, moved away from its place at the top of the norm-hierarchy and cornered in the periphery on an equal footing with other types of social normproduction (Teubner, 1996, p. 12). Global normative phenomena such as Lex Mercatoria, internal legal regimes of multinational enterprises, the social concertation in international labour law and technical standards-setting are thus equal to, but by no means untouched by official law. In Teubner's view, 'it is not so much the contrast with state law that characterizes the new social law, but its instrumentalization for purposes of political regulation, which even goes so far that politics in turn initiates artificial procedures of social norm production' (Teubner, 1991, p. 139). The regulation of European standards-settings in technical harmonization is a nice example.

Standard setting

To ensure the free movement of goods within the Internal Market endless national technical product specifications need to be harmonized at such a level of health and safety protection as to impede Member States from stopping imports of products from other Member States. With the 'new approach',[20] the Commission has given up on that huge task. Instead of drawing up these technical specifications, new approach directives[21] only state the 'essential safety requirements', ranging from vague one-sentence formulas to a couple of pages annexed to the directives. Formally these essential requirements are to be sufficiently specific as 'to enable the certification bodies straight away to certify products as being in conformity'.[22] This, however, is widely acknowledged to be a legal fiction.[23]

The solution is found in the 'private governments' of technical standardization (Voelzkow, 1996).[24] The European standards bodies CEN and Cenelec draw up technical standards, compliance with which confers a 'presumption of conformity' with the essential requirements, reversing the burden of proof. These standards are thus coopted in European legislation. Compliance with them is officially voluntary though in practice highly recommendable given the costs involved with the inspection in certification procedures one has to go through without the 'presumption of conformity'.

There is no ready mass of standards from which to draw: the Commission requests and finances the production of specific standards as well as most of the infrastructure of CEN and Cenelec. However, it has hardly any official control over either the contents of the standards or the standard bodies themselves. As to the standards, their compatibility with the 'essential requirements' is ensured only by 'experts' hired by the Commission and attached to CEN and Cenelec. As to the standard bodies, their relations with the Commission are governed by a document which is not even a contract but is qualified as 'guidelines for cooperation',[25] in which the Commission basically gives a monopoly in the standards-setting business to CEN and Cenelec in exchange for a pledge to produce standards as requested by the Commission if possible within the desired time limit.

The set up is a strongly contested patchwork of private rules governing highly sensible issues of safety, health, and the environment (e.g. Falke, 1996). The Commission is well aware of this and even slightly embarrassed, and has tried to institutionalize the system proposing a Standardization Council presiding over the process consisting of representatives of national governments, standards bodies and Commission representatives (Commission, 1990). This proposal was laughed away by the standardization community, and the Commission shied away from its ambitions confining itself to 'assist and promote democratic self-management of standardization' (Commission, 1991).

The artificially created social law by the Commission in an effort at organized decentring thus proves to be too thick to be simply institutionalized in public legal frameworks. The denationalized non-state legality of technical standards has acquired by now far-reaching autonomy.

CONCLUSION

This chapter has made an effort to map out possibilities for concepts of legal pluralism in the study of different areas of European legal integration. It will not have gone unnoticed that I have not submitted any positive definite conception of legal pluralism able to explain in one brush the process of European integration. This chapter's tales of integration have tried to emphasize the importance of an open concept of legal pluralism as advocated by Ost and Van de Kerchove, shying away from determined territorial frames, from determined criteria of 'legal' identity and from determined relations of equivalence or independence between different legal systems (Van de Kerchove and Ost, 1994, pp. 144–5). Such a concept of legal pluralism should reveal at least that much could be learned about European legal integration by decentring two hallmarks of traditional legal discourse on Europe. One is 'law', or a certain conception of law, and the other is 'Europe', or a certain conception of Europe. Both are imprinted with a memory of statehood. I have argued that that 'state' no longer exists, a phenomenon quite independent from European integration. What I mean by decentring Europe then, is to accept that European legal integration is a process that takes place in a wider transformation of law and legal relations. The important question then becomes how European legal integration acts on and is acted upon by these other phenomena. This, I have argued, could end up teaching us a lot about 'law' and 'Europe' in European legal integration. Normatively, this should help us think, with David Kennedy,

> of the international not as a departure, but as continuation of the terrain upon which law participates in ongoing social, cultural, and economic conflicts and negotiations. Under such a conception, internationalization would have no necessary or particular impact on the disciplining and distributive activities of the institutional and normative fabric. If institutions other than the state are to be stressed in a new international order, the stress should be less on efforts to reinvigorate the public than on imagining a broader set of sites for negotiation and struggle over distribution and social policy (Kennedy, 1994).[26]

NOTES

1 Behind this 'innocent observation' lies quite a conceptual battle. Van de Kerchove and Ost chose this formulation, which I follow, because it accommodates not only a plurality of different systems but also systems that are different in *kind*. Moreover, 'this conception does not require any supplementary condition, neither in terms of the identity of subjects of those systems (in many cases those subjects will be different) nor in terms of difference of those systems' contents (their contents can be at least partially identical), nor in terms of relations between those systems (in particular, such a relationship is not necessarily one of equivalence or independence' (van de Kerchove and Ost, 1994, p. 134).

2 Case 26/62, [1963] ECR 10.

3 Case 6/64, [1964] ECR 585.

4 Joint Cases C-6/90 and C-9/90, [1991] ECR I-5357.

5 Case C-106/89 [1990] ECR I-4135.

6 BVerfGE 89, 155; English translation in *Common Market Law Reports* [1994] 57.

7 See Case 11/70, *Internationale Handelsgesellschaft*, [1970] ECR 1133; Case 4/73, *Nold II*, [1974] ECR 507, and, as regards the ECHR, Case 222/84, *Johnston*, [1986] ECR 1651.

8 Case 11/70, *supra*, motivation 3.

9 Council Directive 89/552/EEC on the coordination of certain provisions laid down by law, regulation or administrative action in Member States concerning the pursuit of television broadcasting activities, OJ L 298/23 1989.

10 Joint Cases 60 and 61/84, [1985] ECR 2604.

11 Case 260/89, [1991] ECR 2951.

12 In discussing classic legal pluralism, Roger Cotterrell speaks of 'intellectualized nostalgia' for 'the neighbourhood norms and customs of a pre-modern world replanned out of existence by the lawmaking activities of the state' (Cotterrell, 1995, pp. 306–7).

13 Commission Proposal for a Council Regulation on the statute for a European Cooperative Society, OJ C 99/17 1992.
14 See Montolio (1991).
15 Case T-61/89, [1992] ECR II-1931.
16 Ibid., motivations 46–8.
17 Ibid., motivation 52.
18 The British Presidency of the Council wasted no time in agreeing and adding its preference-order of instruments: 'Other things being equal, directives should be preferred to regulations and framework directives to detailed measures. Non-binding measures such as recommendations should be preferred where appropriate. Consideration should also be given where appropriate to the use of voluntary codes of conduct.' Conclusion of the Presidency, European Council, Edinburgh, 12 December 1992, Bulletin EC 12-1992.
19 Thomas Wilhelmsson has adapted this version to European law and completely turns European legal discourse on its head by submitting that harmonization of national law leads not so much to a new unity of law as to disintegration of national law (Wilhelmsson, 1995).
20 See Council Resolution of 7 May 1985 on a new approach to technical harmonization and standards, OJ C 136/1 1985.
21 See Council Directives 87/404/EEC on simple pressure vessels (OJ L 220/48 1987), 87/378/EEC on toy safety (OJ L 187/1 1987), 89/106 EEC on construction products (OJ L 40/12 1989), 89/336/EEC on electromagnetic compatibility (OJ 1989 L 139/19 1989), 89/392/EEC on machinery safety (OJ L183/1 1989), 89/686/EEC on personal protection equipment (OJ L 399/18 1989), 90/384/EEC on non-automatic weighing instruments (OJ L 189/1 1990), 90/385/EEC on implantable medical devices (OJ L 189/17 1990), 90/396/EEC on gas burners (OJ L 196/15 1990), 91/263/EEC on telecommunications terminals (OJ L 128/1 1991), 92/42 on hot-water boilers (OJ L 167/17 1992), 93/15 EEC on explosives for civil uses (OJ L 121/20 1993), 93/42/EEC on general medical devices (OJ L 169/1 1993), and Council and Parliament Directives 94/9/EC on protective systems in explosive atmospheres (OJ L 100/1 1994) and 94/25/EC on recreational craft (OJ L 164/15 1994).
22 See the Model Directive annexed to the New Approach Resolution, section B/III/1, OJ C 136/4 1985.
23 And necessarily so, since it would be quite impossible to formulate essential requirements with such precision. The Implantable Medical Devices directive, see *supra* n. 21, for example, offers the following 'essential requirement': 'The solutions adopted by the manufacturer for the design and construction of the devices must comply with safety principles taking account of the generally acknowledged state of the art'. (Annex 1, II, 6, OJ L 189/22 1990.)
24 A scheme to be extended to policies concerning biotechnology, the environment, foodstuffs and the range of new information technology services caught in the phrase 'information society'. See Commission (1995).
25 This precious document is available as CEN/Cenelec Memorandum No. 4.
26 Quote sadly left out of the final version of Kennedy (1994).

REFERENCES

Abel, Richard A. (ed.) (1982), *The Politics of Informal Justice*, 2 vols, New York: Free Press.

Arnaud, André-Jean (1991), *Pour une pensée juridique européenne*, Paris: PUF.

Arnaud, André-Jean (1995), 'Legal Pluralism and the Building of Europe', in H. Petersen and H. Zahle (eds), *Legal Polycentricity: Consequences of Pluralism in Law*, Aldershot: Dartmouth.

Belley, Jean-Guy (1986), 'L'État et la régulation juridique des sociétés globales. Pour une problématique du pluralisme juridique', *Sociologie et sociétés*, **18**.

Cohen, Joshua and Joel Rogers (1992), 'Secondary Associations and Democratic Governance', *Politics and Society*, **20**.

De Combrugghe, Dominique (1993), 'La Future Réglementation Communautaire sur le Statut de l'Association, de la Coopérative et de la Mutualité Européennes, *Revue de Marché Unique Commun*.

Commission of the European Communities (1984), *Television without Frontiers, Green Paper on the Establishment of the Common Market for Broadcasting, Especially by Satellite and Cable*, COM (84) 300 final.

Commission of the European Communities (1990), *Action for Faster Technological Integration in Europe*, Commission Green Paper on the Development of European Standardization, COM (90) 456 final.

Commission of the European Communities (1991), *Standardization in the European Community* (Follow-up to the Commission Green Paper), Communication from the Commission to the Council and the European Parliament, COM (91) 521 final.

Commission of the European Communities (1992), *The Principle of Subsidiarity*, Communication of the Commission to the Council and the European Parliament, SEC (92) 1990 final.

Commission of the European Communities (1995), *On the Broader Use of Standardization in Community Policy*, Communication of the Commission of the Council and the European Parliament, COM (95) 412 final.

Cotterrell, Roger (1995), *Law's Community*, Oxford: Clarendon.

Cover, Robert M. (1983), 'Foreword: Nomos and Narrative', *Harvard Law Review*, **97**.

Curtin, Deirdre (1993), 'The Constitutional Structure of the Union: A Europe of Bits and Pieces', *Common Market Review*, **30**.

Dabormida, Renato (1989), 'Derecho Cooperativo Europeo y Ordenamiento Comunitario: ¿Hacía la Armonización o la Uniformación de las Legislaciones en el Seno de la CEE?, *CIRIEC España*, **7**.

Dezalay, Yves (1992), *Marchands de droit. La restructuration de l'ordre juridique international par les multinationals du droit*, Paris: Fayard.

Ehrlich, Eugen (1913), *Fundamental Principles of the Sociology of Law*, Cambridge Mass.: Harvard University Press.

Van Empel, Martijn (1992), 'The 1992 Programme: Interaction between Legislator and Judiciary', *Legal Issues of European Integration*.

Everling, Ulrich (1994), 'The *Maastricht* Judgment of the German Federal Constitutional Court and its Significance for the Development of the European Union', *Yearbook of European Law*, **14**.
Falke, Josef (1996), *The Role of Non-governmental Organizations in the Regulation of Risks to Health and the Environment*, EUI Working Paper RSC 96/9, Florence: European University Institute.
Fitzpatrick, Peter (1984), 'Law and Societies', *Osgoode Hall Law Journal*, **22**.
Fitzpatrick, Peter (1992), *The Mythology of Modern Law*, London: Routledge.
Foucault, Michel (1980), 'Two Lectures', in M. Foucault, *Power/Knowledge*, C. Gordon (ed.), New York: Pantheon.
Galanter, Marc (1981), 'Justice in many rooms', in M. Cappelletti (ed.), *Access to Justice and the Welfare State*, Alphen a/d Rijn: Sijthoff.
Galanter, Marc (1992), 'Law Abounding: Legalisation Around the North-Atlantic', *Modern Law Review*, **55**.
Gibson, James L. and Gregory A. Caldeira (1996), 'The Legal Cultures of Europe', *Law and Society Review*, **30** (1).
Griffiths, John (1986), 'What is legal pluralism?', *Journal of Legal Pluralism*, **24**.
Gurvitch, Georges (1932), *L'Idée du Droit Social*, Paris: Sirey.
Harding, Christopher (1992), 'Who Goes to Court in Europe? An Analysis of Litigation against the European Community', *European Law Review*, **17**.
Harlow, Carol (1992), 'Towards a Theory of Access to the European Court of Justice', *Yearbook of European Law*, **12**.
Henry, Stuart (1983), *Private Justice – Towards Integrated Theorizing in the Sociology of Law*, London: Routledge & Kegan Paul.
Höland, Armin (1993), 'Die Rechtssoziologie und der unbekannte Kontinent Europa', *Zeitschrift für Rechtssoziologie*, **14**.
Hondius, Frits W. (1988), 'Regulating Transfrontier Television – The Strasbourg Option', *Yearbook of European Law*, **8**.
Jacobi, Bertil, and Peter L. Vesterdorf (1993), 'Co-operative societies and the Community rules on competition', *European Law Review*, **18**.
Joerges, Christian (1989), 'Paradoxes of Deregulatory Strategies at Community Level', in G. Majone (ed.), *Deregulation or Re-regulation? Regulatory Reform in Europe and the United States*, London: Pinter.
Joerges, Christian (1997), *Scientific Expertise in Social Regulation and the European Court of Justice: Legal Frameworks for Denationalized Governance Structures*, in Ch. Joerges, K.-H. Ladeur and E. Vos (eds), *Integrating Scientific Expertise into Regulatory Decision-Making*, Baden-Baden: Nomos.
Kennedy, David (1994), 'The International Style in Postwar Law and Policy', *Utah Law Review*.
Van der Kerchove, Michel and François Ost (1994), *Legal System between Order and Disorder*, Oxford: Clarendon Press.
Lang, John Temple (1990), 'Community Constitutional Law: Article 5 EEC Treaty', *Common Market Law Review*, **27**.
Lenaerts, Koen and Patrick van Ypersele (1994), 'Le principe de subsidiarité et son contexte: étude le l'article 3B du Traité CE', *Cahiers de Droit Européen*, **30**.

Luhmann, Niklas (1993), *Das Recht der Gesellschaft*, Frankfurt: Suhrkamp.
Macaulay, Stewart (1986), 'Private Government', in L. Lipson and S. Wheeler (eds), *Law and the Social Sciences*, New York: Russell Sage Foundation.
MacCormick, Neil (1993), 'Beyond the sovereign state', *Modern Law Review*, **56**.
MacCormick, Neil (1996), 'Liberalism, Nationalism and the Post-sovereign State', *Political Studies*, **44**.
Mancini, G. Federico (1989), 'The Making of a Constitution for Europe', *Common Market Law Review*, **26**.
Mayntz, Renate (1991), *Modernization and the Logic of Interorganizational Networks*, MPIGF-Discussion paper 91/8, Köln, Max-Planck Institut für Gesellschaftsforschung.
Mayntz, Renate (1993), 'Governing Failures and the Problem of Governability: Some Comments on a Theoretical Paradigm', in J. Kooiman (ed.), *Modern Governance – New Government-Society Interactions*, London: Sage.
Merry, Sally Engle (1988), 'Legal Pluralism', *Law and Society Review*, **22**.
Micklitz, Hans-W. (1991), 'Organisierte Rechtsdurchsetzung im Binnenmarkt', in G. Winter, (ed.), *Die Europäischen Gemeinschaften und das Öffentliche*, ZERP-Diskussionspapier 7/91, Bremen: Zentrum für Europäische Rechtspolitik.
Montolio Hernándex, José María (1991), 'Estatuto Cooperativo Europeo', *REVESCO*, **59**.
Moore, Sally Falk (1973), 'Law and Social Change: The Semi-Autonomous Field as an Appropriate Subject of Study', *Law and Society Review*, **7**.
Reich, Norbert (1986), *Förderung und Schutz diffuser interessen durch die Europäischen Gemeinschaften*, Baden-Baden: Nomos.
Sarat, Austin and Susan Silbey (1988), 'The Pull of the Policy Audience', *Law and Policy*, **10**.
Scharpf, Fritz W. (1994), 'Community and Autonomy. Multilevel Policy-Making in the European Community', *Journal of European Public Policy*, **1** (2).
Schepel, Harm and Rein Wesseling (1997), 'The Legal Community: Judges, Lawyers, Officials and Clerks in the Writing of Europe', *European Law Journal*, **3**.
Schmitter, Philippe C. (1992), 'Representation and the Future Euro-Polity', *Staatswissenschaften und Staatspraxis*, **3**.
Schwartz, Ivo E. (1986), 'Broadcasting and the EEC Treaty', *European Law Review*, **11**.
Schwartz, Ivo E. (1989), 'Fernsehen ohne Grenzen: Zur Effektivität und zum Verhältnis von EG-Richtlinie und Europarats-Konvention', *Europarecht*, **24**.
Schwartz, Ivo E. (1990), 'La liberté d'expression (Art. 10 CEDH) et la libre prestation de services (Art. 59 Traité CEE) dans le domaine de la radiodiffusion telévisuelle', in A. Cassese and A. Clapham (eds), *Transfrontier Television in Europe: The Human Rights Dimension*, Baden-Baden: Nomos.
Selznick, Philip (1992), *The Moral Commonwealth – Social Theory and the Promise of Community*, Berkeley: University of California Press.
Shaw, Jo (1996), 'European Union Legal Studies in Crisis? Towards a New Dynamic', *Oxford Journal of Legal Studies*, **16** (2).
Snyder, Francis (1990), *New Directions in European Community Law*, London: Weidenfeld & Nicolson.

Snyder, Francis (1993), 'The Effectiveness of European Law: Institutions, Processes, Tools and Techniques', *Modern Law Review*, **56**.

Snyder, Francis (1994), 'Soft Law and Institutional Practice in the European Community', in S. Martin (ed.), *The Construction of Europe – Essays in Honour of Emile Noël*, Deventer: Kluwer.

Sousa Santos, Boaventura de (1985), 'On Modes of Production of Law and Social Power', *International Journal for the Sociology of Law*, **13**.

Sousa Santos, Boaventura de (1992), 'State, Law and Community in the World System: An Introduction', *Social and Legal Studies*, **1**.

Sousa Santos, Boaventura de (1995), *Toward a New Common Sense – Law, Science and Politics in the Paradigmatic Transition*, London: Routledge.

Streeck, Wolfang (1983), 'Interessenverbände als Hindernis und Vollzugsträger öffentlicher Politik', in F.W. Scharpf and M. Brockmann (eds.), *Institutionelle Bedingungen der Arbeitsmarkt- und Beschäftigungspolitik*, Frankfurt: Campus.

Streeck, Wolfgang (1992), 'Inclusion and Secession: Questions to the Boundaries of Associative Democracy', *Politics and Society*, **20**.

Streeck, Wolfgang and Philippe C. Schmitter (1985), 'Community, Market, State – and Associations? The Prospective Contribution of Interest Governance to Social Order', in W. Streeck and P.C. Schmitter (eds), *Private Interest Government: Beyond Market and State*, London: Sage.

Streeck, Wolfgang, and Philippe C. Schmitter (1991), 'From National Corporatism to Transnational Pluralism', *Politics and Society*, **19**.

Tamanaha, Brian Z. (1993), 'The Folly of the "Social Scientific" Concept of Legal Pluralism', *Journal of Law and Society*, **20**.

Teubner, Gunther (1989), 'How the Law thinks: Toward a Constructivist Epistemology of Law', *Law and Society Review*, **23**.

Teubner, Gunther (1991), 'Autopoiesis and steering: how politics profit from the normative surplus of capital', in In R.T. 't Veld *et al.* (eds), *Autopoiesis and Configuration Theory: New Approaches to Societal Steering*, Dordrecht/Boston/ London: Kluwer.

Teubner, Gunther (1992), 'The Two Faces of Janus: Rethinking Legal Pluralism', *Cardozo Law Review*, **13**.

Teubner, Gunther (1997), 'Global Bukowina: Legal Pluralism in the World Society', in G. Teubner (ed.) *Global Law Without a State*, Aldershot: Dartmouth.

Teubner, Gunther (1993), 'The "State" of Private Networks: The Emerging Legal Regime of Polycorporatism in Germany', *Brigham Young University Law Review*.

Teubner, Gunther (1996), *Breaking Frames: The Global Interplay of Legal and Social Systems*, paper presented at the Joint LSA/RCSL Meeting, Glasgow, July 1996.

Teubner, Gunther and Helmut Willke (1984), 'Kontext und Autonomie: Gesellschaftliche Selbststeuerung durch reflexives Recht', *Zeitschrift für Rechtssoziologie*, **5**.

Toth, A.G. (1994), 'A Legal Analysis of Subsidiarity', in D. O'Keeffe and P.M. Twomey (eds), *Legal Issues of the Maastricht Treaty*, London: Chancery.

Trubeck, David M. and John P. Esser (1989), 'Critical Empiricism' and 'American

Critical Legal Studies: Paradox, Program, or Pandora's Box?', in D.M. Trubek and Ch. Joerges (eds), *Critical Legal Thought: An American-German Debate*, Baden-Baden: Nomos.

Voelzkow, Helmut (1996), *Private Regierungen in der Techniksteuerung-Eine sozialwissenschaftliche Analyse der technischen Normung*, Frankfurt a.M.: Campus.

Ward, Ian (1995), 'Identity and Difference: The European Union and Postmodernism', in Jo Shaw and Gillian More (eds), *New Legal Dynamics of European Union*, Oxford: Clarendon Press.

Wieacker, Franz (1990), 'Foundations of European Legal Culture', *American Journal of Comparative Law*, **38**.

Wilhelmsson, Thomas (1995), 'Legal Integration as Disintegration of National Law', in H. Petersen and H. Zahle (eds), *Legal Polycentricity: Consequences of Pluralism in Law*, Aldershot: Dartmouth.

Willke, Helmut (1986), 'The Tragedy of the State – Prolegomena to a Theory of the State in Polycentric Society', *Archiv für Rechts- und Sozialphilosphie*, **72**.

Willke, Helmut (1992), *Ironie des Staates*, Frankfurt: Suhrkamp.

4 Europe's Emprise: Symbolic Economy and the Postmodern Condition

James Henry Bergeron

INTRODUCTION

The critical movement in European legal studies, engaging as it does with the current ideas and topical discourses of other disciplines, is treading a path which leads almost inexorably to the question of European law's 'postmodernism'. This 'postmodern question' has been raised in critiques of the European Union which sees its crisis of legitimacy as grounded in a waning of Enlightenment optimism (Weiler, 1996; Smart, 1992) or perceive in its institutional complexity or fragmentation the elements of a postmodern political institution (Ward, 1996; Ruggie, 1993, Arnaud, 1991; Sousa Santos, 1992; cf. Curtin 1993). This should not surprise considering the preoccupations of EU law with teleological reasoning and the creation of a jurisprudence which straddles the fault lines of state and individual, politics and economy, culture and commodity, all products of Enlightenment rationality which have been subject to the postmodern gaze.

In contrast, I argue in Chapter 1 for an interpretation of the EU as a robust expression of the modernist faith, conceiving the jurisprudence of the Court of Justice as an ambitious attempt to bolster the flagging myth of modernity by elevating it to a higher and more abstract plane, while using that myth as the organizing principle of European Community law. From this perspective, the institutional fragmentation of the EU does not essentially deny its individualizing, universalizing, and ultimately modernist calling. Indeed, as Fitzpatrick points out, such incompleteness and fragmentation more deeply grounds the claims of Europeanism by acting as a spur to progress (Chapter 2, this volume).

That answer is not the whole answer, since the EU does exist in a place and a period of time when significant changes are occurring in the perception of meaning, culture and identity, changes often referred to as postmodern in nature. But the relevance of the postmodern perspective, I will contend below, consists in explaining the trajectory of social structures and forces below the 'level' of European institutions, such as language and symbolism, as well as those far beyond, such as capitalism and globalization. This is not a 'postmodernism' which constitutes an epistemic break with modernity, so much as one which flows out of the logic of modernity. In this sense, the 'postmodern condition' – modernity's child – represents a context within which the EU exists, but against which the EU defines and justifies itself, and which it attempts to incorporate into a new 'modernity'.

As Fitzpatrick and I have argued, the metanarrative of modernity used in the creation of the EU contains within it an alterity in the form of the nation. This alterity, it will be contended below, is an essential but unacknowledged element in the operation of the European internal market where an ever greater number of goods are mythically inscribed with the lineaments of nationality. This inscription of nationality is achieved through the manipulation of forms of mythic speech and visual representation, and realized in symbols or traces of 'nation' as a form of commodity. But it is equally inscribed in the negative inference of nation as a restraint from which the commodity is liberated by virtue of EU law. The EU structures trade as a free trade between nations, involving goods legally characterized by their free movement across national boundaries, liberated from the claims of nation. Such developments are a regional reflection, it is suggested, of the global integration of aesthetic and cultural production into commodity production which Jameson sees as the dominant cultural form of late capitalism (Jameson, 1991). Although driven by the 'logic' of modernity and made possible only by modernity's operative myths of reason and progress, the internal market engages with the 'postmodern' condition inasmuch as the structure of global production which the EU and its market now inhabits increasingly requires the subject matter of exchange to be a commodity symbolically inscribed with, among other things, the sign of 'nation'.

The role of EU law well illustrates these dynamics. EU law is thoroughly modern in its function of opening markets, expanding the legal realm of its rational European legal subject and breaking down national barriers to the production and acquisition of goods. This modernity is at its height where the law encounters commodities whose inscribed national symbolism is protected by pre-existing law, as is the case with national restrictions on the quality marking and appellation of origin of goods. In such cases, discussed below, the Court of Justice redefines, universalizes and 'Europeanizes' the symbol, which is reified onto an even more abstract plane of 'pure' nationality. The Commission and Council, in contrast, treat the symbolic commodity as a form of intellectual property right and limit the symbol to particular national producers. Although contradictory in terms of market liberalization, both approaches are 'modern' in the sense that they seek to achieve an unambiguous connection between commodity and symbol, achieved through a reification of nationality, in the face of a growing cultural heterogeneity which calls the possibility of nation into question.

This 'postmodern' symbolic economy has become essential to the operation and legitimacy of the European internal market. The internal market allows the supra-nation to preserve, in mythic purity, the 'nation' which is Europe's Other but to which Europe always refers. And the rational structure of exchange mythically inscribes the irrational desire for nation, as well as other objects of culture, with the sign of reason and civilization. Unlike all other customs unions, only the EU has been able to present globalization, the decline of national and regional hegemony, cultural pluralism, hybridity, and so on, as the result of a rational, constitutional design – as a new form of coherent identity – rather than that of a global capitalism and postmodern culture run wild. The cultural effects of globalization, of which the internal market is one instance, are subsumed within an overarching Western claim to power and rationality denied to non-Western Others, for whom the same cultural effects are seen as the result of natural and irrepressible forces.

After laying the groundwork for discussion in an explanation of how I am employing the contentious language of modernity and postmodernity, the analysis will proceed by pondering the relationship between symbol, commodity and myth and will lay out a semiological explanation of the symbolic economy. The symbolic economy is then considered in terms of its historical context and in its relations with modernist and postmodernist forms of cultural production. Finally, the symbolic nature of the European internal market and the role of EC law will be addressed.

MODERNITY, POSTMODERNITY AND THE MARKET

It is important to define at the outset of this study the sense in which the concepts 'modernity' and 'postmodernity' are being used. Considering that a huge literature has been developed exploring these contestable concepts, I can make no attempt here to defend exhaustively a particular interpretation, and seek only to address those aspects of modernity and postmodernity that I have adopted and which are of most relevance to this study. 'Postmodernity' is here used to describe a disenchantment with the philosophical structures and grand narratives of modernity, and a consequent awareness of the implosion of concepts of unitary being, ultimate truth and rationality (Lyotard,

1983). Linked to this philosophical change, and it is submitted laying the foundation for it, is a change in the mode of cultural production. As Jameson puts it, the distinctiveness of postmodernism is in its meaning and social function in the economic system where 'aesthetic production today has become integrated into commodity production generally' (Jameson, 1991, 56). This expansion of the reach of the market – Jameson's 'cultural logic of late capitalism' – relates in turn to a recognition of the growing commodification of cultural forms (Friedman, 1994), a depthlessness or superficiality in all cultural objects with the resulting impossibility of an avant-garde critique of the existing order (Jameson, 1991) and the centrality of pastiche or simulacra in cultural production (Friedman, 1994; Jameson, 1991; Baudrillard, 1993).

'Modernity', by contrast, implies a form of identification based on a structure of alterity and contained within a global and capitalist economic order. As a form of identification, modernity relates to a structure of thought, self-consciously Western, which views the isolated individual as a transcendent and universal being in a path of infinite progression, a being in relation to an Other which is not (Fitzpatrick, 1992). It combines an explicit attachment to instrumental rationality of means with a denial of the emotional, irrational and often collective nature of human ends, a denial particularly strong in high-modernist discourses such as economics and law.

Classical economics views the market as a process whereby rational, self-interested individuals enter into exchange relationships as a means of satisfying specific material needs and maximizing utility in a competitive environment governed by the laws of supply and demand. Likewise, the law of contract defines exchange as a rational meeting of minds of the parties. It is not for the court, so the mantra goes, to make bargains for the parties and therefore the law tries to avoid an enquiry into the objects of exchange. It is enough that the parties value them.

The nature of these 'needs' is seldom defined, the problem being plastered over by the concept of individual 'utility' and an intimation that asking the question somehow invades the sovereign liberty of the individual to make 'rational' choices (cf. Jevons, 1870). The contradiction lies in that these needs most often take the form (as Hobbes noted) of pride, status and power, or else in the idolatrous pursuit of sexual arousal, national pride, aesthetic pleasure, or other forms of emotive attachment to objects which is often considered cult-worship or iconolatry when practised by non-Europeans, but receives the more civilized name of culture at home.

At the heart of modern economic theory, then, is a clash between a proposed universal human rationality and the need for particular subjectivity in the pursuit of ends which cannot be deemed rational, a contradiction mediated through recourse to the myth of the individual. This myth functions by transferring the presumed 'objectivity' of the individual onto the material world itself, which is considered to possess fixed and objective meaning, while subjectivity is allowed to function as the individual's utility-maximizing choice. The desire of the individual is transposed onto the object of desire, which is then viewed as possessing this characteristic as an inherent, natural quality (cf. Marx, 1974a, 1974b; Durkheim, 1961). Market relations in modernity are thus made to appear as the intersection of nature and reason in that the economic process is based on a relationship between a subjective rationality which is common to humanity yet which is not culturally or historically contingent and a natural world of objective material goods.

The transposition of human irrationality onto the material world is part of the larger phenomenon of a separation of the concept of self from its representation. As will be discussed below, this separation constitutes a distinctive mode of cultural production in modernity which allows for the emergence of public and private space, the breakdown of ascribed hierarchies of social rank and the freeing of previously restricted symbols of wealth and status which become commodities in themselves (Friedman, 1994; Baudrillard, 1993). Just as the myth of progress is founded on a temporalized alterity based upon the myth of the transcendent individual, this separation of self and representation relies on the mythical function of symbols to ground free-floating values in material goods, and thus to allow the reification of human irrationality as inherent qualities of material objects.

Alterity is central to the structure of modernity, indeed it is modernity's defining attribute. As Fitzpatrick has pointed out, the construction of the individual is possible only through the negation of the primitive Other, the recourse to a myth of temporalized alterity being the only means by which the contradictions inherent in the transcendent claims of that individual could be resolved (Fitzpatrick, 1992). The two inherent contradictions of greatest concern here are that between rational means and irrational ends, and the mediation between the self and its representation through symbolism. In the context of modernity, the mythical reconciliation of these depends upon the myth of progress, based on an assumption of an inherent rationality which is not yet fully achieved, to privilege the space of reason and self over that of desire and representation. And rationality requires, ironically, the symbolic infusion of economic life.

Thus the alchemy of modernity subsumes attributes contradicting the high-modernist vision of rationality, transcendence and universality, transubstantiating the lead of 'primitivism' into the gold of civilized behaviour. Hobbes's unruly and possessive individual in the state of nature becomes the civil merchant capitalist of the commonwealth, while the modernist mode of cultural production turns culture into fashion, iconolatry becoming civilized under the sign of rational exchange. In the context of the EU, the colonization of modernity as a political model consists of appropriating this high-modernist vision for the legal subject of EU law, relegating the nation to an alterity from which the EU proceeds (see generally Chapters 1 and 2 of this volume). In this way the European legal order replicates the myth of progress. But since the idea of nation is also linked to culture and reason – a contradiction mediated again through myth – nation is also implicated in the alterity of reason/desire and culture/commodity. It is with these latter aspects of the modernist myth that this chapter will deal.

SIGN, SYMBOL AND MYTH

The separation of the concept of self from its representation founds both the liberal vision of economic rationality as well as its semiological critique (Jameson, 1991). Both are plagued by the essential arbitrariness of value caused by the separation of essence and appearance. But while the liberal vision avoids the issue by transposing culture into nation as described above, structuralism and post-structuralism reconceived the space between matter and meaning as inhabited by the mythical structure of symbolism.

In his *Course in General Linguistics* (1974), Ferdinand Saussure posited the structural separation of language into signifiers and signifieds. Rejecting an essential or absolute relation between words and meaning, semiology pursued the search for meaning in terms of relations between signs. Thus 'bread' signifies a foodstuff made from wheat. But it equally depending on the cultural context, signifies life, Christian redemption, wealth or prosperity etc. As a signifier, 'bread' is both under-inscribed and over-inscribed with meaning: under-inscribed in that the signifier has no essential or absolute signified; over-inscribed in terms of the multitude of significations the same signifier is capable of carrying.

For Roland Barthes, this structural separation between signifier and signified is the essential condition for mythic speech:

> … myth is a peculiar system, in that it is constructed from a semiological chain which existed before it: it is a *second-order semiological system*. That which is a sign (namely the associative total of a concept and an image) in the first system, becomes a mere signifier in the second … Myth sees in them only the same raw material; their unity is that they all come down to the status of a mere language. Whether it deals with alphabetical or pictorial writing, myth wants to see in them only a sum of signs, a global sign, the final term of a first semiological chain. And it is precisely this final term which will become the first term of the greater system which it builds and of which it is only a part. (Barthes, 1972, pp. 112–3)

To illustrate using Barthes's own example, a magazine cover depicting a Black man in French army uniform smartly saluting the French tricolour contains both a first-order and second-order semiological system. In the first-order chain of signifiers, the Black man, military uniform, the flag and the salute signify complex and contradictory values, histories, geographies, biographies and so on. But in the second-order system – at the level of myth – the signified becomes the sign of empire, 'a mixture of Frenchness and militariness' (Barthes, 1972, p. 119). In shifting from the first- to second-order chain, the signified of the first chain becomes distorted, radically reduced, made artificial or 'placed at a distance' as Barthes puts it. The full meaning of the first-order sign is not directly precluded or destroyed – it is still there – but becomes subordinated to the motivations of the second-order sign which reduces the complex contingency of the first-order signified. 'When it becomes form, the meaning leaves its contingency behind; it empties itself, it becomes impoverished, history evaporates, only the letter remains' (Barthes, 1972, p. 120). It is this function of absorbing first-order signs and distorting their meaning in a second-order symbolic which is the essential aspect of mythical speech:

> We reach here the very principle of myth: it transforms history into nature. We now understand why, *in the eyes of the myth-consumer*, the intention, the adhomination of the concept [the second order signified] can remain manifest without appearing to have an interest in the matter: what causes mythical speech to be uttered is perfectly explicit, but it is immediately frozen into something natural; it is not read as a motive, but as a reason. (Barthes, 1972, pp. 129–30) [his emphasis]

And in so doing, the signification of the myth is transformed from value to fact:

> ... any semiological system is a system of values; now the myth-consumer takes the signification for a system of facts: myth is read as a factual system, whereas it is but a semiological system. (Barthes, 1972, p. 131)

This alchemic property of the myth, or second-order symbolic, to transform a perception of constructed value into one of natural fact, is of wide application in human affairs, comprehending virtually all forms of writing and representation which involve (and all such forms necessarily involve) signs which are first-order symbolics. But this property is of particular importance, for our purposes at least, in the way it infuses signs and signifieds where the sign is a physical object or representation, and the signified connotes irrational desires such as status, nation and identity in terms like Frenchness, military-ness, or Europeanness. In those cases, it is the myth-effect which allows for second-order concepts of the -ness sort to appear as concrete meaning, as natural, as facts. It allows us to say, in the context of a motivated representation or context, that a certain good, High Tea for example, connotes Englishness, contains Englishness as a natural quality of its being and implies that Englishness is itself a fact. It is this process of reification which allows the irrational to be transposed onto nature as inherent qualities of material goods, thus propping up the myth of the rational individual. And in so doing, reducing the underlying complexity of the symbol (High Tea is impossible without tea leaves from Asia and Africa, sugar from Jamaica, silver and porcelain from God knows where, and so on) to an abstract purity.

The argument for a symbolic nature of goods explains their attractiveness to the consumer in ways which go beyond mainstream economics. It is common knowledge in the advertising industry that investment in 'brand image' will raise the price which a commodity will normally command, an image only tangentially related to the 'utilitarian' definition of the product. In effect, the product (and particularly the brand-name or trade-mark) becomes the signifier in relation to the image as second-order signified, and takes on what Baudrillard calls a sign-value (Baudrillard, 1972).

To take a current example from British television, a Dulux paint advertisement shows a nice-looking, middle-aged (middle-class) man painting the exterior of his eighteenth century Georgian farm-house deep in rural England, swearing 'to do right by these four walls' to the background strains of Holst's 'I Vow to Thee My Country'. Dulux becomes the signifier for a complex of signifieds – the landscape, the house, the music, each with its own complex and contingent genealogies, histories and associations, but together and in the context of the advertisement and its motivation, these are subsumed by the overwhelming second-order symbolic of Englishness which now inhabits Dulux.

The assumption of the Dulux advertisement is that people will recognize the cultural clues provided, will read the myth and will desire to associate themselves with the myth's signified by purchasing this product over others. Because the myth allows its second-order symbolic of English-ness to be perceived as natural, as a fact, it becomes possible to possess that symbolic as property in the ownership of the commodity, achieved through rational exchange. In effect, the rationality of the means of acquisition provides the motivated context within which the character of that which is coveted is transformed. Within the myth of modernity, the act of acquisition rationalizes or civilizes what would otherwise be seen as an irrational desire for objects, and by a logical inversion, establishes the reality of the symbolic entity (Englishness) as a fact. Instead of an acknowledged instability or complexity, a pure image of rationality and a pure symbolic image of desire is created. This results in the individual being driven to 'possess' the symbol, and using rational, that is, economic, means to do so. Thus the myth of modernity, the law of exchange and the structure of symbolism combine to establish the foundation for a symbolic economy.

THE STRUCTURE OF THE SYMBOLIC ECONOMY

Having laid the semiological foundations of a symbolic economy, it is necessary to turn our attention to its operation in history. The presence of a pervasive symbolism in society does not necessarily imply a symbolic economy, or always the same kind of symbolic economy. A key factor which determines that economy is the way in which signs interact both with the changing nature of production and the structure of society.

A central aspect of modernity has been the collapse of the aristocratic unity of social status and appearance, the decline of an order in which signs were immovably attached to persons (Friedman, 1994, p. 216; Baudrillard, 1993). Thus costume, titles, names, heraldry, succession, even land at first, exist as signs of an immutable social order defined and protected by law. In such a system, there is no symbolic economy as there can be no symbolic exchange. The breakdown of this unity facilitates the emergence of a concept of the 'self' which is distinct from its social representation, and with it, modern fashion.

> The counterfeit (and, simultaneously, fashion) is born with the Renaissance, with the destruction of the feudal order by the bourgeois order and the emergence of overt competition at the level of sign distinction. There is no fashion in a caste society, nor in a society based on rank, since assignation is absolute and there is no class mobility. Signs are protected by a prohibition which ensures their total clarity and confers an unequivocal status on each. Counterfeit is not possible in the ceremonial, unless in the form of black magic or sacrilege, which is precisely what makes the mixing of signs punishable as a serious offence against the very order of things. (Baudrillard, 1993, p. 50)

In bourgeois society, the struggle for access to signs of status reflects the prevailing ideology of market competition. The sign becomes emancipated and begins to 'move'.

With the advert of Fordism another major change occurs in the structure of consumption. The advent of mass production could be sustainable only given an ordered system of mass consumption, mostly of luxury products, directed by a grammar of signs. As a result, the mode of 'conspicuous consumption' which Veblen had attributed only to the upper classes in a nineteenth-century capitalist economy now became extended to the whole of society (Veblen, 1973; Baudrillard, 1970). Thus society produces needs through socialization, managing consumer demand and stabilizing the mass economy. Consumption replaces production as the driving force in the creation of social status and identity.

This is also the period of European economic hegemony. Under that hegemony, it was European production which created a creolization or hybridization of cultures around the globe. But European societies themselves, controlling the terms of trade to their advantage, could incorporate such foreign cultural products as they allowed in as curiosities within the grand narrative of Western superiority (Friedman, 1994, p. 100)

For Baudrillard, the advent of mass production leads to a qualitative change in the nature of commodities.

> A new generation of signs and objects arises with the Industrial Revolution – signs with no caste tradition that will never have known restrictions on their status, and which will never have to be *counterfeits*, since from the outset they will be products on a gigantic scale. The problem of their specificity and their origin is no longer posed: technics is their origin, they have meaning only within the dimension of the industrial simulacrum. (Baudrillard, 1993, p. 55) [his emphasis]

Unlike the pre-industrial production of unique goods, the commodity-form of mass production is an object which is identical to all other objects in the production process. Within a mode of production based on this identicality of all objects in the series, each series must be identifiable by some signifier which can uniquely identify all objects in the series. The signifier can no longer be the original commodity-form itself, it must take the form of an attaching sign. Further, the increasing similarity of competing series of goods, again brought about by the mode of mass production, requires a much greater emphasis to be placed on symbolic aspects of the goods, a need met by the tradename, trademark, advertising slogan and other signs for the series. Thus identicality makes the symbolic more, not less important. Meaning becomes not under-inscribed but over-inscribed. Consider how ineffective the great bulk of current advertising for beer, soft drinks, automobiles and airlines would be without the sign, with reliance only on the material form of the good. Although still attached to a commodity-series, the signifier is becoming no longer the commodity-form itself but the name, image or appellation.

The transformation of the commodity signifier is completed by the emergence of the 'postmodern' cultural condition. The advent of multi-media advertising, computer imagery, and so forth allows for an aggregation of symbolic messages, of sexuality, nation, status, beauty, identity and others almost *ad infinitum*, attached to the signifier. Now over-inscribed with meaning, the signifier attaches itself directly to the intended second-order symbolic (for example, 'Dulux' = Englishness) with little reference to the paint. This process is aggravated by the globalization of production and the radical expansion of commodity production into the realm of culture generally, identified by Jameson as the cultural dominant of late capitalism (Jameson, 1991). In its effort to further expand the reach of the global market, the new form of cultural capitalism which emerges in the post-1945 period brings together cultures, communications technology and global commodity markets to inscribe commodities with diverse cultural and national symbolisms.

> What has happened is that aesthetic production today has become integrated into commodity production generally: the frantic economic urgency of producing fresh waves of ever more novel-seeming goods (from clothing to aeroplanes), at ever increasing rates of turnover, now assigns an increasingly essential structural function and position to aesthetic innovation and experimentation. (Jameson, 1991, pp. 4–5)

This process of direct valorization of the signifier, linked with the hegemonic expansion of the economic order into all forms of cultural production, is reflected in Baudrillard's third-order simulacrum – a replacement of series production with generation through models.

> We are dealing with third-order simulacra here. There is no more counterfeiting of an original, as there was in the first order, and no more pure series as there were in the second; there are models from which all forms proceed according to modulated differences. Only affiliation to the model has any meaning, since nothing proceeds in accordance with its end any more, but issues instead from the model, the 'signifier of reference', functioning as a foregone, and the only credible, conclusion. (Baudrillard, 1993, p. 56)

The growing over-inscription of meaning in commodity signifiers under the cultural dominant of late capitalism, made possible by modern communication and information techniques, has led to an autonomous existence for the sign separate from its former commodity-form. It is the sign which is now primary, as a model from which forms proceed and are modulated. As Debord puts it, 'the image has become the final form of commodity reification' (Debord, 1968, cf. 1990). The name now precedes the thing. This is (again) made possible by the myth-effect, wherein the first-order signifier of a commodity ('Pepsi') connoting, health, youth, fun etc., in effect naturalizes those qualities, as facts, inherent in the sign itself. It is this 'autonomous' existence for the sign which allows Pepsi or Guinness to launch their series of designer sportswear, Singaporean black markets to sell bulk quantities of copied Izod and Ralph Lauren polo shirt insignias for sewing onto 'common grade' clothing, Manhattan street sales of fake Rolex watches to knowing purchasers, or the earth-moving equipment firm Caterpillar to produce an extensive series of shoes and leather goods under its logo. When the Lexus automobile was first advertised on British television, without any reference to, or depiction of, an automobile in the advertisement, a new threshold was crossed in the direct commodification of abstract signifiers. The symbolic economy has reached fruition, in that the movement of goods is replaced by the movement of signs.

Globalization under this late-capitalist cultural dominant is no respecter of Western sensitivities or cultural values. On the contrary, the pre-existence of a modernist identity-space is an essential element in perceiving the postmodern condition (or at least the West's postmodern condition), because the postmodern can have no meaning without the modern as its referent. Since the symbolic 'quality' of material objects are mere transpositions of the irrational within the myth of modernity, a universalization and naturalization of particular cultures, a growing cultural pluralism is perceived instead as a radical instability and heterogeneity in the meaning of objects and things generally. In the context of the West, this anxiety reflects the declining economic hegemony of Europe, and the encounter with new cultural products (and peoples) from America, Asia, Africa and elsewhere that cannot be rationalized within the pre-existing notions of one's own 'national' identity or the (by definition inferior) identity of the Other (Friedman, 1994, pp. 86–7, cf. Bell, 1976).

These developments have important implications for law. One role of law in modernity is to regulate commodity exchange, on the assumption of a naturally affixing signifier that is not itself the product of creation through investment and advertising. With the rise of the autonomous sign as a species of property and form of capital, the law must expand its function to protect the sign as a commodity 'form' in itself. This action brings the law to the coal-face of the postmodern condition, since it must either acknowledge the constructed and unstable nature or the signifier in its efforts to protect it, or else absorb and incorporate that instability within a claim to stability provided by law's own modernist metanarrative. The latter is the project of the internal market, which attempts to inscribe a reified 'nation' into the structure of the law, as the Other of modernist rationality. To those developments we now turn.

THE NATION IN LAW TRIUMPHANT: EUROPE'S SYMBOLIC MARKET

The formal project of European integration works on the premises of the myth of modernity. The abolition of tariff and non-tariff barriers, and harmonization of economic regulation, is expected to result in a widening of the common market and efficiency savings which will magnify the material possibilities offered to the utility-maximizing consumer, creating jobs and growth in the process (cf. Cecchini, 1988). Indeed, the general gist of EU law relating to the free movement of goods across national borders and to provision of national assistance to domestic enterprises is that 'regressive' national rules and loyalties, expressed in restrictions on trade, national monopolies and the grant of exclusive rights to state and semi-state bodies, must not be allowed to impede the needs and goals of that utility-maximizing individual (see generally Chapter one). And again, the objectivity of the 'goods which move' is balanced by the 'rational subjectivity' of the consumer. As such, the formal logic of European integration is rooted in a rejection of the role of nation in economic affairs in favour of 'Europe', an identity and politics formed in negation. Consider the following classic statement:

> Integration can best be looked at from the negative side. The Community's efforts to integrate national markets are basically attempts to limit the influence of national governments on production and consumption activities throughout the Community. The desire to limit the influence of national governments stems from economic as well as political concerns. National measures restrict people in their economic activities throughout the Community, often at the expense of common welfare. As national governments regulate according to the desires of their constituencies alone, many national measures contain some protectionist bias. (Wils, 1993, p. 476)

But from the perspective of the semiological critique developed above, the development of the internal market tells a different story. The essence of the trade freedoms granted by the EC Treaty relate to the free movement of goods from and to other Member States, in other words, other nations. The Treaties structure this trade as a free trade between nations, involving goods legally characterized by their liberation from the restraints of nationality. Nation is thus always-already inscribed into the operation of the internal market. The operation of Arts 12–13 and 30–37 EC comprising the free movement of goods rules, although denying the continuing validity of national economic protectionism, has preserved the validity of nation itself. The complexity (and indeed impossibility) of nation is reduced, as Barthes might say, to being a mere signifier in a new third-order mythical chain –

the law of the internal market itself – which stands as the sign of reason and law transcending nation. But inherent in that reduction is a kind of preservation of the nation in mythic purity. This preservation is essential – nation must exist in alterity to the EU, so that EU law can transcend it. This is the modernist emprise at its most robust and its most Romantic.

The symbolic economy with which EU law engages is likewise dominated by the reference to nation. British Steel posters advertise its support of economic development in India (ghosts of the Raj and the white man's burden) invoking the Britishness of the steel and mythically confirming the reality of both nations in mythic purity. Similarly, automobiles made in Germany are marketed as a superior form of product by virtue of their Germanness, as is Japanese high-technology. Airlines carry the identification of national culture as well as the national flag, while the realms of fashion, cosmetics, perfume, food and drink are completely permeated with references to nationality, from Givenchy to McDonald's, Aquascutum to Asti Spumanti. While not claiming universality for the identification of nation and commodity (sexuality is another pervasive symbol), nationality has become a substantial part of the consumer economy.

This widespread symbolic invocation of nationality in commodities is thoroughly modern but engages with the postmodern. It reflects the continuing irrationality of consumption, the idolatrous desire to possess the God of nation and to see the world in terms of nation, the marketplace becoming a kind of carnival of delights. It also represents, as Jameson noted, the point where all production is culture, and vice-versa. But this pervasive iconolatry is subsumed within the rationality of exchange, becomes tamed and civilized. It is seen as representing, not tribalism, but fashion and sophistication. The modernist myth of rationality is preserved through the symbolic reification of 'nationality' as an abstract quality of commodities, the desire for possession of which is rationalized under the sign of exchange.

It is here that the law of the European internal market comes into its own in providing the rational-legal infrastructure within which exchange takes place. The abolition of customs duties and quotas, the expansive jurisprudence of the European Court in expanding the boundaries of the free movement of goods, the extensive role of EU legislation in standardizing national trade regulations, place the EU at the centre of a system providing the rational means by which 'nationality' is preserved as a symbolic referent, an ideal frozen in abstract purity, as if in amber.

Consider the development of EU law prohibiting the imposition of customs duties or charges having an equivalent effect on intra-Community trade. Art. 9 EC prohibits such charges 'between Member States ... on imports and exports'. In Case 24/68 *Commission* v. *Italy* [1969] ECR 193, the European Court defines the concept of 'charges having equivalent effect' as charges imposed on goods 'by virtue of the fact that they cross a national border'. Throughout the case-law relating to the free movement of goods, a cardinal distinction is drawn between the treatment of 'domestic' and 'imported' products. The entire structure of the law is based on this binary distinction, as the subject goods must assume before the law an identity as either a domestic or foreign good.

The picture painted by the myth of the internal market of a simple and stable relation between commodity and nation, imports and exports, or domestic and foreign production ignores the globalization of production. Many modern commodities are the result of raw materials, manufacturing processes, and assembly, packaging, transport and advertisement services which include several if not dozens of different global locations. With capital goods such as aeroplanes and automobiles, the number of contributors can be truly daunting. It is thus becoming less and less possible to talk 'rationally' about the existence of 'national' goods at all. The relationship of EC law to the symbolic economy of the internal market demonstrates an attempt by a system of law with totalizing pretensions to stabilize decentred significations of nationality within its own metanarrative.

The European internal market engages with this particular threat to nation mainly through two means: the idea of 'Community goods' and the concept of 'Community content'. Under Art. 9 EC, goods which enter the customs union of the EC and which comply with all EC tariffs, quota, inspections and formalities, are considered to be 'Community goods'. This creates the possibility, especially in the case of products requiring complex assembly, that a 'Community' good might possess minimal Community 'content'. EC law has responded to this by defining Community (and in most cases, therefore, national) goods as those where the 'last substantial process' of production or assembly was carried out in the Community,[1] or where a minimum percentage of Community's 'content' – commonly about 40% of the total value – exists in the final product.[2] The process of global production is to some extent hidden in these internal market rules. German textiles are transported to Poland for cutting and stitching, packaged in Germany and sold as German clothing. The imprimatur of Germanness is granted nonetheless. The effect is to diminish to some extent the impact of globalization on the national image of commodities, and to prop up the modernist strategy of rational trade reifying its Other in the form of nation.

One exceptional area where the internal market faces resistance in employing its grand narrative of modernity and nation is that of goods whose symbolic national imagery is already determined by national law. In these cases, it is not enough for EC law to alter the structure of trading rules, for example, by prohibiting the imposition of customs duties or import quotas. Here, the internal market demands that the symbolic structure of the commodity itself be altered in order to make it more 'market friendly'. It is no accident that so many of the cases in EU law relating to the free movement of goods, and especially those cases which are deemed most worthy of commentary, analysis, repetition and story-telling, are symbolically inscribed with the lineaments of nation which the EU claims to transcend. Liqueurs, pasta, wine and beer, *aceto*, *brioche* and *jenever*, national souvenirs and objects symbolic of quality national workmanship and traditions, hold an important place within the free movement of goods case-law, the founding-stone of the internal market's symbolic economy.[3] These signifiers exist as a second-order symbolic which allows goods to possess nationality or other cultural meaning as a natural property.

The debate over this area of the law, on both sides of the divide, assumes the naturalness of that symbolic order. For the critics of the case-law (mostly in the popular press and political organizations), the European Court's subversion of national culture through such judgements is plausible only because such goods are believed to possess national characteristics of the '-ness' kind (cf. Lasa, 1991, pp. 409–10). Similarly, to the proponents of the law (mostly lawyers and Commission officials), such judgements stand as a triumph of cultural integration and 'European construction' precisely because such goods are seen as possessing concrete cultural meaning. In both cases meaning is seen as fixed.

Consider the judgement of the Court of Justice in Case 193/80 *Commission* v. *Italy* [1981] ECR 3019. An Italian law prohibited the sale of products containing acetic acid not originating in the acetic fermentation of wine. The same law required that the term *aceto* be limited only to wine-based 'vinegars'. The effect of the rule was to prohibit access of cider or malt-based vinegars, commonly produced in Northern Europe, to the Italian market. The prohibition on importation was rejected as a clear violation of the Court's Art. 30 case-law on equally applicable measures which favour 'typically national' products.

The more interesting question arose on the designation issue. Rejecting the argument of the Italian government that Italian consumers, 'by time honoured tradition', associate *aceto* only with wine-vinegars, the Court referred to the EC's Common Customs Tariff classification as proof [*sic*] that the term vinegar was not limited to wine-vinegar alone. Vinegar was held to be a generic term, and with it, *aceto*:

> It follows that vinegar is a generic term and it would be incompatible with the objectives of the common market and in particular with the fundamental principle of the free movement of goods for national legislation to be able to restrict a generic term to one national variety alone to the detriment of other varieties produced, in particular, in other member states.

> However, it is not to be ruled out that *following the implementation of the rules at issue* Italian consumers have become accustomed to the term 'aceto' being used in commerce for wine-vinegar alone. If that is the case then the concern of the Italian government to protect consumers may be justified. Such protection may however be provided by other means enabling national and imported products to be treated alike, in particular by the compulsory affixing of suitable labels giving the nature of the product sold and containing a description or additional information specifying the type of vinegar offered for sale, provided that such a requirement applies to all vinegars including wine-vinegar. *Such a course would enable the consumer to make his choice in full knowledge of the facts* and would guarantee transparency in trading and in offers to the public by providing an indication of the raw material used to make the vinegar. [my emphasis]

In declaring that the meaning of *aceto* must be expanded to encompass other forms of vinegar, the Court directly regulates and stabilizes the sign as a new generative model capable of multiple subsequent applications by redefining it within the law's grand narrative. That narrative, in this situation, takes the form of a rejection of the irrational and an assumption that the rational consumer can make an informed choice when presented with full information, provided by proper labelling. It is not national culture but protective national law, according to the Court, which explains the popular association of *aceto* with wine-vinegar.

In the *Second Aceto* case, the Italian government in effect called the European Court's modernist bluff. A new Italian rule was promulgated allowing sale of cider and malt-based vinegars as *agro di*, to be followed by the name of the raw material from which the vinegar was obtained.[4] *Agro di vino* would designate wine-vinegar, although *aceto* was also required to be used. *Agro* was a new term created by Italian law to designate 'generic vinegar' In effect, the Italian government attempted to do explicitly what the Court had done implicitly, that is, to create a new sign through an official alteration in the language.

The Court's rejection of the new Italian scheme is revealing. It is not enough that the consumer could 'make his choice in full knowledge of the facts' through use of a new generic term and that *aceto* was now explicitly limited to that product (wine-vinegar) which popular usage had long associated with it. It was *aceto* itself, and the myth of Italian-ness, quality, tradition and so on, of which it acted as the signifier, which was the target of the law to exploit just as it was the goal of the Italian government to conserve. In effect, the Court imposes a new order of mythical speech where *aceto*, a first-order symbolic for Italian wine-vinegar, and second-order symbolic for nation, becomes extended to a third-order myth, of which *aceto* is the symbol and for which the judgement is the context. That myth is the myth of

EC law itself, its ability to reconcile nation and market, desire and reason. The effect of the third-order myth is to treat *aceto* as fully Italian, yet fully liberated from the bounds of nationality. Once again, an explicit valorization of market rationality hides the preservation of *aceto* as a signifier of nationality.

But there is more than a preservation here. The 'logic' of the internal market requires that *aceto* henceforth not refer only to vinegar made from wine, and thus in practice, not refer only to vinegar made in Italy. Yet the name carries its symbolism of nation with it. Indeed, that was the whole reason why foreign access to the name was sought. The ironic result is that, within the logic of the internal market, *aceto* achieves its purest form of national symbolism in the very act of severing any territorial connection to Italy.

By its judgement, the European Court provides an example of EC law's reduction of complexity and potential instability under its own modernist metanarrative, that is, a robust defence of free trade and the rights of the rational legal subject of the Treaties, while preserving nation as the alterity of the internal market. Both the rational subject and *aceto* are reified in a more pure form, denying the actual instability occurring in both due to the onset of cultural hybridity wrought by trade.

Most of the classic cases dealing with appellations of quality and origins, or product names, involve some variant of the approaches considered in the *Aceto* cases. In all of these, the European Court has employed its expansive reading of Art. 30 EC to stabilize, simplify and 'Europeanize' the ever more contradictory aspects of nation symbolized in goods.[5] But the Court acts at the level of national rules limiting access to symbols of nationality. At the level of European legislation aimed at the harmonization of laws, significant attempts have been made by the Member State governments meeting in the Council to recreate a fixed relationship between sign and place or product.

The earliest, and still most significant focus on such activity relates to wine. This is unsurprising since wine is so closely linked to locality and region, and defined in terms of an extremely sensitive scale of quality and taste. But the assignment of value to these fine shades of difference in taste, colour, aroma, and so on, remains a fundamentally social process. The identification and emphasis placed on these characteristics, coupled with the huge expansion in mass consumption of wine in Europe in the last thirty years, demonstrate wine's new function as a symbolic commodity. Indeed, since wine (and other foodstuffs) can combine symbolic sensations of sight, smell and taste, they stand as prime examples of such commodities.

In 1970 the European Commission enacted a Regulation harmonizing standards for 'quality wines produced in specified regions' (known as quality wines psr).[6] Under this and amending regulations, certain wines, and only those wines, are allowed to display quality designations such as 'qualitaetswein', 'appellation d'origine controlee', 'champagne', 'denominazione di orgine controllata', and so on. The system established by these regulations establishes a loose set of common standards for quality and allows producers from specified regions, defined down to the individual vineyard, an exclusive right to use the appellation of quality. Further, only designated wines (in other words, only designated producers) may avail of the name of the specified region. Non-quality wines, other beverages, and the raw materials for wine-making, even if from the region, are prohibited from using the name.

Since each Member State establishes its own list of specified regions, the appellation of quality is expressed in the national language, and indeed the name of the wine must be printed in the language of the country of origin, the system acts as an indirect indicator of national origin. And this is essential to the market since it is a quality wine of a certain nationality, region or locality, as against a quality wine in the abstract, which is itself the commodity.

A similar market system has been established for sparkling wines, limiting the use of names and geographical appellations of origin to wines produced in specified regions and to loosely harmonized quality standards.[7] The most controversial subject in this area has been the restriction of 'champagne' as a term relating to a 'production method' only to sparkling wines produced in France, thus barring use of the appellation *méthode Champenoisé* by other, particularly Spanish, sparkling wines. Likewise, *cremant* is now reserved for particular French and Luxembourgeois quality sparkling wines, *winzersekt* for German, *asti* for Italian and *cava* for Spanish sparkling wines. The imposition of nationality through law is evident.

In one sense the approach of the Court of Justice in the appellation of origin cases is flatly contradicted by that of the Community legislator in the wine regimes. Instead of a Europeanization of the sign which allows it to function as an abstract symbol of nationality dissociated from connection with territory, the legislative structure limits and fixes signs to their national or regional sites of origin by force of European law. Clearly, the action of the Community legislator would have been a violation of Art. 30 EC had it been attempted by a Member State. The wine regime reflects the continuing power of nationalism at the domestic level – of the nation not as the Other, but as the Self. Thus the EU and the nation are struggling for the same terrain, an example of the 'competing nationalisms' described by Fitzpatrick in Chapter 2.

The divergence of approach between the Council and the European Court also speaks to the hierarchy of discourses within the EU legal structure. The

Council represents, from the point of view of the EU lawyer, a political regime based on compromise, a body often incapable of taking the 'hard decisions' necessary to bring about the completion of the European internal market (see Craig and De Búrca, 1995, pp. 52–3). The Court, by contrast, is often held to represent the pro-integrationist ideal in its purest form. The divergent treatment of 'cultural goods' therefore also establishes an 'internal' dynamic within EU law wherein the progressive case-law of the European Court is privileged over the retrograde behaviour of the Council.

But it would be a mistake to view these two approaches as totally at odds with each other. Both seek the same end of providing fixed meaning to, and thus determining property rights over, destabilized signifiers of value. Within the narrative of EC law, we now 'know' what *aceto* is, because the law has specified it as a commodity but has removed national boundaries from its definition, leaving only reified connotations of nationality. The judgement of the European Court becomes a third-order text signifying order and rationality, and civilizing the desire for nation under the sign of rational exchange.

We equally know what champagne is, because the law has specified that as well. But in the area of Council action, the commodity remains legally bound to a particular place. This law runs counter to the 'high modernist' jurisprudence of the European Court. But it is nonetheless 'law' – it legitimises the iconolatry of nation under the sign of constitutional process and positive legality. In its new legal incarnation, *aceto* is undisturbed by attachment to non-wine vinegars, while champagne can revel in French pride, without regard for the many foreign imitators producing close substitutes, because those imitators no longer have legal access to the *méthode Champenoisé* sign. In both cases, the function of law is to regulate and protect the signifier as the commodity-form in itself. In the context of the internal market, this action supports the modernist separation and mutual preservation of reason and nation in ever more abstract forms.

CONCLUSION: GLOBALIZATION AND THE EMPRISE OF EUROPEAN INTEGRATION

Recent literature on globalization has emphasized the interdependency and interculturality of relations between global forces and local conditions (Featherstone, 1995; Nederveen Pieterse, 1995; Robertson, 1992). From this perspective, the global-local relationship is not so much one of antagonism as mutual constitution. In particular, it is within a global framework that the idea of the local is itself constituted (Robertson, 1995). It has been pointed out that a prime early example of this 'glocalisation' was the development of the European nation-state (Greenfield, 1992). But it is also clear that the current trend in global cultural, economic and information flows is away from the primacy of the nation-state, one important instance of which is the growing recognition that the temporal vision of modernity is, indeed, a myth. In its place, globalization theory and cultural studies are emphasizing a view of modernity as a spatial entity, a component part of a presently existing world order (or disorder) (Featherstone and Lash, 1995). And although the world order/disorder might have a historical dynamic, it is no longer the temporalized myth of modernity.

One constant in the otherwise contentious field of globalization studies is a recognition of the universal impact of the global economy and its inculcation of a broadly defined 'postmodern culture'. States throughout the world have experienced, in different ways, the cultural effects of global trade, cultural hybridity, the fragmentation of identity, creolization, and so on, whether weak or powerful, whether connected to customs unions or not, whether adopting laissez-faire or protectionist economic and cultural policies.

In the context of EU studies, this is an important point, since it is very seldom made. It implies that the globalization of production and onset of the 'postmodern condition' would have occurred in Europe in any event, even if the Common Market had not come into existence. It would have occurred differently, of course. It would not have been as managed at the regional level. It might have led to a more truly global cultural heterogeneity, and on different terms *in Europe*, as against one which is biased towards a *European* cultural heterogeneity. But it would have occurred. It is not therefore true to say that the EU has brought about the 'postmodern condition' in Europe, although the internal market facilitated it, particularly between the EU member states.

In terms of the modernist emprise, what the project of European integration did accomplish was to present the experience of globalization, cultural fragmentation, the perceived instability of meaning and identity, and so on, as the result of a conscious design. The Preamble of the EC Treaty speaks of 'an ever closer union' of the European peoples resulting primarily from the establishment of a common market, implying social integration mediated through exchange and social mobility. This idea, a central plank of Community political strategy, incorporates the 'postmodern condition' as the achievement of a European act of rational will and constitutional planning, rather than as globalization gone wild. As we have seen, the structure of the internal market, the national symbolism which inhabits large parts of the consumer economy, and the reifying action of EC law when presented with the possibility of instability in the meaning of symbolic commodities, all mythically produce an abstract sphere of rational exchange, and another of pure nation. The formal project of the EU attempts to incorporate globalization and the postmodern within a discourse of rationality and market freedom, while as an alterity, preserving a simplistic vision of the nation-state within a new myth of modernity.

This is a very Western coup. The cultural fragmentation and economic globalization which is viewed as an irresistible force, overwhelming 'primitive' cultures in the 'developing world', becomes rationalized and enters into the constitution of European Being as the results of European statesmanship, determination and the truth of liberal economics. In this perhaps defining sense, the project of the EU is a modernist one, in that it ultimately preserves the myth of European superiority and the alterity of the primitive Other, even in the face of postmodern dislocation and fragmentation.

'Emprise' is an archaic term referring to an enterprise or undertaking that is noble and chivalrous in intent. It speaks to the desire for crusade and sacrifice, the impulse to impose a true vision on a recalcitrant or heretical world, a project of empire. But emprise also connotes a call to rational action subsumed within the loftiness of the ultimate goal. The internal market is the emprise of European modernity under the growing strains of a cultural postmodernity which is modernity's child. But now the original function is reversed: it is the irrational and confused which is subsumed within the lofty call to reason, the postmodern propping up the modern. Lyotard once noted that one cannot be modern without once having been postmodern (Lyotard, 1983). In the context of the EU, the kind of modernity which acts as the legitimation of European integration ever more assumes the 'postmodern condition' as a condition precedent. Thus the EU is not a postmodern institution, but a modernist one which has used postmodern culture as an Other by which it can justify itself in negation.

NOTES

1 Art. 5 of Council Regulation 802/68 on the determination of origin of goods for customs purposes, JO L 1968, L148/1, cf. Council Regulation 1769/89 on certificates of origin, OJ L 1989 L174/11. See Case 49/76 *Überseehandel* v. *Handelskammer Hamburg* [1977] ECR 41, Cases 34/78 & 114/78 *Yoshida* [1978] ECR 115 & 151, and Case 26/88 *Brother International* v. *HZA Giessen* [1989] ECR 4253.

2 See, for example, Art. 13(10), Council Regulation 2423/88, OJ L 1988 L209/1.

3 See Case 120/78 *Rewe-Zentral AG* v. *Bundesmonopolverwaltungfuer Branntwein* [1979] ECR 649 (*Cassis de Dijon* liqueur), Case 12/74 *Commission* v. *Germany* [1975] ECR 181 (wine), Case 407/85 *Drei Gloken GmbH and Kritzinger* v. *USL Centro-Sud and Provincia* [1988] ECR 4233 (pasta), Case 178/84 *Commission* v. *Germany* [1987] ECR 1227 (beer), Case 193/80 *Commission* v. *Italy* [1981] ECR 3019 (*aceto*), Case 130/80 *Fabriek* [1981] ECR 27 (*brioche*), Case 182/84 *Miro* [1985] ECR 3731 (*jenever*), Case

207/83 *Commission* v. *United Kingdom* [1985] ECR 1201 (national quality goods). See Chapter 1 for a discussion of these cases.

4 Case 281/83 *Commission* v. *Italy* [1985] ECR 3397.

5 See fn 1 above and the discussion in Chapter 1.

6 Commission Regulation (EEC) 817/70 of 28 April 1970 laying down special provisions for quality wines produced in specified regions, JO L 1970 L99/20, amended by Commission Regulation (EEC) 1698/70, JO L 1970190/4, Council Regulation (EEC) 338/79, OJ L 1979 L54/207, Council Regulation (EEC) 823/87, OJ L 1987 L84/59, Council Regulation (EEC) 2392/89, OJ L 1989 L232/13.

7 Council Regulation (EEC) 3309/85 of 18 November 1985 laying down general rules for the description and presentation of sparkling wines and aerated sparkling wines, OJ L 1985 L320/9, amended by Council Regulation (EEC) 2333/92, OJ L 1992 L231/9, Commission Regulation (EC) 554/95, OJ L 1995 L56/3.

REFERENCES

Arnaud, A. (1991), *Pour une pensée juridique européenne*, Paris: PUF.

Barthes, R. (1972), *Mythologies*, trans. A. Lavers, London: Jonathan Cape.

Baudrillard, J. (1970), *La société de consommation*, Paris: Gallimard.

Baudrillard, J. (1972), *For a Critique of the Political Economy of the Sign*, trans. Charles Levin, St Louis: Telos.

Baudrillard, J. (1993), *Symbolic Exchange and Death*, trans. Iain Hamilton Grant, London: SAGE.

Bell, D. (1976), *The Cultural Contradictions of Capitalism*, London: Heinemann.

Cecchini, P. (1988), *The European Challenge – 1992*, London: Gower.

Craig, P. and De Búrca, G. (1995), *EC Law, Text, Cases and Materials*, Oxford: Clarendon Press.

Curtin, D. (1993), 'The Constitutional Structure of the Union: A Europe of Bits and Pieces', *Common Market Law Review*, **30** (17).

Debord, G. (1968), *La Société du spectacle*, Paris: Buchet-Chastel.

Debord, G. (1990), *Comments on the Society of the Spectacle*, London: Verso.

Durkheim, E. (1961), *The Elementary Forms of Religious Life*, New York.

Featherstone, M. (1995), 'Localism, Globalism and Cultural Identity' in Dissanayake and Wilson (eds), *Global/Local: Cultural Production and the Transnational Imaginary*, Durham NC: Duke University Press.

Featherstone, M. and Lash, S. (1995), 'Globalization, Modernity and the Spatialization of Social Theory: An Introduction' in Featherstone, Lash and Robertson (eds), *Global Modernitie*, London: SAGE, 1.

Fitzpatrick, P. (1992), *The Mythology of Modern Law*, London: Routledge Press.

Friedman, J. (1994), *Cultural Identity and Global Process*, London: SAGE.

Greenfield, L. (1992), *Nationalism: Five Roads to Modernity*, Cambridge MA: Harvard University Press.

Jameson, F. (1991), *Postmodernism, or The Cultural Logic of Late Capitalism*, Durham NC: Duke University Press.

Jevons, W.S. (1870), *The Theory of Political Economy*, London.

Lasa, H. (1991), 'Free Movement of Foodstuffs, Consumer Protection and Food Standards in the European Community: Has the Court of Justice Got it Wrong?', *European Law Review* **16** (391).

Lyotard, J. (1983), 'Answering the Question: What is Postmodernism?', in Hassan and Hassan (eds), *Innovation/Renovation*, Madison: University of Wisconsin Press, 71.

Marx, K. (1974a), *The German Ideology*, London.

Marx, K. (1974b), *Capital*, 3 vols, London.

Nederveen Pieterse, J. (1995), 'Globalization as Hybridization' in Featherstone, Lash and Robertson (eds), *Global Modernities*, London: Sage, 45.

Robertson, R. (1992), *Globalization: Social Theory and Global Culture*, London: SAGE.

Robertson, R. (1995), 'Glocalization: Time-Space and Homogeneity-Heterogeneity' in Featherstone, Lash and Robertson (eds), *Global Modernities*, London: SAGE, 25.

Ruggie, J.G. (1993), 'Territoriality and Beyond: Problematizing Modernity in International Relations', *International Organisation*, **4** (1).

Saussure, F. de (1974), *Course in General Linguistics*, trans. W. Baskin, London: Fontana.

Smart, C. (1992), 'Europe Today and the Post-Modern Paradox' in Nelson, Roberts, Veit (eds), *The Idea of Europe: Problems of National and Transnational Identity*, Berg, 26.

Sousa Santos, B. de (1992), 'State, Law and Community in the World System: An Introduction', *Social & Legal Studies*, 1.

Veblen, T. (1973), *The Theory of the Leisure Class*, Boston: Houghton Mifflin.

Ward, I. (1996), *A Critical Introduction to European Law*, London: Butterworths.

Weiler, J.H.H. (1994), 'Fin-de-siècle Europe: On Ideals and Ideology in Post-Maastricht Europe', in Curtin and Heukels (eds), *Institutional Dynamics of European Integration, Essays in Honour of Henry G. Schermers*, Vol. II, Dordrecht: Martinus Nijhoff, 23.

Wils, W.P.J. (1993), 'The Search for the Rule in Article 30 EEC: Much Ado About Nothing?' *European Law Review* **18** (475).

PART II
EUROPEAN IDENTITY IN EU LAW

5 Understanding the EU/EEA as Systems of Functionally Different Processes: Economic, Political, Legal, Administrative and Cultural

Inger-Johanne Sand

INTRODUCTION: THE PROBLEMS OF CREATING AND UNDERSTANDING NEW POLITICAL AND LEGAL ORGANIZATIONS AND SYSTEMS

The European Community and Union have from the signing of the Rome Treaty step by step evolved as a new type of political and legal association, from the beginning of the 1960s under the concept of supranationality. This concept means that there are powers or competences vested in the institutions which both have 'supremacy' vis-à-vis the Member States and 'direct effect' vis-à-vis the citizens of the Member States. This would imply that there are possibilities for relatively effective legislative and sanction systems on other organizational levels than those of the nation-states. The development of the EC/EU has been an exception to the otherwise 200-year-long era and reign of the democratic and sovereign nation-states in Europe. In this epoch political and constitutional sovereignty have been vested as national. Cooperation beyond the nation-state has been founded on the sovereignty of the participating states, and it has been done voluntarily. Other legal treaties and political cooperations which have been entered, have thus had much less effective legislative and sanction systems.

Discussions concerning the identity of the new international and supranational organizations have been predominantly concerned with defining their politico-legal status somewhere between the ideas of a confederation or a federation of states (Moravcsik, 1993). In the legal sciences attention has been given to discussions of the characteristics of supranationality as a legal concept, and how this has evolved (Weiler, 1991). There are disagreements both in the political and legal sciences as to what both the EC/EU and the EEA are as political and legally constituted organizations. They have been described as having both supranational and international elements. They have been described as both coherent and effective supranational organizations, and as organizations with unclear, inefficient and incoherent relations between their different institutional elements (Joerges, 1993, Snyder, 1993).

These organizations are often treated as given entities and defined in general terms according to the status they have at any specific time. The European Community and Union are however continually ongoing projects – in process. They are also organizations constituted by several different types of institutions and systems of communication – political, legislative, judicial and administrative. The different institutions and competences of the Union have also evolved in different tempi and at different stages. Thereby the different institutions have related to each other in different ways at different times. The construction of such complex organizations is not done in the manner of full coordination of all institutional elements. I would suggest that when analysing the identity of the new European institutions more focus should be given to studies of the processes of the evolvements of the EC/EU and the EEA and to the interactions between the political, legal, economic and administrative elements of the institutions in these processes. Focus should also be given to the non-simultaneity of these processes and to the partly contradictory elements within the configuration of different competences of the institutions. Analysis of the processes should not only help explain how they have emerged, but also more specifically why they have emerged. This should contribute to more specific knowledge of what these organizations are, and how they might be evaluated as political and constitutional organizations.

A central characteristic of the EC/EU is that they have developed as organizations with really existing constitutions, but without explicit and deliberative constitutional debates. Vital constitutional changes have taken place more as the result of accumulated minor changes than of major and deliberative decisions. It may seem that the organizations have evolved step by step by the accumulated help of economic forces, political decisions and judicial acts, and at times with consequences unintended in the specific situation.

The goals and competences of the EC/EU/EEA are fairly wide and vaguely defined. This has given rise to different sets of practice and implementations in the EU institutions and in the Member States. The situation is often accounted for by referring to elements which are part of the normal state of politics – tactics, contradictions, compromises (with hidden disagreements), sudden changes and contingencies. There are also the differences in regulatory cultures among the Member States.

As a result of, and running parallel to, the political process is however the process of creating a legal system with supranational and effective qualities. The political and the legal systems are closely connected in the legislative system, and they are thus mutually dependent on each other, but they also serve qualitatively different functions. The problems of the political processes resulting in compromises and vague or unclear definitions will also affect the legal system, but in qualitatively different ways than the political system. A compromise or an unclear formulation might for example be very useful and productive on the political arena. On the legal scene, however, it might contribute to differing, unclear or incoherent interpretations.

Compromises and contradictions are thus inherent parts of political communication and may be handled by political rationality. The political processes do not have to be coherent. Within the legal system, however, these aspects of supranational communication give rise to more serious problems. Coherence, predictability and equality before the law, in some kind of form, are vital aspects of the idea of a legal system and its rationality. The legal system in the EU has, however, to some extent created its own ways of compensating for its unfinished and in-process character, its lack of coherence and for the contradictions and compromises on the political level. The European Court of Justice has risen to the occasion and contributed considerably to the creation of an independent and fully comprehensive legal system with its rulings of supremacy, direct effect, mutual recognition, its inclusion of human rights and its primary emphasis on the principle of efficiency in the implementation of the goals of the Treaty. The legal system has thus, to some extent, filled in some of the gaps of the politically legislative system and its 'silences' and compromises. The administrative level has created new sources of law in the forms of delegated legislation, interpretative protocols, written opinions etc. naming these soft-law when necessary for the construction of a more coherent legal system, i.e. for the possibilities of making legal decisions according to the traditions of a more coherent and rule-of-law-oriented systems. In this manner the legal system has tried to create its own coherence materially as well as procedurally – independently of the incoherences and compromises of the political system. These are not unknown features in the interplay of national political and legal systems. Political compromises and legal discretionary norms may be productive and efficient, but they also create gaps in meaning-contents and are thus open to criticism and contradictory interpretations. On the

EC/EU-level this is a more problematic feature because the social and political background is much more heterogeneous, and there is a lack of the type of social concensus often seen in long established nation-states. Political compromises and the uses of discretionary elements in law take place on a more open and socially less established field when used on the European level. They are thus more open and sensitive to difficult interpretations and problems when implemented.

The construction of new political and legal systems are complex projects. What I want to focus on here is that vital parts of the problems of incoherence and undecidedness within and between the political, legal and administrative systems might originate from the fact that there are more systematic differences and problems of communication than often admitted between the functionally different systems of politics, law, economics and administration which are all parts of the process of constructing new organizations and institutions (Luhmann, 1984 and 1991, chap. 8). They must handle the same goals, the same treaties and the same texts, and they refer to the same political processes. They 'talk' about the same items, but in such different ways that very systematic and serious misunderstandings, incoherences and gaps are created. The more heterogeneous social and political background of the EU members may also enhance these communicative problems compared to nation-states.

What I will propose in this chapter is that the tendency, legally as well as politically, to treat and to conceptualize the EU as one entity, one organization, may contribute to a failure to see the real complexities and the incoherences of the organization and the way it changes. It will be argued that it will enhance the analytical and critical quality of our studies if we consistently analyse the organization as ongoing processes which are functionally and communicatively differentiated. The political, legal, economic and administrative systems of communication are interacting and mutually interdependent of each other, but they do not communicate directly, only indirectly. Differentiated and communicative analysis is one of the vital keys to a deeper understanding of the dynamics of these types of organizations.

INSTITUTIONAL CHANGES: FROM NATION-STATE TO THE MANY-LAYERED COMBINATIONS OF STATE- AND SUPRA-NATIONALITY

The constitutional and political institutions of the European nation-states have evolved over time and been constructed within the traditions and principles of liberalism, democracy, the rule-of-law and national sovereignty.

More or less stable and common patterns of political and legal institutions and of relations between these institutions have been established. From these traditions and from social movements have also evolved different national traditions of economic regulation and regimes of social welfare. These political, legal and economic institutions have been vital for the existence of the European societies, and their respective traditions have been vital for the legitimacy of the nation-states.

Our expectations as to the possibilities and limitations of political, legal and economic action and our ways of communicating about them have thus been very much embedded and shaped by these traditions and their concepts. The institutions have been predominantly national and very much defined by the structures (and limitations) of national sovereignty. Nation-states as well as their institutions have come, to some extent, to be taken for granted even where they have been significantly changed by external pressures such as internationalization, professionalization or business interests, or by internal institutional changes. We have so far not developed the analytical skill of describing and evaluating changes in these new structures of governance in a sufficiently radical way. We hypostasize them as democratic and nationally sovereign even if these institutions have been drastically changed.

With the entry of the EC/EU/EEA we are seeing new types of legal and political institutions which do not fit easily into the previous patterns of either nation-state or international organizations based on voluntary consent. Parts of their competences are supranational with direct effect and superiority vis-à-vis the national legislatures, and parts have a more traditional international design. Their competences have also become increasingly wide – covering important areas previously monopolized by national legislatures – and increasingly significant vis-à-vis the citizens. This accentuates the problems of unclear definition and rather vague limitations in the treaties. The EU institutions have both increased their competences and seem to have some sort of a de-facto institutional autonomy vis-à-vis the Member States even if the Member State representatives are still formally the decisive players within the new institutional frameworks. The systems of political decisions and legal regulation in Europe are now not predominantly taking place on the nation-state levels, but rather in a many-layered system of national and supranational institutions and negotiations – which is so interactive and complex that it to some extent defies a formal and accurate description.

The EU institutions and the new mixtures of supranational and national institutions, and the manner in which these have emerged, do however differ from the traditional nation-state institutions in ways that are vital for their political as well as their legal and legitimatory functions. These differences and the questions they raise need to be addressed in order to assess more closely what kind of political and legal institutions that are emerging. Some of these differences and questions may be summed up in the following way:

(1) The EU, in its present form, has come a long way towards having some of the same institutional functions as the nation-states, and taking over parts of their legislative competence. The EU institutions do not, however, have the same democratic basis and structure and thereby they lack the legitimacy of the nation-states and their institutions. Political negotiations take place in much more heterogeneous environment than in the Member States. The relationship between the political and the legal has been changed in ways that are complex and difficult to comprehend. Vital aspects of what has traditionally been acknowledged as traditions and precondition of legitimate regimes are not present, or they appear in changed forms. This includes direct and popular elections to the effective legislatures, common languages, some kind of common cultural and social history, specific traditions for the separation of political and legal institutions, constitutionally and politically accountable legislators and traditions of participation and transparency in the legislative process etc. In the main legislative body of the EU, the Council, there is a double indirectness in democratic representation compared to national institutions: the Council is not directly accountable to one parliamentary body, while the national representatives may only be held responsible individually by their own national governments or parliaments. The European parliament is elected popularly, but thus far it is a huge institution with much distance to its electorate, unclear competences and with vital language problems internally. The consequences of the distance, lack of common political culture and the indirectness of representation are not sufficiently appreciated. The consequences of all these changes in vital and legitimate political and constitutional institutions are unknown to us, and they are by definition also hard to assess.

(2) What makes the EC/EU further problematic as an organization is the combination of a lack of democratic legitimacy with wide competences, unclear definitions and vague boundaries. The unclear definitions of key concepts are also interpreted and implemented by several authoritative institutions on the European and nation-state levels simultaneously. These problems are more severe in the EU/EEA than in the nation-states because there is less consensus at the European level as to the background of the interpretation of vital concepts and values.

(3) Even if the construction of the EU has had several political goals, the most vital focus and the main political instrument of the EU has been the

creation of a single market with strong emphasis on the principles of free competition and economic liberalism. These goals have also constituted a semi-constitutional principle in the EU due to their position in the treaties (Joerges, 1993). The predominant part of the EU's regulatory competences is aimed at constructing and regulating the free market. Imbalance in these regulatory aims may also lead to distortions in the interpretation of regulations concerning or bordering social, ecological or other fields.

(4) The EU has been constructed in a relatively short span of time. Its institutions have also been explicitly constructed by political, legal or professional élites, and without the participation of a larger and more comprehensive public sphere. The Member States are also quite culturally, geographically and socially heterogeneous. There is a lack of a common public sphere and of common political and public debates in Europe. All these facts may have some consequences for both how the institutions have been created and whether they are accepted as legitimate.

(5) The EU treaties and institutions have not evolved along any clear, smooth and well-defined line or political goals and aims. The history of the emerging of the EU treaties and institutional competences is rather full of sudden changes and incoherencies in the relation of the institutions. There has not always been a consistent line between the political goals which have been set and the practices of the institutions. Some instances of institutional behaviour are not easily explained.

This combination of immense institutional changes and innovations, unknown consequences and incoherent and over-complex histories ask for more radical and comprehensive analyses than a descriptive analysis focusing on the organization as a whole. The complexities of the processes of change demand critical, comprehensive and deconstructive types of analysis. The new institutions should be seen as unfinished and complex processes which need to be taken apart in order to reach some kind of understanding of them.

COMPLEXITY AND THE GAPS OF THE EU – ANALYSED AS A PROCESS BETWEEN POLITICAL, LEGAL, ADMINISTRATIVE AND ECONOMIC SYSTEMS OF COMMUNICATION

According to the systems theory of Niklas Luhmann, society is organized around and constructed by different social functions and their respectively differentiated systems of communication (Luhmann, 1984, 1993). These different systems of communication are normatively closed to each other, but cognitively they are open and may cover the same social areas and objects. Politics, law and economics serve as primary functions for the coordination and integration of modern and differentiated societies, and they appear in these societies as systems of communication. These systems have different sets of codes and rationalities and will communicate differently according to these. When establishing and constructing new political organizations these communicative systems will be essential. They will also correspond to explicitly different social functions within the organizations. These functions will deal with the same items or subjects (the market, social regulation, environment etc.), but because of different functions in relation to the same social areas, they will communicate in systematically different ways about them. One way of analysing and understanding the constructed supranational institutions and processes of the EU/EEA might be to use the theories and concepts of systems theory and of communicative and social differentiation in order to grasp the complexities, the contradictions, the gaps and the incoherences of how these institutions have evolved.

A short summary of this line of argumentation would be: the political, the economic and the legal are different functions and different types of communication within the EU. The main instrumental and practical goals of the treaties are economic. They have been decided upon on a background of both political negotiations and advice from economic experts and interest groups. The decision-making processes leading up to the treaties, the directives etc. are political. They are parts of a political process and based on political rationalities. This will include the uses of political power and elements of compromises, rhetorics and wide discretions. Political decisions are then transformed as texts into legal treaties, directives, etc. These texts are legislation and could also be called the 'structural coupling' between politics and law. The implementation of political decisions takes place with the institutions and the instruments of law and administration and by their respective rationalities. This will include the uses of rule-of-law norms and standards of efficiency. With goal-oriented political decisions much power and discretion is delegated to legal and administrative authorities or experts and thus to the rationalities and communications of these systems.

Politics, law, economics and administration are represented by qualitatively different types of communication and correspondingly different rationalities. They are also, however, as laid out above, continuously interacting and mutually interdependent on each other. My thesis is that this interdependence of qualitatively different systems will systematically contribute seriously to misunderstandings, incoherences and contingencies in communication and in institution-building. This is not necessarily wrong, but it is vital that these differences in functions and in modes of communication are pointed out, observed and used in our analysis of institutions in process. The differences in modes of communication may have contributed to the production of other types of regulations and institutions than were politically intended. A lack of clear intent and the use of compromise on the political level may have contributed to contingent results. Without such differentiated and reflexive analysis we may as scientists and commentators come to contribute to a reification of very preliminary steps in organizations, contingent or unintended consequences or to any type of rhetoric or compromise which the politicians at any time may want to proclaim. A differentiated analysis is vital for the possibility of a critical analysis of such institutions.

I would now like to expand this argument further. The goals of the EC/EU are decided on a political level. The primary general and political goals of the EC/EU have been economic cooperation in the form of one single, free and competitive market and peace-keeping in Europe. It is however the creation of one common market with a ban on uncompetitive measures which has been the main instrumental goal of the treaties. The principles of economic liberalism and free competition have from the start been the most basic parts of the introductory and principled articles and goals of the treaties. The amendments to the treaty of 1985 (the SEA) were predominantly about increasing the efficiency of the common and free market. With the Maastricht treaty the material competences are increased and diversed, but the principle of economic liberalism is still underlined as the most basic principle, among many, cf. Art. 3a, and the realizing of one single and free market is still the most basic and instrumental goal.

The political emphasis on increased economic cooperation and an effectively free market has been established not only by pure negotiation, but also as the result of advice from economic experts and pressure from business and industrialist interest groups. The economic expertise will base their advice on economic theories and dogmas and economically based pictures of reality. These will tend to emphasize certain aspects of society, and to disregard others. This means that there will be a problem of translation from the economic to a more general societal and political language when politicians use the advice of economists. Similar problems will arise vis-à-vis other professionals. Political authorities should base their decisions on fully comprehensive views of society. By seeking the advice of economists, lawyers and other professionals they will systematically risk being influenced in partial and imbalanced ways. Expert advice is however often a necessity and a good thing, but it is often used without politicians having the necessary understanding or awareness of the problems of different discourses and of how to evaluate or translate such advice.

Even if they are influenced by others, political decisions, treaties, directives and other regulations will always be the result of political processes among political actors. Hence the political rationality of being in or out of power will be the predominant guideline. Political actors seek power and to win discussions or negotiations. This will be the case even when negotiations are complex. Compromises and negotiated solutions are vital parts of the political power play. Politicians may also be working with very unclear or contradictory goals when necessary in the political struggle. Political decisions will thus normally be influenced by power play, tactics, rhetorics and compromises as well as 'legitimate' ideals. This will however often lead to reductionist ideas or 'blind alleys'.

The implementation of the EU treaties and regulations and in particular the single and free market has been delegated, as in other organizations, from the political to the administrative and legal authorities. This will unavoidably mean wide and discretionary delegations of power. The process of implementing political decisions, will partly mean the transforming of political discourse into legal or administrative texts and partly delegating it to specific administrative and judicial authorities to implement these texts or regulations in practice and vis-à-vis the other social actors involved. It will also imply delegating important parts of the legislative process to the same administrative authorities. Functionally this means that many political decision are left to be further developed legislatively, judicially and administratively not only by other types of actors than the political, but also by other types of communication with correspondingly different rationalities. Judicial and administrative actors are given political or quasi-political functions.

Legislation is then the structural coupling or translation between law and politics. There are however no clear solutions as to how political compromises or intendedly unclear formulations should be treated legally. There are rather communicative processes between politics and law which will include gaps, misunderstandings and incoherences, some of which may be productive, others unproductive and problematic.

Political decisions have been formed within a scheme of political rationality and codes. Now the same discourse is transformed into a legal or administrative text. The language is the same, but it is thus taken over by the operations of different rationalities and codes – for the purposes of implementation and juridification, without which the political processes would be severely reduced in their effects. A political decision transformed into a treaty or directive will, because of the finality of the text, keep its elements of discretion, vagueness or compromise, but often without sufficiently clear guidelines as to how the political compromises should be treated legally. The text will in the further process be used in different ways. Used as legal texts within the administrative or judicial branches or by private parties there will be demands of coherence, equality before the law and legal guidelines of interpretation. Thus the political system does not 'own' their decision any more. They are taken over, used and transformed according to other communicative rationalities and the function which they take care of. The results of these implementation processes might change the directions of political decisions significantly. They may become more, less or something quite different than was intended. The political system may, however, change or repeal these practices later, on a political level.

The administrative rationality of the EU has been dominated by the principles of efficiency and professionalism. The legal institutions have used the principles of rule-of-law, coherence and proportionality, but also, very predominantly, the principle of efficiency. Within the EU the function of both the administrative and the legal branches is to 'make things work', to implement the material goals of the treaty as efficiently as possible. We have thus seen a combination of, on the one side, a strong emphasis on efficiency in the implementation of the broad political goals of economic policy and coordination and on the other hand the construction of both a comprehensive and coherent legal system developed according to legal rationality and a vast and efficient administrative bureaucracy. The principles of economic efficiency and of legal comprehensive rationality have been combined unintentionally, but to strong effect. The different rationalities have been combined operationally into something that may be considered more than what was originally intended and more than the sum of the parts.

It has been the function of the judiciary to interpret the more precise meanings of the texts for the purposes of legal and administrative implementation. Part of this interpretation concerns definitions and boundaries vis-à-vis national legal systems. The European Court of Justice has in several cases used the opportunities it has been given to establish the EC/EU-law as an autonomous and comprehensive legal system. The Court has declared the supremacy and direct-effect of EC/EU-law vis-à-vis the national regimes, without explicit treaty basis. The Court has chosen to interpret the principle of free competition with emphasis on an optimally efficient implementation of it vis-à-vis the pronounced treaty texts. It went on to establish the principle of mutual recognition of different national regulations. It has favoured a liberal interpretation of Art. 235 extending and stretching it far beyond a narrow legal interpretation of what has seemed 'necessary' in order for the market to function. The Court has made choices within the framework of fully acceptable legal interpretations of the treaties and their discretionary legislation, but not 'forced' upon it by the specific wordings of the treaties. The Court has thus favoured particular considerations to the detriment of others (Weiler, 1993b).

The experience of the ECJ demonstrates that the judiciary has chosen interpretative paths which have been more influenced by the traditions of autonomous and fully comprehensive legal systems than by a desire to limit the competences of the EC/EU institutions. The results may be considered as 'more' than what was necessarily embedded in the political wordings and intentions of the treaties. This does not imply that the Court has wilfully acted against the political texts or intentions, but rather that wide discretions in the treaties have been delegated to the legal and administrative authorities to decide on without sufficient political guidelines as to what kind of legal and political system they would want to construct. The legal system has thus contributed, partly due to its own rationality, to an extension of the politically established organizations, beyond the explicit wordings and the known intentions of the treaties.

The administrative systems of the EU have also been delegated wide discretionary powers of legislation and in implementing these they have also contributed heavily to the contents of legislation according to the principles of goal-oriented efficiency. From the basis of political compromises and general principles, the administrative branch has chosen to endorse optimally efficient implementation of the principles of free competition and other means of integration. Within the Commission and its diverse committee-systems there has emerged a distinct attitude of pro-Europe and pro-integration attitude. The administrative branches have been given a task, and they have made an effort to complete it. The administrators have performed professionally according to the tasks given, and they have tended to optimize the goals and the task delegated. The results may be more than the politicians had intended, as stated above, or, as in some cases, less because the implementation processes on the national levels have met with greater problems than anticipated such as the diverse national regimes and cultures of practical or legal implementation.

The liberal use of Art. 235 by the Commission has contributed to a step-by-step extension of what has been deemed 'necessary' elements in the completion of a common and effective market. There have been issued several directives where one might be rather unsure of whether they have been meant as 'necessary' for the functioning of the market, or whether they have in reality been intended as extensions of the competences given in the treaty (and thus really going beyond what is allowed in the treaty). It is however beyond doubt that the extensive use of Art. 235 has contributed to the later following formal extensions of the competences of the treaty.

From 1986 and onwards the EC made a qualitative jump forward in goal-oriented efficiency by the implementation of the SEA, particularly the qualified majority voting system. The efficiency of the implementation of the legislation was enhanced. This could however again be seen as the combined effects of the material competences developed up to 1985 and the increased procedural competences of the SEA. Incremental steps in legislation may make the decisions seem more minor and less dramatic. The combinations may however have consequences which are more comprehensive or other than intended.

'Behind' the political, the legal and the administrative ways of communication we will however also find the scientific languages and modes of communication within the Commission as well as in independent experts in the committees, working groups etc. Scientific or professional analysis will often be the background against which legal and political papers or proposals are drawn up. They will often have a decisive effect as to how problems are defined and structured, and as to what solutions are suggested. The experts will often define preconditions which it may be difficult for the politicians to understand or evaluate independently. We have here another example of the problems of translation from one communicative mode to another – from the scientific to the legal, administrative or political modes of communication. When scientific reports are used by political, legal or administrative institutions, these actors may read and use the reports in different ways, with different aims and in quite different contexts than those for which they were originally written. Parts may be taken out of context and used in different ways than had been intended. Thus distortions of intentions and of communication may be the result.

How the new supranational organizations emerge by way of combinations of different functions and modes of communication is not easily understandable. We need badly to understand how these new, complex and incoherent organizations are created. We are among other things looking at how these different types of communication and rationalities used on the construction of new organizations combine. The political language cannot be regarded as the authorized or primary language which describes how these processes emerge. We need to analyse processes of change across the boundaries of several social or political functions and several modes of communication. What we are looking for are new and complex combinations.

The supranational character of the EU organizations also implies that political compromises imbedded in rhetorical language often will be the rule-of-the-day, and that there will be both geographical and cultural distance between the supranational and the national institutions, not to mention the distance to the national electorates. There may thus tend to be a much more distanced and less efficient political control of supranational institutions than of the national institutions.

The problem here is not only that competences step-by-step get extended or changed by legal or administrative procedures, but that the extension of competences have gone from narrowly market-oriented to far more comprehensive social and environmental regulations. Such expanded competences will make harder the demands on the legitimacy of the legislative procedures of the political regimes than in the more narrow type of regulations. Goal-oriented and wide political decisions have led to more extensive regimes of regulation than was explicitly intended and thereby also give rise to more extensive demands for legitimacy, so far much unattended by the politicians, as well as by the lawyers.

Some of these mechanisms would also be at work in the changes of national regime. A significant difference is however that within a supranational organization there will be significantly more heterogeneity and less social consensus within the areas regulated than in the nation-states. Crises of legitimacy will therefore be more easily invoked by extended competences and regulations on a supranational than on a national level. Gaps and incoherences between different functions and communicative systems become much more severe when the cultural and social background of the institutions are as heterogeneous as in the EU. The question might be asked whether there is insufficient common cultural background, history, values and languages within the area to compensate for the incoherences and gaps emerging in the interaction between the more functional types of communication used in the construction of political or legal institutions.

CONCLUSION: SOME CRITICAL POINTS ON THE POSSIBILITIES OF LEGITIMACY OF SUPRANATIONAL POLITICAL AND LEGAL SYSTEMS

To summarize:

(1) The EU/EEA have been constructed over a relatively short period of time and with different traditions of state- and nationhood among their members. There will be even less social consensus in the EU than within each Member State. The scope of the ambitions, combined with the relative heterogeneity of the members, has contributed to an increased complexity, incoherence and fragmentation in the processes of creating supranational political organizations and legal systems compared to national ones. The lack of social consensus in the European area might result in gaps and incoherences within the political organizations as well as in the legal systems which are vitally important, but which also may be concealed and intransparent in the political and legal processes. Regulations with discretionary formulations which may work and be acceptable on the national levels, may contain too complex and wide compromises which may be

problematic when functioning on the more heterogeneous European level. The combination of heterogeneity and a lack of social consensus on the one hand, and political compromises and legal discretions on the other hand, may be quite demanding. The legal systems of supranational organizations may come to conceal too wide gaps in the meaning contents between the political and vague compromises on the one hand and the legal regulations in function on the other hand. The combination of political and legal rationalities might be too complex, for the demands of legitimacy.

(2) The most basic principle of the treaties is economic liberalism and the primary instrument is the implementation of a free market. Simultaneously there are processes and intentions of creating much more comprehensive legal systems. Questions may be raised as to what kind of legal system may be created with economic principles as its primary constitutional basis and not more in a more explicit way general social and constitutional goals such as democracy, human rights and social welfare. Are these last mentioned considerations key and necessary elements for us to acknowledge something as a 'legal' system, within the boundaries of modern Western societies? Is the explicit and constitutional balancing of social and democratic values as well as economic necessary in order to speak of a legitimately acknowledged legal system?

(3) The national legal systems have been results of democratic legislation enacted by popularly elected bodies and with accountable executive authorities. Within the EU the representation of legislative democracy is doubly indirect: enacted by representatives of national executives which again might be regarded as representatives of the directly elected national bodies. There are also no efficient systems of accountability. The democratic legitimacy of the EU legislation is thus less and quite different from that of national legislation. The question might be asked as to what this does to the general popular legitimacy of the political and legal systems and their operations.

HOW DO WE KNOW WHAT A DEMOCRATIC INSTITUTION IS?

Within the context of the more limited nation-states we do have some patterns and standards for evaluating what democracy is, and for what is popularly accepted as democratic and legitimate institutions. The new supranational institutions are emerging within a different context. The increased internationalization of trade, finances, cultures etc. confront us with a new situation and with new challenges as to the existing structures of governance and regulation, and thus also as to what democratic structures are, and what they might be within a more internationalized context. There are however no existing and consensual patterns of thought as to what democratic structures may be within these new contexts and the challenges they raise. There is a need of some type of more internationalized regulations and political cooperation, but we do not know how to set or evaluate democratic or other standards for them.

For scientists reflection on this may be performed on several orders. The first-order reflection for scientists would be the analysis of what the political actors themselves regard as democratic and how their disagreements should be analysed. The second order would be how we as scientists will analyse and reflect on how the political actors communicate on the theme of democracy and governance. The third order would be how we as scientists will reflect more independently on how to communicate on the standards or patterns of democratic structures within a new context. The political actors themselves will, however, be unsure of what they mean by democratic structures, and we will be correspondingly unsure both of our analysis of their communications and of our own evaluation of it. The result of this is that we operate within a manifold communicational risk when we talk about or try to evaluate democratic structures under such new conditions. These social risks can of course not be evaded, but it seems vital that we are somehow aware of them and the attending uncertainties when we try to communicate about these new and hopefully democratic institutions.

REFERENCES

Joerges, Christian (1993), 'European Economic Law, the Nation-State and the Maastricht Treaty', in *Democratic and Legal Problems in the European Community, IUSEF* no. 12, Center for European Law, University of Oslo.

Joerges, Christian (1996), 'Taking the Law Seriously: On Political Science and the Role of Law in the Process of European Integration', *European Law Journal*, **2** (2).

Luhmann, Niklas (1984), *Soziale Systeme*, Frankfurt: Surkamp.

Luhmann, Niklas (1991), *Soziologie des Risikos*, Berlin: de Gruyter.

Luhmann, Niklas (1993), *Das Recht der Gesellschaft*, Frankfurt: Surkamp.

Moravcsik, Andrew, (1993), 'Preferences and Power in the European Community: A Liberal Intergovernmentalist Approach', *Journal of Common Market Studies*, **31** (4).

Snyder, Francis (1990), *New Directions in European Community Law*, Weidenfeld & Nicolson, London.

Snyder, Francis, (1993), 'The Effectiveness of European Community Law: Institutions, Processes, Tools and Techniques', *Modern Law Review*, **1**.

Streeck, Wolfgang (1995), 'Neo-Voluntarism: A New European Social Policy Regime?', *European Law Journal*, **1** (1).

Weiler, Joseph (1991), 'The Transformation of Europe', *Yale Law Journal*, **100** (8), 1991.
Weiler, Joseph (1993a), 'Europe After Maastricht – Do the New Clothes have an Emperor?', in *Democratic and Legal Problems in the European Community, IUSEF*, **12**, Center for European Law, University of Oslo.
Weiler, Joseph (1993b), 'Journey to an Unknown Destination: A Retrospective of the European Court and Justice in the Arena of Political Integration', *Journal of Common Market Studies*, **31** (4).
Weiler, Joseph, (1995), 'The State "über alles". Demos and Telos in the German Maastricht Decision', in Due, O. *et al.* (eds), *Festschrift für Ulrich Everling*, Baden-Baden.

6 Culture in the Evolution of European Law: Panacea in the Quest for Identity?*

Valsamis Mitsilegas

> The most tangible and influential reality of Europe as a whole is not merely its geographical, political, economic and social features, but also, essentially, its culture. (European Parliament, 1995)

PROLOGUE

'It is necessary to be clear about what we mean by "culture", so that we may be clear about the distinction between the material organization of Europe and the spiritual organism of Europe. If the latter dies, then what you organize will not be Europe, but merely a mass of human beings speaking several different languages' (Eliot, 1962, p. 119). When these words of T.S. Eliot were broadcast on the London Radio Station right after the end of the Second World War, perhaps no one could conceive their significance regarding the role of culture in the building of Europe. However, the founders of the European Economic Community have practically ignored the significance of the cultural dimension of Europe; therefore, the EEC Treaty has scarcely dealt with culture, limiting the Community basically to its economic scope.

It has been argued that 'a Europe' reduced to a market is indeed nothing (Varenne, 1993, p. 233). Even if this is too extreme, the socio-political evolution is within the European Continent, and especially at the Community level, did nonetheless confirm Eliot's fears. In the light of the new

* The author is grateful to Jim Bergeron, Maria Drakopoulou and Peter Fitzpatrick for their invaluable comments on earlier versions of this chapter.

realities shaped by these evolutions, expressed in particular by the transition from an Economic Community to a Union among the peoples of Europe, the Treaty aiming to establish this Union included specific provisions regarding culture which appears as a new legal term in the EU edifice.

The inclusion of the notion of culture in the Treaty on the European Union is of particular significance because, for the first time in the history of European integration, culture must be viewed at two levels; first, culture must be viewed as an evolving legal term whose inclusion in the Treaty on the European Union has the potential to alter significantly the character of European law; at the second level, going beyond strictly legal considerations, culture must be viewed as a decisive factor in European integration. In the construction of a Union among the peoples of Europe, the notion of culture appears as a predominant force in forming a European identity serving as a factor of legitimacy for this newly established Union.

The need to view culture at this second level is justified when understanding the underlying theoretical framework of the relationship between culture and identity. The analysis of this framework will be followed by an analysis at the first level, with the evolution of culture in European law being assessed on the basis of primary EC legislation and European Court of Justice case-law. The aim of this two-level analysis is to provide a credible assessment of the actual and potential role of culture for the construction of the European Union.

'IDENTIFYING' CULTURE

Renato Rosaldo starts his *Culture and Truth* with the assumption that in 'these days questions of culture seem to touch a nerve because they quickly become anguished questions of identity' (Rosaldo, 1989, p. ix). The ambiguity surrounding the variety of doctrinal discourses on culture and identity not only forms complex questions but makes the tasks of answering them seem Herculean. Difficulties arise both from divergences in defining culture and identity and from discrepancies on delimiting the relationship of these notions.

Hence, while in a number of discourses it has been put forward that, in terms of ethnic identity, an ethnic group is usually perceived to be a group of people identifying themselves as distinct from the broader population by virtue of their culture, language, history, traditions and political past (Parman, 1993, p. 191), such determination of culture as a constructive force of identity is 'capsized' by the assumption that 'culture would first of all include a sense of identity, a notion of an "I" and of a "we", which implies a boundary to the other(s)', (Therborn, 1995, p. 12) as culture and the consciousness of culture are coexistent (Heller, 1992, p. 12) and a consciousness of culture requires the identification of the carrier of culture (ibid.).

Notwithstanding their different starting point the previously mentioned arguments highlight the symbiotical relationship of culture and identity. Both terms involve a 'group of people', a 'carrier', an 'I' and a 'we', as 'distinct' from the 'other'. The only way to understand questions on culture and identity and provide credible answers is to take into account a basic inherent element of their symbiosis: that of 'differentiation'.

'Culture may be uncovered wherever people differentiate people' (Strathern, 1995, p. 156). Marilyn Strathern accurately summarizes the anthropological view of culture as 'differential', acknowledging that culture attributes a set of social behavioural and representational properties to a given population (Friedman, 1994, p. 72). Culture becomes distributive by attributing to this population a set of characteristics shared by some but not by others (Barth, 1989, p. 134). Therefore culture shows itself as 'inevitably inclusive' (in the extent to which certain values are shared) or as exclusive (in the extent to which they are not) (Strathern, 1995, p. 161).

In understanding the exclusive character of culture, the notion of Otherness plays a crucial part. The 'Other' is identified as not having certain properties: In this manner, culture serves as a mechanism for identification of the Other, and at the same time constructs an identity for the self and for the 'Us' who realize through the antithesis with the Other our communion with certain characteristics or attributes. Thus culture serves to construct a collective identity. On the other hand, in order to accept this distribution of characteristics, one has to possess a minimal degree of self-consciousness. It is by assessing one's own identity that one can realize the commonality of attributes that is shared with others: differentiation becomes the key for the formation of a self-identity, which through the distributive mechanisms of culture becomes a collective identity.

This 'Janus-faced' placement of culture enlightened by and casting light on images of identity at the same time becomes particularly opportune in the interplay of identities in the European Union. In the symbiotic and at times conflicting relationship between the national identities of the EU Member States, viewed under a methodological individualist assumption as being 'born whole' hence encompassing a self-identity (Featherstone, 1995, p. 144) and the repeatedly evoked collective 'European' identity, culture will strike the balance in a series of existential issues for the future of the Union.

Are the peoples of the EU Member States conscious of an individual national identity, enabling them to accept a series of common 'European' characteristics? Does culture have the power to attribute such characteristics and by differentiating between the people of the Union and others, to form an identity for this Union? A contextual overview of the evolving and at times conflicting relationship of culture and European law will serve to provide answers to these crucial issues for the development of the European Union.

CULTURE AND THE EUROPEAN COMMUNITY: THE ANTE-MAASTRICHT STATUS

Culture in the EEC Treaty

The European legislator appeared reluctant to include expressly the term 'culture' in the EEC Treaty, focusing on the construction of an economic Community. Cultural aspects appear only indirectly, in Art. 36 of the Treaty, exceptionally allowing prohibitions or restrictions on imports, exports or goods in transit justified on grounds of the protection of national treasures possessing artistic, historic or archaeological value.

This indirect reference to culture remains limited to an economic sphere, as the same Article expressly provides that such prohibitions or restrictions shall not constitute a means of arbitrary discrimination or a disguised restriction on trade between Member States. Furthermore, thorny issues arise due to the terminology of Art. 36: the term 'national treasures' is more accurately translated as such in the text of the Treaty only in some of the official languages of the Community, whereas in a considerable number of other languages the term is translated as 'national cultural heritage' or 'national cultural good' (Voudouri, 1992, pp. 39–40).

Abandoning Art. 36, as well as the 'incidental' provision of Art. 131, referring to the 'economic', social and cultural development' of the overseas countries and territories associated with the Community, culture is nowhere to be found in the Treaty of Rome. However, even in the context of the economic goals pursued by the Community, cultural concerns appeared at a Community level through the case-law of the European Court of Justice that placed culture in the Community legal order.

Culture in the jurisprudence of the European Court of Justice

The Community system was marked by 'a clear but unexpressed resolution to separate the economic and cultural spheres' (De Witte, 1993, p. 156). Thus the elliptic provisions of Art. 36, referring to the protection of national treasures possessing artistic, historic or archaeological value, along with Art. 131, seem to be incidental provisions in the framework of the Treaty, leaving plenty of space for 'creative' intervention by the European Court of Justice. The Court, on the other hand, has been obliged to deal with cultural concerns plenty of times, as it is impossible to disassociate culture from the rest of society. The Court had to face cases related to the compatibility of culture protection with the basic freedoms of Community law and with competition law.

A present ...

Hence, in *Cinétheque SA and Others* v. *Fédération Nationale des Cinémas Français* (Joint cases 60 and 61/84, ECR [1985], p. 2605) the Court, ruling on the compatibility of national measures having cultural finalities with the free movement of goods, held that it must be conceded that a national system which, in order to encourage the creation of cinematographic works irrespective of their origin, gives priority for a limited initial period to the distribution of such works through the cinema (system that, according to the Court, may create barriers to intra-Community trade) is so justified (*Cinetheque*; point 23).

Furthermore, the Court, judging whether the prohibition of Sunday trading was compatible with the free movement of goods, held that this field is a matter for the Member States to regulate, as such rules reflect certain political and economic choices in so far as their purpose is to ensure that working and non-working hours are so arranged as to accord with national or regional socio-cultural characteristics (see case *Torfaen Borough Council* v. *B and Q plc* [1989], p. 3851, point 14. Also cases *Syndicates CGT de l'Aisne* v. *Sidef Confarama* [1991], p. I-997 and *Ministère Public* v. *Marchandise* [1991], p. I-1027).

In the 'Tourist Guides' cases, the Court dealt with national restrictions on the free movement of services, based on cultural finalities. Although the term 'culture' was not expressly used by the Court, it was held that the general interest in the proper appreciation of the artistic and archaeological heritage of a country (*Commission* v. *Hellenic Republic* [1991], p. I-735, point 21), in the conservation of the national historical and artistic heritage (*Commission* v. *Italian Republic* [1991], p. I-709), and in the proper appreciation of places and things of historical interest and the widest possible dissemination of knowledge of the artistic and cultural heritage of a country (*Commission* v. *French Republic* [1991], p. I-659), can constitute an overriding reason justifying a restriction on the freedom to provide services (quotation identical to all three cases).

Cultural policy is mentioned expressly in the 'audiovisual' cases concerning national measures taken by the Government of the Netherlands in the audiovisual sector. Answering to the contention of the Dutch Government that these measures were justified by reasons of cultural policy, the aim of which was to safeguard the freedom of expression of the various (in particular social, cultural, religious and philosophical) components making up the Netherlands (*Commission* v. *Netherlands* [1991], p. I-4069, point 29. See also the '*Gouda*' case [1991], p. I-4007, point 22), the Court held that a cultural policy understood in that sense may indeed constitute an overriding requirement relating to the general interest which justifies a restriction on the freedom to provide services (*Commission* v. *Netherlands*, point 30, '*Gouda*', point 23).

As regards the compatibility of cultural policy provisions with the free movement of persons, the Court, in the Groener case (*Groener* v. *The Minister of Education and the City of Dublin* [1989], p. 3965), examining 'the policy followed by Irish governments ... designed not only to maintain but also to promote the use of Irish as a means of expressing national identity and culture' (*Groener*, point 18), held that the EEC Treaty does not prohibit the adoption of a policy for the protection and promotion of a Member State which is both the national language and the first official language (*Groener*, point 19).

The Court had to examine cultural justifications in relation to competition law. In the joint cases *Vereeniging ter Bevordering van het Vluamse Boekwezen, VBVB, and Vereeniging ter Bevordering van der Belangen des Boekhandels, VBBB* v. *Commission* (joint cases 43 and 63/82 [1984], p. 19), the Court held that 'the specific nature of books as an object of trade must justify certain special conditions in the matter of distribution and price' ('VBVB', point 46). Moreover, in the Leclerc case (*Association des Centres distributeurs, Edouard Leclerc and Others* v. *Au Blé Vert Sàrl and Others* [1985], p. 17), facing the French government's justifications of national measures aiming 'to protect books as cultural media from the adverse impact that untrammelled competition in retail prices would have on the diversity and cultural level of publishing' (*Leclerc*, point 16), the Court held that 'as Community law stands, Member States' obligations under Article 5 of the EEC Treaty, in conjunction with Arts 3(f) and 85, are not specific enough to preclude them from enacting legislation of the type at issue on completion in the retail prices of books' (*Leclerc*, ibid., point 20).

A first outlook on this mosaic of cases before the Court concerning culture present in the ECJ case-law either directly, or, more often, an indirect way thus demonstrates that the European judge is ready to acknowledge cultural preoccupations as overriding reasons of general interest, able to impose restrictions on fundamental principles of Community law.

... Absent

However, a careful examination of the Court's attitude towards culture leads to different assumptions. The Court, judging on controversial issues of Community competence, excluded cultural considerations from its ruling. This attitude is clearly illustrated in the Grogan case (*Society for the Protection of Unborn Children Ireland Ltd* v. *Stephen Grogan and Others* [1991], p. I-4685), where the Court avoided to judge upon the balance between 'moral and philosophical imperatives' (Terms used by the Advocate General, point 26) and the free movement of services, and issued a judgement based on purely economic criteria.

Similar was the attitude of the Court in the Leclerc case (1985, p. 17) with regard to cultural considerations in EC competition law. The Court, examining the compatibility on French measures aiming 'to protect books as cultural media' (*Leclerc*, p. 20) from untrammelled competition with Community competition law, seemed reluctant to provide an answer *in concreto*. However, it was deemed necessary to consider whether 'such legislation is consonant with the other specific Treaty provisions, in particular those concerning the free movement of goods' (Leclerc, point 20; see also the 'second' Leclerc case, 1985, p. I-2515, point 9).

The fact that the Court, contrary to the Grogan approach, actually examined cultural considerations both in the Leclerc case and the rest of the aforementioned cases does not signify that the Court is ready to accept culture as a prominent consideration for Community law. In spite of the in principle acceptance of cultural policy restrictions to Community law, such restrictions could only be justified under severe qualifications.

First of all, according to the constant case-law of the European Court of Justice, national measures pursuing 'cultural' aims can prevail upon Community law principles under the condition that they are non-discriminatory and satisfy the proportionality test.[1] Furthermore, and most significantly, national measures pursuing cultural policy goals are justified as exceptions to the fundamental Community law freedoms. The restrictive interpretation of the Court as regards the scope of these exceptions, does not leave much space for culture justifying measures contrary to the economic freedoms well established in the Treaty.

This assumption is vividly illustrated in the Leclerc case (1985 V-2515), where the Court, after having held that 'since it derogates from a fundamental rule of the Treaty, Art. 36 must be interpreted strictly and cannot be extended to cover objectives not expressly enumerated therein' (*Leclerc*, point 30), it refused to justify French measures protecting book publishing as an exception to the free movement of goods, excluding the protection of creativity and cultural diversity in the realm of publishing from the scope of Art. 36.

The Court maintained this strict approach as regards the compatibility of national measures justified by cultural policy grounds restricting the free movement of services. In the *Bond van Adverteerders and others*. v. *The Netherlands State*, (352/85 [1988], 2085, it held that such restrictions, which simultaneously pursue economic aims cannot be justified since economic aims ... cannot constitute grounds of public policy within the meaning of Art. 56 of the Treaty (Bond van Adverteerders, point 34).

Thus, in spite of the absence of relevant provisions in the EEC Treaty, the European Court of Justice came across a number of cases involving culture. However, the Community judge followed much the approach of the Community legislator. When culture was not excluded from the EC law framework, its presence was subordinated to paramount economic criteria. Although it was accepted that culture could in principle override Community economic freedoms, the Court, facing the specificity and the diversity of cultural policy in relation to economic standards, attempted to shape cultural considerations according to these standards. No water was given for the flowering of culture trying to grow within the EEC cement: thus the flower remained feeble – in the well-built walls of the market, culture was still a present-absent.

CULTURE AND THE EUROPEAN COMMUNITY: THE IMPACT OF MAASTRICHT

Culture in the EC Treaty (as amended by TEU)

The new provisions

A significant step towards the transformation of the European Economic Community to a Union is achieved through the Maastricht Treaty. In this transformation the European political and legislative authorities have realized the importance of culture as a fundamental element of identity, both at national and European level. Thus, in the Preamble to the Treaty on the European Union, express reference is made to a new stage in the process of European integration as well as to the signatories' desire to deepen the solidarity between their peoples while respecting their history, their culture and their traditions.

These new objectives established in the Treaty on the European Union have had a significant impact to the extent that, in sharp contrast with the ante-Maastricht cultural wasteland, the amended Treaty contains a series of provisions explicitly referring to culture. Thus, Art. 3(p) of the amended EC Treaty expressly provides that the activities of the Community shall include 'a contribution ... to the flowering of the cultures of the Member States'.

This provision would have had solely a theoretical value had it not been accompanied by Art. 128 of the EC Treaty, inserted by Art. G(37) of the European Union treaty. This Article establishes a new Community cultural competence the first time expressly provided for in the Treaty. According to this Article, the Community shall contribute to the flowering of the cultures of the Member States, while respecting their national and regional diversity and at the same time bringing the common cultural heritage to the fore (Art. 128(1) of the Treaty). The Article goes even further providing that the Community shall take cultural aspects into account in its action under other provisions of the Treaty (Art. 128(4) of the Treaty). However, the Article continues excluding any harmonization of the laws and regulations of the Member States (Art. 128(5) of the Treaty), stating that the Council shall adopt recommendations (Art. 128(5) of the Treaty).

The Maastricht contribution to the primary EC legislation as regards culture does not end in Art. 128. Quite surprisingly, the European legislator chooses to insert culture in a traditional economic fortress, that of competition rules. Hence, Art. 92(3) of the Treaty, referring to state aids able to be considered compatible with the common market, expressly mentions aids to promote culture and heritage conservation (Art. 92(3) of the Treaty).

This framework of Arts 9p, 92(3)d and 128 of the Treaty is completed by the provisions of Arts 36 and 131 which remained unaffected by the Maastricht amendments.

Issues and complexities

Culture? The problem in asserting the role of Arts 3p, 92(3)d and 128 of the EC Treaty, stems from the difficulty in providing a concrete definition of 'culture'. The latter has been viewed in many perspectives: as an 'endless multidimensional construction, a gathering of ateliers, workshops, opera houses, theatre halls, academies, attics, cellars, grand arenas and corners of pedestrians ways' (Spath, 1989, p. 235), but also as a more complex notion including the concepts of a human condition which implies a value, a specific way of life, an ethnic entity pure and simple and a regionally meta-ethnic entity (Kahler, 1968, pp. 15–16). While culture is perceived by some as a notion limited to the arts and other manifestations of human intellectual achievement regarded collectively (*Concise Oxford Dictionary of Current English*, 1991) others view it as essentially 'a transformation of nature, of society' (Storme, 1994, p. 28).

This ambiguity in perceiving culture, emanating from the inherent polysemy of the term and the variety of doctrinal approaches to cultural phenomena, is emphasized by divergences in approaching the relationship between the notions of culture and civilization. With culture being defined as a means of 'cultivating' of 'gardening as a mechanism of social reproduction' (Bauman, 1989, pp. 81–95), it is questionable whether culture in the EC Treaty is to be perceived as a 'gardening' procedure which, by identifying the European Union with civil virtues, will attempt to civilize others within or potentially within this Union (or whether one should accept the antithesis of culture and civilization, as one distinguishes between soul and society, freedom and voting rights, art and literature (Mann, 1983)).

The text of the treaty throws further shadows on the issues, especially when examining the wording of the various official versions of the treaty in the languages of the different member states (Missir di Lusignano, 1994, p. 184). Thus, while the EC Treaty refers to 'culture' in English and French, it refers to 'civilization' (*politismos*) in Greek. It remains to see how 'culture' will be defined post-Maastricht and what the implications of this definition will be for the *acquis communautaire* built by the case-law of the European Court of Justice (Lane, 1993, p. 957).

Culture of the Member States? Both Articles 3p and 128 of the Treaty refer to 'cultures of the Member States' of the European Community. Does the latter mean that to make use of these provisions one has to distinguish 15 cultures in the Community, one for each Member State?

Article 128(1) helps towards an answer to this issue, when speaking of a contribution to the flowering of the cultures of the Member States, while respecting their national and regional diversity.[2] Apart from the emphasis placed on regional diversity, allowing to include 'regional' cultures to the scope of these provisions, this position is strengthened by a liberal grammatical interpretation of this provision, conceiving the 'cultures of the Member States', also to 'cultures of a Member State'. However, with the latter not being clear, major issues continue to exist, particularly regarding the cultures of minorities in the Member States. These cultures are not covered by the regional diversity provision, as many of these minorities are originally non-European and do not form a region in a State, being dispersed throughout its territory.

Common Cultural Heritage? Article 128(1) of the Treaty provides that 'the Community shall contribute to the flowering of the cultures of the Member States while ... bringing their common cultural heritage to the fore'. This common cultural heritage is accompanied by a respect for the 'national and cultural diversity' of these States.

This choice of the European legislator justifies the argument that 'in theory the development of a community of Europeans is not inconsistent with the maintenance of ethnic enclaves, cultural distinctiveness and other elements of diversity in the daily affairs of average Europeans' (Howe, 1995, p. 28). However, the overwhelmingly wide notion of 'common cultural heritage' leaves open both the delimination of the term 'cultural heritage' and the path to be followed for this heritage to be considered 'common'. The argument in favour of a synthesis of national, regional and minorities heritage of the Member States crashes onto the rocks of views emphasizing striking cultural differences between these states, regions and peoples.

In the quest for a 'common cultural heritage' the temporal factor is also crucial, as it is essential to assess whether the European Union seeks for a 'common culture' existing after the EEC foundation taking into considerations specific late-twentieth-century political, economic and ideological conditions, or whether this common culture encompasses stereotypical Western attributes related to race, religion or colour. This is of enormous importance with regard to the accession of future Members to the Union, and the extent that these states are required to receive and contribute to this 'common cultural heritage'.

Cultural Aspects into Account in Community Action? The fourth paragraph of Art. 124(4) of the Treaty provides that the Community shall take cultural aspects into account in its action under other provisions of this Treaty. What is the actual significance of this provision?

First of all, it is surprising to see that the European legislator, in a provision crucial for the effectiveness of the whole framework regarding culture, does not choose to avoid ambiguities by using the term 'culture' in a straightforward manner, but attempts to manoeuvre by utilizing the vague term of 'cultural aspects'. Should the latter term be viewed as a synonym of 'culture', as a specific manifestation of culture or as possessing a different meaning? And if this is the case, how shall this meaning be delimited? (see also Lane, 1993, p. 957).

Further issues arise from the requirement of the Treaty that these cultural aspects are to be taken into account in Community action, as it is not clear whether this requirement is of a political nature, or if it constitutes a rule enhanced with mandatory force (Lane, 1993, p. 957). An answer to this controversy is vital for the assessment of the legal significance of Art. 128 in the EC Treaty if Art. 128(4) is considered to be an 'integration clause' (Lane, 1993, p. 956) being a part of the 'bloc of community legality' (Karydis, 1994, p. 559) cultural aspects acquire a significant role in European integration, a role that remains decorative in the case of 128(4) being deprived of mandatory value (Bekemans and Balodimos, 1993, p. 135).

Culture in the jurisprudence of the ECJ: answers to the complexities of presence or the easy way to absence?

After the entry into force of the Maastricht Treaty the European Court of Justice dealt with a number of cases involving culture. In these rulings the Court did not refer to the new provisions of the Treaty, but continued to view these cultural aspects in the light of their relationship with the free movement of persons, services and capital. In the Lotteries case (*Her Majesty's Customs and Excise* v. *Gerhart Schindler and Jorg Schindler* [1994], p. I-1039), the Court held that it is not possible to disregard the moral, religious or cultural aspects of lotteries, like other types of gambling, in all the Member States (point 60), adding that the particular factors characterizing lotteries:

> justify national authorities having a sufficient degree of latitude to determine what is required to protect the players and, more generally, in the light of the specific social and cultural features of each Member State, to maintain order in society as regards the manner in which lotteries are operated, the size of the stakes, and the allocation of the profits they yield. (Lotteries, point 61)

In reaching this decision, the Court moved strictly within the free movement of services scope. After assessing whether lottery measures fall within the scope of this economic freedom (points 16–37 of judgement), the Court examined the compatibility of such measures with the EC law, by including them in the public policy exception of Art. 59 on the Treaty. In spite of the judgement's references to moral, religious and cultural considerations entouring lotteries (see *inter alia* point 60), no reference was made to the culture provisions of the Treaty.

Similar was the reasoning in the Bosman case (1995, p. I-4921), where the court viewed nationality clauses restricting the right of nationals of one Member State to take part, as professional players, in football matches in another Member State in the spectre of the free movement of workers. The Court after including them in the freedom of movement framework, examined whether these clauses, which according to the plaintiffs 'are justified non-economic grounds', serving to maintain the traditional link between each club and its country, a factor of great importance in enabling the public to identify with its favourite team and ensuring that clubs taking part in international competitions effectively represent their countries (points 122 and 123 of judgement) are justified as a public policy exception to the economic freedom of movement within Art. 48 of the treaty.

The new 'culture' provisions have thus not yet influenced the Court in creating a new ethos in the interpretation of other Treaty provisions, with the result that cultural aspects are to be taken into account in Community action vis-à-vis EC fundamental economic rules.

EUROPEAN LAW VIS-À-VIS EUROPEAN IDENTITY: THE ROLE OF CULTURE

Culture as another EC competence ...

Thinking of Europe, Edgar Morin realized that Europe has no entity but only inside and through its multiplicity (Morin, 1991, p. 34). This point has been upheld by the European legislator, in the effort to create a Union out of an Economic Community and is reflected in the new provisions regarding culture in the Maastricht Treaty. These provisions speak about the 'flowering of the cultures of the Member States', the respect of 'their national and regional diversity' and the bringing to the force of their 'common cultural heritage' (Art. 128(1) of the EC Treaty). They speak about the promotion of culture and heritage conservation (Art. 92(3)d of the EC Treaty). And they aim to create a Community that shall take cultural aspects into account (Art. 128(4) of the EC Treaty).

From a legal perspective, the achievement of these objectives constitutes for the Community a wish rather than an imperative goal. Thus, the Council, in achieving these objectives, shall adopt incentive measures (Art. 128(5) of the EC Treaty) or unanimous recommendations. More effective measures on culture are viewed as a taboo, as any harmonization of the laws and regulations of the Member States is excluded (Art. 128(5) of the Treaty) and the role of the Community remains subsidiary, as its action shall aim only to encourage (co-operation between Member States), to support and to supplement (action of the Member States) (Art. 128(2) of the EC Treaty).

Under these circumstances, Art. 128, already burdened with a vague legal terminology and a lack of clarity regarding its exact context, is rendered practically ineffective. Its strength lies mainly in the clause inserted in the fourth paragraph of the Article (providing that the Community shall take cultural aspects into account in its action under other provisions of this Treaty), a provision whose value may range, according to various interpretations, from an integration clause influencing the whole of the Community legal construction to a simple declaratory provision deprived of any mandatory effect.

The situation is not ameliorated by the European Court of Justice, reluctant to expressly use the new provisions of the Treaty. An outlook on the post-Maastricht jurisprudence of the Court demonstrates that the new legal framework had had practically no influence in its ratio. Cultural policies aiming to preserve national diversity still bump into the barrier of the pursuit of an economic aim, and with Arts 92(3)d and 128, apart from a series of peripheral measures having a limited scope,[3] remain inapplicable.

... Or as a symbol?

Notwithstanding the foregoing analysis, the narrow view of culture strictly as a 'decorative' Community competence constitutes a rather short-sighted evaluation, disregarding the role that culture can play in the evolution of the European Union. The latter underlines the need to abandon an infertile legalistic approach and to associate the insertion of the 'culture' provisions in the Maastricht Treaty with the telos of an 'ever closer Union between the peoples of Europe', that the Treaty on the European Union is deemed to pursue (Preamble of TEU).

In the process of the creation of a Single Union of people, the European legislator faces an enigma: in view of the predominance of the nation-state as the prevalent form of legitimate polity in Europe, to what extent can a new, supranational policy such as the European Union appear legitimate in the eyes of people who feel paramountly members of nation-states?

The solution of this legitimacy enigma, lies to a great extent with the development of the Union as an imagined community. In a similar fashion to the building of the nation-states, the European Union is challenged to provide to the people of its Member States 'a quasi-religious sense of belonging and fellowship which is attached to those who are taken to share a symbolic space' (Featherstone, 1995, p. 108). This sense of belonging and fellowship requires the existence of distinct characteristics of 'European-ness' shared within these people. It is these underlying characteristics that will form a collective identity legitimizing the European Union.

The inclusion of culture in the Maastricht Treaty serves exactly this purpose. When Art. 128 accepts a 'common cultural heritage' of the EU Member States, it does nothing but put in force the distributive mechanisms of culture. The latter is used to confirm the existence of a set of common attributes, of a 'common heritage' based on culture, shared by everybody in the Union. Culture offers something common, this sense of belonging and fellowship of 'us', the people of Europe in the symbolic space of the European Union; and a collective identity is thus constructed.

In evoking culture as a mechanism of constructing a European identity, the makers of the Treaty appeared cautious not to overlook the role of individual Member States in the Union. Hence, Art. 128, along with acknowledging this 'common cultural heritage', at the same time requires respect for national and regional diversity and highlights the aim of the flowering of the cultures of the Member States.

Apart from relieving worries for the creation of a European Super-State, allowing thus the step of the explicit reference to a common culture in the EC Treaty, the emphasis on the national and regional diversity of the EU Member States, and the acknowledgement of their culture, implies the existence of a consciousness of identity in these states. By taking these elements for granted, the Treaty perceives these nations as 'born whole', ready to accept this common cultural heritage which will lead to the formation of a collective European identity.

EPILOGUE

The presence of culture in the Treaty on the European Union is of pivotal significance, to the extent that it has the power to influence the future of this Union, by entitling the latter with a distinct identity. In this attempt of the European authorities, culture, either appearing in the Treaty as a 'common heritage', or through its 'flowering' in individual Member States, remains Janus-faced. By encouraging the coexistence of a common heritage with national and regional diversity, the use of culture in the Treaty reflects a philosophy of integration encapsulating the Morinian principle of unity through multiplicity or 'unitas multiplex' (Morin, 1991, p. 34).

However, this philosophy remains incomplete: notwithstanding the contribution of the notion of culture in delimiting how a collective European identity is to be constructed, it fails to decipher what will form this identity and who is deemed to evoke it. Will, for instance, the delimination of 'us' be based – as in other Treaty provisions (Art. 8 of TEU on Citizenship of the Union: see *inter alia* Martiniello, 1994, p. 29) – strictly on the element of nationality or will this expand to factual criteria such as that of residence in the territory of the Union? And what exactly is this common heritage shared by the people of Europe?

Further issues arise from the ambiguous attitude of the European legislator towards culture. In spite of the 'usefulness' of the latter as a constitutional identity symbol, it is not evident whether this symbol is to be used also as a legally binding provision in European law. On the one hand, Art. 128 is formed according to the subsidiarity principle, leaving culture to Member States and giving Community action in this field only a supplementary character, and, on the other, it contains a paragraph that may be perceived as an integration clause, rendering culture a decisive factor influencing European law and policy.

In the absence of any substantial legislative or jurisprudential intervention, it remains to be seen how culture will function as a 'European' symbol and as a legal term. What should be borne in mind, is that the context of this term can no longer remain static in a narrow 'Western-White-Christian' model. In a constantly changing landscape, the only way of legitimizing a 'European' culture is for it to be readjusted. In agreeing with John Keane, who pointed out that 'a European public spirit ... requires deep respect and support for those new cultural identities ... produced by the post-1945 wave of migration into Europe of nearly twenty million people, the largest single recorded movement of people in human history' (Keane, 1992, p. 59), it is essential to extend this respect to these new cultures, abandoning a static focus of culture in abstractions of nations or regions. This 'common cultural heritage' is not to be viewed as an amalgam of values accepted on a majority basis and on quantitative criteria. By disregarding the multicultural features of the Union, the enhancement of diversity is rendered meaningless.

With such thoughts in mind, one hopes that the European authorities will not act as a modern Oedipus, killing out of ignorance his multicultural father, for the sake of a 'traditional' mother-Europe of the past. In this case ignorance cannot be forgiven and blindness will become death for any form of Union.

NOTES

1 See *inter alia* Cinetheque 1985 points 22, 23, *Commission* v. *Hellenic Republic*, points 18, 19, *Commission* v. *Italian Republic* [1991], points 17, 18, *Commission* v. *French Republic* [1991], points 14, 15, *Commission* v. *Netherlands* [1991], points 31, 42, 43, '*Gouda*' [1991], points 23, 24, '*Groener*' [1989], point 19, *Bond van Adverteeders*, points 36, 37.

2 See also the amendments to the Proposal for a European Parliament and Council Decision establishing a Community action programme in the field of cultural heritage – the Raphael Programme (COM 95) C 287/161, in which cultural heritage is defined as 'the expression of national, regional and local identities'.

3 See, for instance, the Commission Proposal for a European Parliament and Council Decision establishing a Community action programme in the field of cultural heritage – Raphael COM(95) 110 final, 95/0078(COD), and the amended Commission Proposal for a European Parliament and Council Decision establishing a programme to support artistic and cultural activities having a European dimension – Kaleidoscope 2000 COM 95 final, 94/0188(COD).

REFERENCES

Albanese, Ferdinando (1991), 'Ethnic and Linguistic Minorities in Europe', *Yearbook of European Law*, 313.

Barth, Fredrik (1989), 'The Analysis of Culture in Complex Societies', *Ethnos*, **54** (1–2), 119.

Bauman, Z. (1989), *Legislators and Interpreters*, Cambridge: Polity Press.

Bekemans, Leonce (1994), 'Economy and Culture in European Society – Methodological Considerations', *History of European Ideas*, **19** (1–3), 267.

Bekemans, Leonce and Balodimos (1993), 'Le Traité de Maastricht et l'éducation, la formation professionelle et la culture', *Revue du Marché unique Européen*, 99.

Bracconier, Stephane (1995), 'Politiques culturelles locales francais et principe communautaire de libre-concurrence', *Revue Trimestrielle du droit Européen*, **31** (4).

Cloos, J., Reinesch, G., Vignes, D. and Weyland, J. (eds) (1994), *Le Traité de Maastricht*, Brussels: Bruylant.

Constantinesco, Vladimir (1993), 'La structure du Traite Instituant l'Union Europeenne', *Cahiers du droit Européen*, **29** (3–4), 251.

Derrida, J. (1992), *The Other Heading*, Bloomington: Indiana University Press.

De Witte, Bruno (1993), 'Cultural Legitimation: back to the Language Question', in Soledad Garcia (ed.), *European Identity and the Search for Legitimacy*, London: Pinter Books for the Eleni Nakou Foundation and the Royal Institute of International Affairs.

Eliot, T.S. (1962), *Notes Towards the Definition of Culture*, London: Faber & Faber.

European Commission, *Proposal for a European Parliament and Council Decision Establishing a Community Action Programme in the Field of Cultural Heritage*, RAPHAEL, COM (95), 110 final, 95/0078 (COD).

European Commission, *Amended Proposal for a European Parliament and Council Decision Establishing a Programme to Support Artistic and Cultural Activities having a European Dimension*, KALEIDOSCOPE 2000, COM (95) 373 final, 94/0188 (COD).

European Parliament, *Amendments to the Proposal of a European Parliament and Council Decision Establishing a Community Action Programme in the Field of Cultural Heritage*, RAPHAEL, DOC A4-0225/95, OJ 1995, C.287/161.

Featherstone, M. (1995), *Undoing Culture: Globalization, Post-Modernism and Identity*, London: Sage Publications.

Fitzpatrick, Peter (1998), 'New Europe and Old Stories: Myths of Identity and Legality in the European Community', in Peter Fitzpatrick and Jim Bergeron (eds), *Europe's Other: European Law between Modernity and Postmodernity*, Aldershot: Ashgate.

Friedman, J. (1994), *Cultural Identity and Global Process*, London: Sage Publications.

Geddes, Antony (1995), 'Immigrant and Ethnic Minorities and the EU's Democratic Deficit', *Journal of Common Market Studies*, **33** (2), 201.

Grossfeld, Bernhard (1992), 'The Internal Dynamics of the European Community Law', *The International Lawyer*, **26** (1), 125.

Hedetoft, Ulf (1994), 'National Identities and European Integration "From Below": Bringing People Back In', *Journal of European Integration*, **18** (1), I.

Hellenic Centre of European Studies (1993), *Hellenic Cultural Identity and European Unification* (*Ellininki Politistiki Tautotita ke Europaiki Enopoiisi*), Athens: Estia.

Heller, Agnes (1992), 'Europe: An Epilogue?', in Brian Nelson, David Roberts and Walter Veit (eds), *The Idea of Europe: Problems of National and Transnational Identity*, New York, Oxford: Berg.

Howe, Paul (1995), 'A Community of Europeans: the Requisite Underpinnings', *Journal of Common Market Studies*, **33** (1), 27.

Kahler, Erich (1968), 'Culture and Evolution' in Montagu Ashley (ed.), '*Culture: Man's Adaptive Dimension*', Oxford University Press, 3.

Karydis, Georges (1994), 'Le juge communautaire et le préservation de l'identité culturelle nationale', *Revue Trimestrielle du Droit Européen*, **30** (4), 550.

Keane, John (1992), 'Questions for Europe', in Brian Nelson, David Roberts and Walter Veit (eds), '*The idea of Europe: Problems of National and Transnational Identity*', New York, Oxford: Berg.

Laffey, J. (1993), *Civilization and its Discontented*, London Black Rose Books.

Lane, Robert (1993), 'New Community Competences under the Maastricht Treaty', *Common Market Law Review*, **30** (5), 939.

Martiniello, Mario (1994), 'Citizenship of the European Union. A critical View', in Rainer Baubock (ed.), *From Aliens to Citizens: Redefining the Status of Immigrants in Europe*, Avebury, 29.

Missir di Lusignano, Livio (1994), 'Communauté et Culture', *Revue du Marché Commun et de l'Union Européen*, **376** (3/94), 181.

Morin, E. (1991), *Penser l'Europe* (Greek edition), Athens: Exantas.

Parman, Susan (1993), 'The Future of European Boundaries: A Case Study', in Thomas M. Wilson and M. Estellie Smith (eds), *Cultural Change and the New Europe*, Boulder, San Francisco, Oxford: Westview Press.

Reif, Karl Heinz (1993), 'Cultural Convergence and Cultural Diversity as Factors in European Identity', in Soledad Garcia (ed.), *European Identity and the Search for Legitimacy*, London: Pinter Books for the Eleni Nakou Foundation and the Royal Institute of International Affairs.

Rencontres Internationales de Geneve (1986), *L'Europe aujourd'hui*, Neuchatel: Ed. de la Baconniere.

Rosaldo, R. (1989), *Culture and Truth: The Remarking of Social Analysis*, London: Routledge.

Smart, Barry (1992), 'Europe Today and the Post-Modern Paradox', in Brian Nelson, David Roberts and Walter Veit (eds), *The Idea of Europe: Problems of National and Transnational Identity*, New York, Oxford: Berg.

Smith, Antony (1992), 'National Identity and the Idea of European Unity', *International Affairs*, **68** (1), 55.

Spath, L. (1989), *1992: Der Traum von Europa*, Deutsche Verlags: Anstalt.

Storme, Marcel (1994), 'Droit et Culture dans la Societe Contemporaine', in Lambros Kotsiris (ed.) *Law at the Turn of the 20th Century – International Conference, Thessaloniki, 1993*, Thessaloniki: Sakkoulas.

Strathern, M. (ed.) (1995), *Shifting Contexts: Transformations in Anthropological Knowledge*, London, New York: Routledge.

Therborn, G. (1995), *European Modernity and Beyond*, London: Sage Publications.

Varenne, Herve (1993), 'The Question of European Nationalism', in Thomas M. Wilson and M. Estellie Smith (eds), *Cultural Change and the New Europe*, Boulder: San Francisco; Oxford: Westview.

Veikos, A. (1993), *Nationalism and National Identity ('Ethnikismos ke ethniki tautotita')*, Athens.

Voudouri, D. (1992), *The Protection of Cultural Heritage under the Perspective of the Single European Market ('I prostassia tis politistikis kleronomias ipo to prisma tis eniaias europaikis agoras)*, Papazissis.

Wallerstein, E. (1991), *Geopolitics and Geoculture*, Maison des Sciences de l'Homme and Cambridge University Press.

Ward, Ian (1994), 'In Search of a European Identity', *Modern Law Review*, **57** (2), 315.

Wilson, Thomas M. (1993), 'An Anthropology of the European Community', in Thomas M. Wilson and M. Estellie Smith (eds), '*Cultural Change and the New Europe: Perspectives on the European Community*', Oxford: Westview Press.

7 The Common Foreign and Security Policy of the EU: Reinforcing the European Identity?

Sionaidh Douglas-Scott

INTRODUCTION: THE 'LEAST KNOWN' PILLAR

Much is being written these days about that elusive concept, a European identity. The question of what this European identity might be has become more pertinent in the wake of the deeper integration of the European Union espoused by the Maastricht Treaty and the call for a 'return to Europe' by central European countries after the revolutions of 1989 and 1990. In this context it is therefore interesting to observe that the Maastricht Treaty provisions for a common foreign and security policy of the EU have been introduced with the aim of asserting and reinforcing the European identity. Thus, in the Preamble to the Maastricht Treaty the parties are:

> RESOLVED to implement a common foreign and security policy including the eventual framing of a common defence policy, which might in time lead to a common defence, *thereby reinforcing the European identity* and its independence in order to promote peace, security and progress in Europe and the world. [italics added].

Continuing in the same vein Art. B paragraph 2 of the Maastricht Treaty, sets, *inter alia*, the following objective for the Union:

> ... *to assert its identity* on the international scene, in particular through the implementation of a common foreign and security policy including the eventual

> framing of a common defence policy, which might in time lead to a common defence. [italics added].

This common foreign and security policy (CFSP) was introduced by way of the provisions in Title V, Art. J of the Maastricht Treaty. This is perhaps the least well-known 'pillar' of the Union and, unlike some other sections of the Treaty, there was little discussion of it in the media in the run-up to Maastricht. Nor, indeed, has the policy been conspicuous for its success since the Treaty came into force.

The aim of this chapter is twofold – initially, to consider what meaning the concept of a European identity might have and secondly to consider how the introduction of this 'second pillar' of the EU, the provisions on a CFSP, might help to shape or strengthen it.

This chapter will argue that, at present, the European self-image is confused and in need of greater definition if the EU is to assert itself as a powerful force in the way aspired to by the Treaty provision set out above. It will also be argued that the Maastricht Treaty in general, and the CFSP in particular, do little to improve this situation. Not only is there a crisis in European identity but also within the EU's constitutional and institutional structure. However, in distinction from some commentators who take this lack of unity and consistency to be a bad thing, I argue that we should be suspicious of assertions of a strong, unified, European foreign policy and the silencing of plurality of claims that such a policy would bring with it.

THE EUROPEAN IDENTITY

The notion of a European identity is a highly contested and complex concept. 'Europe' is a geographical expression, with political significance and immense symbolic weight, but without clearly defined or agreed boundaries. The word has been used and misused, interpreted and misinterpreted and is subject to many metaphors and images, for example, the 'common European home' of Gorbachev's rhetoric or the reference to Central Europe as 'a kingdom of the spirit' (Garton Ash, 1989).

Europe and the other

Attempts to articulate a European identity have frequently been given by means of an antithesis or common European enemy. And so Europe has often been defined in relation to the 'Other' – to what it is not (Derrida, 1992). Historically, Europe began with its differentiation from Asia, and, for a long period in its existence, its defining ethos was Christendom (although, of course, Christianity has often been a divisive force in Europe). Edward Said has shown how Europeans created the Orient to perform the task of the Other (Said, 1995). This negative form of identification proceeds with a vocabulary of Otherness – for example, 'the Barbarians' 'the heathen' or 'despotism' (Burke, 1980, p. 22). The non-European world was still conditioning a European sense of identity in the second half of the twentieth century when the politicians who set out to rebuild Europe immediately after the Second World War had to work within framework set by Russian hostility and American sponsorship, rather than strongly 'European' guidelines.

More recent examples can also be given. Increasingly porous boundaries can pose a threat to the identity of Europeans. Physical borders, along with their legal and political significance, can assume psychological meanings which are eroded when such radical events as the fall of the Iron Curtain and the projects of the EU for 'an ever closer union' take place. A result of such shaken identities may be the triggering of primitive psychological defence mechanisms and the transfer of aggressive emotions onto vulnerable groups (Falk, 1974). Outbursts of racial violence and xenophobia may be symptoms of this, as well as an attempt to single out a non-European Other. Turkey continues to have a difficult and ambiguous relationship with Europe – unacceptable as yet for EU membership (as evidenced by Turkey's unsuccessful application for EEC membership in 1987) and even within parts of western Europe still identifiable as the Other, blamed by nationalists for unemployment and crime and forced to suffer the consequences of otherness by violent attacks. Policies such as the Schengen agreement, which controls admission of third country nationals into Europe, underline the impression that there is still an Other who must be kept at bay. And above all a common foreign and security policy strengthens the perception of an external threat against whom protection is required on a unified European level.

At the same time, however, differentiation from the Other can prove problematic. The ending of the Cold War and application of former Communist countries for membership of both the EU and Council of Europe have also accentuated confusion over European *geographical* identity, for where do the boundaries of Europe stop? For Adenauer, in 1946, 'Asia stands on the Elbe' (Garton Ash, 1993, p. 50). But, in more recent years, Europe's boundaries have shifted several hundred miles eastwards, a move characterized by the re-emergence of Berlin as capital of Germany, a resurfacing of the idea of 'Mitteleuropa' and the renaming of Leningrad as St Petersburg in an attempt 'to regain its lost European identity' (Delanty, 1995, p. 135).

A Europe of institutions

However in the postwar years the expression 'Europe' has been, to a certain extent, appropriated by the EEC and now the EU, by those whose governments had declared a commitment to build a 'European Union' resting on a common aspiration to a European identity and a shared European idea. Thus politicians opposed to certain aspects of the EU are labelled 'anti-European' or 'Euro-sceptic' and the judges of the European Court are said to have '*une certaine idée de l'Europe*'.[1] Art. 237 of the EEC Treaty (now Art. O TEU) stated that 'Any European state may apply to become a member of the Union'. It was therefore of consequence to the applicant governments of post-Franco Spain and post-colonels Greece, as well as to Turkey, whether their countries were included in the accepted definition of Europe.

There is, of course, also a broader institutional Europe – that of the Council of Europe, whose most important achievement remains the European Convention on Human Rights. The obligations of membership of this institution also define a certain conception of Europe which has something in common with the EU, for *market economies and liberal constitutional systems* are conditions of inclusion. This construction of Europe is also being carried forward in the 'Europe agreements' between Central European countries and the EU. The preamble of the Czech (CFSR) 'Europe agreement', for example, speaks of a strong commitment to: 'the rule of law and human rights and to operate a multi-party system with free and democratic elections, and in recognition on the side of the CFSR, that the Community is one of the cornerstones of the system of stability in Europe, based on co-operation.' Such clauses underline the EU's claim to moral standing in international relations. However one should note with care the kind of European identity which this broader Europe of institutions has been constructing. In 1984 in the article 'The Tragedy of Central Europe' Milan Kundera wrote of an identity (central European) which he took to be created by a state of mind – by culture. Kundera stressed that this Europe was in the process of losing its cultural identity – as much under threat from western Europe as from the then Soviet Union. For in 1984 the west was an area where cultural values were ever-diminishing. Certainly ten years on, the focus of the EU's agreements with central Europe is not cultural but technical, economical and institutional – the focus of an instrumentalist modernism, threatening the very cultural values so important to identity. Derrida has criticized this as 'capital' – economic dominion, involving a discourse of technology and capital, built on universalizing ambitions rather than respecting the pluralism of the European heritage (Derrida, 1992, p. 47).

What factors could promote a European identity? Europe is, of course, drawn from different peoples and languages. Given this diversity, people need clear and tangible concepts to develop a sense of belonging – capable of fostering unity in diversity. It is fairly easy to identity with the nation-state with its frontiers, flags, taxes, passports, armed forces and (usually) clearly recognizable national government. However, it *is* possible to identity distinctive European values – such as Greek thought, Roman law, Christianity, the Renaissance, the Industrial Revolution, the Enlightenment, Imperialism, to name but a few (Wistrich, 1994). Edmund Burke wrote of a common European heritage based on common religion, law and customs.[2] Due to this, he thought no European should be a complete exile in any part of Europe. Rousseau wrote: 'whatever people say today there are no more Frenchmen, Germans, Spaniards or even English. There are only Europeans.' (Rousseau, 1793). It was the intention of the founders of the EEC to foster a distinctive 'European identity' to replace warring national identities, and, as the British, French, Germans and Italians had done in their deliberate nation building myths of the nineteenth century, the founders of the EEC set out to create new myths and symbols to replace the old. Some sharp disputes within the EEC concerned just this. For example, disputes between De Gaulle and Hallstein regarding how ambassadors should be received by the EEC reflected De Gaulle's determination to prevent the EEC developing symbols of statehood. There have also been repeated arguments about the role and powers of the European Parliament and its growing status as an alternative focus of legitimacy to national parliaments. Similarly there has been resistance to the Commission's attempt to establish its legal competence over certain matters, such as education and, in particular opposition to 'a more European history'.[3]

There has been debate about the significance of public opinion for European integration. For some writers, especially Karl Deutsch, integration is synonymous with the creation of a 'sense of community' of 'we feelings' and trust (Deutsch, 1953). But, for Lindberg and Scheingold, two neo-functionalist writers, no such massive shift in loyalties is required – rather a 'permissive consensus' (Lindberg, 1963). For some, the perceived lack of a European *demos*, a people sharing a collective identity and loyalty forged by language, history and ethnicity, shows the futility of seeking a European identity (Kirchhof, 1993, considered in Weiler, 1995). According to Smith (1992, p. 62), who argues against the possibility of a trans-national consciousness, 'national identifications possess distinct advantages over the idea of European unity'. The recent attempted designs for a euro-currency, where the customary national figures are replaced with semi-imaginary buildings, compilations and amalgams of the architectural heritage of Europe, for want of an acceptable Euro figurehead, might seem to support this view.

In any case the neo-functionalist strategy favoured by Jean Monnet appears insufficient to construct a European identity for the 1990s. In an attempt to translate a 'permissive consensus' into effective support, EEC institutions began to address the meaning of a 'People's Europe' in the 1980s. The Adonnino report was established in 1984 to outline a series of measures to strengthen and promote the idea of a 'Citizens' Europe'. This report stressed the necessity of 'strengthening the Community's image and identity' in order to 'enhance the sense of belonging and identifying with the Community' (Adonnino, 1984). This was to be achieved by the creation of new symbols of 'Europeanness' – i.e. a European anthem, day (9 May, the day on which in 1950 Schuman gave the speech which led to the Coal and Steel Treaty – hardly a date well-known to the citizens of Europe), driving licence, town twinning, youth exchanges, as well as the flag adopted from the Council of Europe – somewhat hesitant first steps towards the construction of a European identity. But the Adonnino committee's symbols of European identity may have been less successful at fostering effective support for Europe than giving the impression of a European elite trying to legitimate their own ideology. Other Adonnino proposals on citizens' rights found their way into the EC Treaty through the insertion of the new Art. 8A EC by the Maastricht Treaty, which creates the new concept of citizenship of the Union. However, this citizenship is not free-standing in nature but requires the individual concerned to possess citizenship of an EU member state before they are eligible to become a 'citizen of the Union'. In its present derivative form European citizenship does not appear to be a concept capable of fostering a strong European identity, partly because it adds very little to the existing body of EU law. And the existing body of EU law does little to create a European identity at a political level – largely because of the democratic deficit in the EU. While the EU continues to exclude its citizens from so much of its decision-making it cannot be truly representative. Its institutions remain distant and bureaucratic – incapable of fostering and promoting identity, even if Europe does possess the strong cultural traditions mentioned earlier.

Given present difficulties in delineating a tangible European identity, it may be questioned whether the European Community or Union is in fact only, in Anderson's much used phrase, an 'imagined community'. Concepts such as citizenship of the Union or a foreign policy to 'reinforce' the European identity suggest a certain lack of confidence as to the present strength of the European identity and a perceived need to foster and promote one. However, perhaps it is unrealistic to consider any community as occurring naturally rather than being constructed. For example, in the context of the nation-state, Ernest Gellner (1983) has written: 'Nationalism is not the awakening of nations to self-consciousness; it invents nations where they do not exist.' Indeed, for Gellner, who sees the formation of nation-states in Europe as a necessary accessory to the process of industrialization and the needs of nineteenth-century capitalism, the European Union, with its internal market and projected monetary union, must surely be a suitable entity for a supranational state.

However if the 'European' identity is not a natural phenomena, it is instructive to consider the reasons underlying its attempted creation. Why go to the trouble of constructing a strong European self-image rather than maintaining intergovernmental co-operation in certain key areas? To prevent further conflict in the region, to encourage economic prosperity and liberal democracy and to promote these values in the newly emerging democracies? In this way, the rhetoric of European identity may provide a legitimacy otherwise lacking for political strategies that seek to mobilize new kinds of power (Delanty, 1995). A strong foreign and defence policy and profile can be a cynical, if useful, tool in this regard. However, a focus on the unifying aspects of Europe's history and culture has been seen by some as Euro-nationalistic (Wilterdinck, 1993), involving a one-sided emphasis on harmony, unity, continuity progress etc., whereas the divisive, violent and repressive sides of the European tradition (war, imperialism, genocide) are either ignored or treated as not essentially European. Derrida (1992) has suggested that the designers of the European Union have failed to take account of its historicity. The idea of Europe is not unified but surely one of pluralism and difference.

EUROPE ON THE INTERNATIONAL STAGE

It is undeniable that the EU faces problems in defining and practising a credible role for itself. On the one hand, it expects to be an assertive player in the regional setting. On the other, there is concern about its image abroad – about whether it has made the transition from a somewhat passive, beneficent 'civilian power', devoid of imperialistic intent, to a proactive organization capable of creditably initiating, following through and executing a CFSP, with all that this implies politically, economically and financially.

The self-professed image of a 'civilian' power was devised at a time when not only did the EEC (as it then was) lack the military wherewithal to conduct a defence policy but when the notion that the EEC as such should have any military capacity was taboo, following the failure of the attempted European Defence and Political Communities in the 1950s.[4] Thus there was no basis in the original Rome Treaty for foreign policy. However this did not render the EEC incapable of action abroad for it was involved with foreign *affairs*. Consequently, the European Community (as opposed to the EU) has international legal personality (Art. 210 EC). Certain limited treaty-making powers are also expressly conferred by the EC Treaty, for example, under

Art. 113 with regard to the Common Commercial Policy, Art. 238 regarding Association Agreements and under Art. 228 regarding its power to conclude international treaties for example with the World Trade Organisation. It also has the power to receive and establish diplomatic relations. The European Court of Justice has also implied powers in other areas, through the doctrine of parallelism, which states the EC's international relations power should be co-extensive with its internal legislative power[5] – this has meant that external aspects of, e.g. transport or competition are matters of *Community* competence.[6] Additionally, in so far as the EC's competencies in the external relations field are exclusive, Member States are excluded from these fields of activity.[7] In this way, the EC has been able to play an important role in international affairs as in the conclusion of trade agreements which are negotiated by the European Commission on behalf of EU Member States.

The largely trade-based nature of the EC's foreign affairs distinguishes it from the traditional nation-states which were unable to maintain independence or create a strong identity without violence and war. But the integration of Europe, the creation of a European Union and the CFSP are premised on a need to preserve peace. Indeed, as Von Staden points out, the history of the integration process in Europe is marked by a striking paradox (Carlsnaes and Smith, 1994). For, although the major motive underlying the plan for the European Coal and Steel Community in the early 1950s was to guarantee a lasting peace in Europe, or at least between France and Germany, the actual exapnsion of European integration evolved at the level of economic and social needs, rather than 'high' politics (i.e. foreign policy and defence). The military protection of Western Europe became or rather remained the sole responsibility of NATO, with the European countries, except France, accepting the political leadership of the United States.[8]

FOREIGN POLICY : EUROPEAN POLITICAL CO-OPERATION

Therefore, in other aspects of foreign relations, the EU has been until recently inconspicuous. There are many obstacles in the way of a developed, let alone a common, EU foreign policy. The primary problem, as discussed earlier, is that the EU is not a unified state and, indeed, lacks many of the characteristics associated with nation-states which tend to lead to affective support. The idea of EU foreign policy also encroaches most fundamentally on the notion of national sovereignty, especially regarding those states which have long histories of being influential on the world stage in their own right, or have special relationships with particular parts of the world which they are anxious to maintain. Defence, inextricably linked to foreign policy, is particularly problematic, given its close association with national sovereignty, the differing defence capabilities of Member States of the EU and the unwillingness of some of its Member States to use armed force (although there has been some integration of foreign policy within NATO).

Notwithstanding these obstacles, as long ago as 1970 the EEC launched its foreign policy co-operation, under the name of European Political Co-operation (EPC) in the Luxembourg report. This originally operated on a tentative basis, quite outside the institutional structure of the Community Treaties, with the Commission generally excluded from its meetings. The practice of EPC evolved through the various reports and conclusions of the European Councils in Luxembourg in 1970, Copenhagen in 1973, London in 1981 and the Stuttgart Solemn Declaration of 1983, none of which was a Treaty document. An interesting precursor to the aspirations of the CFSP was issued at the Copenhagen summit in the form of a declaration on European Identity which focused on assessing the extent to which the nine Member States were already acting together in relation to the rest of the world and the responsibilities which resulted from this.[9]

However, rigid divisions between EEC and extra-Community practices could not be continued in the light of international events. For example, was the adoption of economic sanctions against a third country a matter for EPC (because it concerned foreign policy) or for the EEC (because it concerned commercial policy, a subject covered by Arts 110–116 of the EC Treaty)? In the context of the Falklands War, sanctions against Argentina were adopted by the EEC after 'discussions in the context of EPC' (Hartley, 1994, p. 24).

The developing importance of foreign policy co-operation was recognized when EPC was accorded its own section – Title III – in the Single European Act (SEA). However unlike certain other policy areas which were also recognized in the SEA such as environment, Title III was not incorporated into the Treaties, mainly because the Member States were unwilling to allow the normal Community decision-making processes to apply to foreign policy. As a result EPC continued to be much looser, and more voluntaristic and incremental in nature, than most other policy areas with which the Community concerned itself. No laws were made within EPC, decisions were arrived at by consensus, and no state could be prevented from engaging in independent action if it so chose.

However, the distinction between the EEC as a 'civilian' power, separating the contractual and economic from the political (to be dealt with under EPC) became ever more unrealistic, especially given that EEC trade policy showed itself susceptible to the vagaries of Member States' national interests and those of their private-sector commercial concerns. In any case, history has intervened to dispel the notion that adherence to such a world picture could continue. The current situation, where the EU is making a positive effort to assert itself on the international scene, owes much to factors beyond its control. It is a product of changing circumstances and regional turbulence at the end of the 1980s, of the break-up of the Soviet Union and Comecom. It is also a product of EPC and the way in which the EEC's external competencies in limited areas as defined by the Rome Treaty developed and became politicized. The power to conclude international agreements and Association agreements (e.g. the recent 'Europe agreements' with central Europe) all augmented the EEC's international presence and visibility *per se*. Furthermore, the whole concept of 'security' itself, comporting notions of military capability and such, has recently in some respects been 'civilianized'. So, for example, the 1990 (Conference on Security and Co-operation in Europe) CSCE Paris Charter provides an interesting example of the tension involved in reconciling security demands perceived in terms of defence and military insecurities and those seen in terms of promoting normative values and attachment to tolerance, liberal democratic values and respect for human rights. More recent initiatives taken under CFSP 'Joint Action' also illustrate this combination, as will be dealt with below.

So, to summarize the argument so far: European identity is uncertain and, to an extent, constructed or imagined. Further, although originally any international identity presented by the EEC was economic in nature (somewhat paradoxically given that one of the objectives of founding the ECSC, EEC and Euratom Communities was to ensure future European security) this former 'civilian' power image of the EEC could no longer continue – it was becoming impossible to separate the economic from the political, i.e. political aspects of foreign trade, use of sanctions etc., difficulties with EPC. Also, defence and security in their turn are becoming more 'civilianized'.

However, confusion in identity and image goes deeper than manifestations in the international arena. It is apparent in the inconsistent structure of the Maastricht Treaty itself, which on the one hand aspires to a Union with a consistent, coherent identity, to which the rhetoric of the CFSP provisions testifies. (This aim is itself questionable, in that it invokes the notion of an imperialistic EU, masking the diversity and historicity of Europe in order to further a particular economic vision.) On the other hand, these aspirations are undermined by the structure and content of the Maastricht Treaty itself, a mixture of the supranational and the intergovernmental, emasculated by opts-outs and special interest pleadings, which, taken together, make a mockery of the notion of consistency in external relations. It is, in short, a Europe of 'bits and pieces' (Curtin, 1993) but one which, nevertheless, aspires to legitimation of the idea of a unified, harmonious Europe.

THE CFSP : NEW WINE IN OLD BOTTLES?

A brief outline of the most salient features of the CFSP will first be given. A closer look at its provisions follows thereafter. This section focusses on the CFSP as it has evolved under the Maastricht Treaty. The Treaty of Amsterdam (in draft only at time of writing) is not considered, although it is unlikely that these new provisions, if implemented, will substantially change the operation of the CFSP.

First, the provisions are intergovernmental in nature, so according to Art. M TEU, they do not form part of EC law, nor may they do anything to affect the body of EC law. Furthermore, they are excluded from the jurisdiction of the European Court of Justice (ECJ) under Art. L. (The provisions should also be read subject to the Declarations adopted by the Intergovernmental Conference, namely No. 27 on voting in the field of CFSP, and No. 30 on the Western European Union as well as the Edinburgh Council Denmark decision, which are annexed to the Maastricht Treaty.) Secondly, the basic obligation on the Union and its Member States is set out in Art. J 1: 'to define and implement a common foreign and security policy, governed by the provisions of this Title and covering all areas of foreign and security policy.' This constitutes a very broad and somewhat vague obligation. Thirdly, Art. J 1 also contains a list of objectives of the CFSP, which can be pursued in two ways, namely, through co-operation under Art. J 2 and joint action under Art. J 3. Fourthly, Art. J 4 concerns defence (a new area of competence for the Union) and security. All questions of the security of the Union are included in the CFSP as is 'the eventual framing of a common defence policy which might in time lead to a common defence'. By Art. J 4(2) it is the Western European Union that is to be responsible for elaborating and implementing decisions of the EU which have defence implications. Joint action is not to be available for issues involving defence (as opposed to purely security implications, Art. J 4(3)). Fifthly, the CFSP must be compatible with the NATO Treaty. Bilateral co-operation within the framework of WEU and NATO is not excluded.

Finally, responsibility for formulating and implementing the CFSP is divided. The European Council, according to Art. J 8, is to define principles and give general guidelines. The Council of Ministers is to take decisions defining and implementing the CFSP and ensuring consistency of the Union's action across the board of the Community pillar and CFSP. The Presidency (and not the Commission as in EC external policy) represents the Union and in principle will present the Union's position in international organizations and conferences.

Clearly not all of these provisions are entirely new – some aspects of the CFSP, particularly those relating to co-operation and common positions, simply replicate what was already in place with European Political Co-operation.

Although the CFSP has been operational only for a short time, concern has already been expressed about its slow and reactive foreign policy decision-making and the frequent failure of member states to agree a common position. Former US Assistant Secretary of State Richard Holbrooke's reaction is typical: 'You have to wonder why Europe does not seem capable of taking decisive action in its own theatre.'[10] European institutions themselves do not seem to have much confidence in the CFSP – the Commission has stated: 'Getting the CFSP under way has been a laborious process.'[11] Certainly, one of the reasons for EU inability to take effective action over Bosnia and other areas must be the unsatisfactory institutional framework established at Maastricht. This section will focus in greater detail on certain aspects of the CFSP, assessing it particularly with regard to its capability of promoting, reinforcing (or undermining) the notion of a European identity.

CFSP objectives and scope – Art. J 1

Art. J 1 provides that:

> (1) The Union and its Member States shall define and implement a Common Foreign and Security Policy, governed by the provisions of this title and covering all areas of Foreign and Security Policy.
> (2) The objectives of the Common Foreign and Security Policy shall be: – to safeguard the common values, fundamental interests and independence of the Union;
> – strengthen the security of the Union and its Member States in all ways;
> – to preserve peace and to strengthen international security, in accordance with the principles of the UN Charter as well as the principles of the Helsinki Final Act and the objectives of the Paris Charter;
> – to promote international co-operation;
> – to develop and consolidate democracy and the rule of law, and respect for human rights and fundamental freedoms.

These very broad objectives are pursued through co-operation under Art. J 2 and joint action under Art. J 3.

The material scope of the CFSP is defined widely but vaguely in Art. J 1 TEU as 'covering all areas of foreign and security policy'. But the Treaty tells us nothing more about what is to be understood by the notion of foreign policy. This therefore raises problems regarding the notion of European identity in the foreign policy arena.

In the absence of any Union definition of foreign policy one can consider Member State practice. But the practices of Member States are not identical. Furthermore, the scope of a 'European' foreign policy may differ from national foreign policy. Formerly, within EPC, the scope of foreign policy matters was determined by agreement or compromise. The Maastricht Treaty did not change these arrangements. Therefore the scope of European foreign policy may turn on Member State special interests and reservations.

Furthermore, although Art. J 1 (3) provides: 'joint action shall be gradually implemented' this is confined to areas where Member States have 'important interests in common'. This recognizes that Member State interests may differ and that there can still be room for autonomous Member State action.[12]

The CFSP and national sovereignty

Under the Maastricht Treaty the EU and its Member States are to define and implement a CFSP which the Member States undertake to support 'actively and unreservedly' (Arts J 1 (1) and (4)). This is no small matter, given the position that foreign policy occupies at the very heart of national sovereignty and the place of national self-interest in determining foreign policy. Art. J 2 (2) provides that where it deems it necessary the Council of Ministers 'shall define a common position. Member States shall ensure that their national policies conform on common positions.' Under Art. J 2 (3) these common positions shall be upheld in international organizations, including those in which not all the Member States participate.

Also of relevance in this context is Art. J 3 (2), which provides that the Council shall define which matters are to be taken by qualified majority in the field of joint action, a provision capable of eventually weakening the intergovernmental nature of the CFSP. Although some Member States, in particular, Germany, are keen to progress to more qualified majority voting, this does not seem likely to happen, given strong opposition on grounds of national sovereignty, especially from the UK, whose White Paper for the IGC stated the strong position: 'The Government does not accept … that the CFSP would be strengthened by the introduction of voting models which overrode the particular concerns of key Member States' and 'The Government believes that the nation-state should be the basic building block in constructing the kind of international order we wish to see.'[13]

However moving beyond the sovereignty of the nation-state need not lead to a uniform European identity either. Neil MacCormick has suggested that: 'To escape from the idea that all law must originate in a single power source, like a sovereign, is thus to discover the possibility of taking a broader, more diffuse view of the law' (MacCormick, 1993, p. 8). Attracta Ingram has written that Europe must build a Union founded on principles of liberal justice taking us beyond the nation-state. A European identity could be created whereby power was removed from the nation-state and relocated at a most basic level (in fact an application of one vision of subsidiarity). In this way there would be a 'self-defining European "us"' (Ingram, 1993, p. 23) of the sort required by Karl Deutsch. Such visions of Europe have more in common with postmodern notions of identity, which encompass respect for plurality, difference and participatory democracy. They have less in common with the concept of identity contemplated in the Maastricht CFSP provisions, which builds on a need for coherence, unity and harmony (without which foreign policy, at least according to more traditional notions would be unworkable).

Action under the CFSP – common positions and joint action

The Treaty introduces the concepts of 'common position' and 'joint action'. The former is very like EPC co-operation. The CFSP requires that Member States 'shall ensure that their national policies conform to the common position' (Art. J 2(2)) and any common position adopted is to be upheld in international conferences and organizations.[14] Of the relatively few common positions so far adopted (less than 30 at the time of writing) the majority concern economic sanctions, covering Libya, Haiti and former Yugoslavia. The rest concern the EU's general objectives and priorities towards Rwanda, Ukraine and Burundi.

The procedure for joint action is set out in Art. J 3. The Council of Ministers is to decide (unanimously Art. J 8 (2)), on the basis of guidelines from the European Council, whether a matter should be subject of joint action. Art. J 3 (4) commits Member States to follow joint action in the conduct of national foreign policy. However, Art. J 3(6) provides for Member States to 'take the necessary measures' in cases of urgency, provided they have regard to the general objectives of the joint action and inform the Council immediately afterwards. At the 1992 Lisbon summit it was agreed that, in assessing whether important common interests were at stake, and in defining issues and areas for joint action, account should be taken of the following:[15]

- geographical proximity of the country/region to the EU;
- important EU interests in the political or economic stability of the region/country;
- existence of threats to security interests of the EU.

Joint actions undertaken so far include former Yugoslavia, support for the Middle East Peace Process, the definition of a Stability Pact in Europe, support for the democratic transition in South Africa, preparation of the conference on the non-proliferation Treaty, control of anti-personnel mines and sending observers to the Russian elections.

Joint action was intended by the Council to be the key instrument for the Union, backed up by common positions on everyday matters. This distinction has not been maintained in practice, with a considerable overlap between the two – joint actions may simply be *ad hoc* administrative measures whereas common positions can cover concrete actions. Resulting confusion strengthens the impression that the CFSP lacks any coherent form. Another noticeable feature of EU foreign policy action so far, noted by the Commission in its report for the IGC, is: 'How their scope shrinks, between the mandate handed down by the European Council and what is finally undertaken.'[16] While the Commission blames this on the requirement of unanimity, the UK Government, in the White Paper, stresses the need for better preparation of Council discussions and proper monitoring of and follow up to action, such as the joint action in Mostar.[17] Either way, the difficulties in achieving agreement reflect the lack of any real leadership for the CFSP in a Europe without hegemony – the plurality which is a key feature of Europe makes action in the foreign field difficult to achieve (Miall, 1994, p. 269).

Defence and security

That the EU might have defence resources available to it in certain circumstances is hardly implied by the relevant TEU article which refers to: 'the eventual framing of a common defence policy which might in time lead to a common defence' (Art. J 4(1)).

This provision is new and marks an important change from EPC, which concerned foreign and security policy but not defence.[18] However, although new, the provision is drafted in terms of compromise – the 'eventual framing' only *might* lead to a common defence.[19]

Furthermore, a clause in Art. J 4(4) is intended to ensure that the specific character of security and defence policy of certain Member States and their obligations under NATO are respected. This may make it very difficult to frame a common policy. The reference to 'specific character' would provide for the neutrality pursued by the certain Member States.

Initially, these aspects of the CFSP should not present major problems for the EU as defence is at present sub-contracted out to the WEU – a long established defence organization – which is identified in Art. J 4 (1) as 'an integral part of the development of the Union' and the WEU is requested in the same provision to 'elaborate and implement decisions and actions of the Union which have defence implications'.

In the Declaration attached to the TEU the potential role of the WEU is described in even more forceful terms:

> WEU will be developed as the defence component of the EU and as a means to strength the European pillar of the Atlantic Alliance. To this end it will formulate a common European defence policy and carry forward its concrete implementation through the further development of its operational role.

Membership of the two Institutions is also more closely aligned, with three EU states, which were not members of WEU when the TEU was signed, changing their status. So, in November 1992 Greece became a member of WEU and Denmark and Ireland observers.

But the increasingly close relationship between WEU and the EU does not mean that the EU can now be said to have a clear defence capability. The EU and WEU are still separate organizations and the defence resources of the EU states are still under national control – even if they do frequently operate within the framework of, or are 'lent out' to, international organizations such as the UN, NATO and WEU. A main issue for the 1996–97 IGC was whether steps should be taken towards integration of the WEU into the EU. The German government was most clearly in favour of a merger and speeding up other moves towards a common defence. On the other hand, opposition to the use of WEU to carry out the EU defence policy came from neutral members, and the UK, which insisted that NATO should be maintained as the bedrock of European defence.

For the present, WEU remains a separate organization and may be likely to continue as such given the accession by further neutral states. However, as the Royal Institute of International Affairs (RIIA) paper points out, such a postponement 'would only put off controversy for a while over the several competing visions for a European defence identity'.[20]

The decision reached by the European Council at Edinburgh, regarding Denmark and defence, illustrates potential problems for defence of the EU. This decision, which is a binding international agreement, emphasizes that responsibility for implementing defence aspects of CFSP falls on WEU at which Denmark is only an observer (although it is a member of NATO). The Decision provides that Denmark 'does not participate in the elaboration and implementation of decision and actions of the EU which have defence implications but will not prevent closer co-operation between Member States in this area'.

This decision creates potential problems. It is possible that, as part of the policy of common defence (with which Denmark is not associated) the Council of Ministers agreed (by qualified majority vote under Art. 228a) on the use of economic sanctions. It would seem that Denmark would be obliged to accept these sanctions as part of its EC obligations, even if it had not been involved in the initial decision to take such a measure. In this way, decisions taken by some of the Member States under the different procedural framework of the CFSP could have an impact on the EC's common commercial policy – an example of the unsatisfactory 'variable geometry' of the Maastricht Treaty.

Institutional incoherence

According to Art. C, TEU:

> The Union shall be served by a single institutional framework which shall ensure the consistency and the continuity of the activities carried out in order to attain its objectives while respecting and building on the 'acquis communautaire'.
>
> The Union shall in particular ensure the consistency of its external activities as a whole in the context of its external relations, security, economic and development policies. The Council and the Commission shall be responsible for ensuring such consistency. They shall ensure the implementation of such policies, each in accordance with its respective powers.

Art. C abounds with the rhetoric of coherence (and also the pretended universalism of the constitutional order which has been deconstructed by Derrida (1992)). However, it is submitted that the Maastricht Treaty presents no such unity and, under different pillars of the Treaty, European Union institutions have to operate under different procedures.[21] The CFSP is primarily intergovernmental in nature, operating by means of common positions and joint actions. It seems a long way removed from the 'new legal order' evoked by the judges of the European Court. These distinctions lead to incoherence. A closer look at the differing institutional roles highlights these distinctions.

The Commission

Under the EC Treaty, it is the Commission which has the right of initiative. However, under the CFSP it is the European Council which has the policy forming role, although the Commission is to be 'fully associated' (Art. J 9) as it was under EPC, and shares a right of initiative with other member states. A new Directorate-General (DG 1A, Common Foreign and Security Policy) was formed to help the Commission deal with its role under the CFSP.

Quite how the EC/CFSP relationship will work out in practice remains to be seen although, as in the past, the influence of the Commission will vary according to circumstances. The Commission, for example, quite recently played an important part in relations with Central and Eastern Europe. Although the 'Europe Agreements' fell within EC competence, the objectives of such co-operation are more likely to be realized if the foreign policies of the Member States are co-ordinated.

The Commission will be in a strong position when CFSP actions involve economic sanctions as policy instruments for the Council of Ministers can only act then on the basis of Commission proposals under Art. 228a EC. But the Commission is less favourably placed regarding 'political' matters – especially if the incumbent Presidency is a large Member State with a big and effective foreign ministry and policies which may conflict with the construction of a European identity.

The European Council

Under Art. J 8 'The European Council shall define the principle of and general guidelines for the CFSP'.

The European Council, which is not a Community Institution, is composed of heads of state and government and the president of the Commission assisted by the foreign ministries. Art. D of the TEU provides that: 'The European Council shall provide the Union with the necessary impetus for its development and shall define the general political guidelines thereof.'[22] The European Council thus has an extremely important role, acting as supreme director of EU activities, although it will have no specific responsibility regarding implementation of the CFSP. The main policy forming role in this area is therefore taken by an intergovernmental, rather than a communitarian, organization. Communiqués from European Council meetings have long contained declarations on a wide range of foreign policy issues but since the Maastricht summit they have also concerned themselves with establishing frameworks in which the CFSP should operate and be developed, i.e. as at the 1992 Lisbon summit and the two Brussels summits in late 1993 which were used to launch the initiative for the Stability Pact.

Council of Ministers

The Council of Ministers is at the heart of the CFSP process. It functions at several levels. Most important for this context is the General Council which consists of Member States' foreign ministers with the Commission in attendance, which meets around once per month with additional special meetings when necessary.

The General Council is the main decision-making body of the CFSP. It operates within the context of such general policy guidelines as have been issued by European Council and makes CFSP decisions – including those on defining common-position or joint actions. As highlighted earlier, different rules operate for voting in the Council of Ministers under the CFSP than under the EC Treaty. Under the CFSP the general rule is for decisions to be taken unanimously.[23] However, within the EC, decisions concluding agreements with third states are generally subject to qualified majority voting.[24] Acts taken under the Common Commercial Policy and adoption of economic sanctions under Art. 228a, are all taken by qualified majority vote. These different voting procedures underline the very different functions of the Council under the CFSP and under the EC Treaty.[25]

The Council Presidency has the particular responsibility to 'represent the Union in matters coming within the CFSP' and to be 'responsible for the implementation of common measures'.[26] The Presidency works closely with previous and successive Presidencies in a so called '*troika*' which ensures smoothness of transition.

Different areas of institutional responsibility under the CFSP and EC pillars underline lack of effectiveness. It is often difficult to determine which Institution is responsible for the Union and this is compounded by the rotating Council Presidency – a problem for non-EU states, as well as the public within the EU, which is rarely aware which body or individual is representing their interests, and, as the Commission noted in its report to the Reflection Group, 'this can only contribute to a certain sense of alienation vis à vis the Union'.[27] A proposal for a figurehead appointment to act as representative of the CFSP, while adding superficial coherence, risks the further fragmentation of the institutional framework.

At present the Member States remain firmly in control of CFSP initiatives, thus apparently undermining the assertion of the sort of European identity aspired to in the Treaty.

The European Parliament

The position of the Parliament further supports the conclusion that the CFSP does not really aid the EU to move beyond the sovereignty of the nation-state. Under Art. J 7:

> The Presidency shall consult the European Parliament on the main aspects and basic choices of the CFSP and shall ensure that the views of the European Parliament are duly taken into consideration. The European Parliament shall be kept regularly informed by the Presidency and the Commission of the development of the CFSP.

Thus the Parliament's role is advisory, in contrast to certain areas of EC external policy, where its role has been strengthened. Under Art. 228(3) certain type of agreements require the assent of the Parliament.[28] The European Parliament's growing influence was illustrated, for example, by its refusal to assent to the Association agreement with the Czech and Slovak federation in 1992, on the ground that the constitutional position of the two states was unclear. It is noteworthy that it was also the Parliament which insisted on the revised EEA agreement being referred to ECJ a second time under Art. 228. However, the European Parliament still remains relatively weak and the democratic deficit created by the lack of an effective Parliament in the EU has been much discussed. An even more serious point is that the Maastricht Treaty, by transferring certain areas (moreover sensitive ones, such as foreign and security policy, international terrorism and drug trafficking) from national to intergovernmental competence, threatens liberal democracy by removing such matters from the control of the national legislatures without ensuring the sort of scrutiny generally provided under the Community legal system (i.e. by the European Parliament and European Court of Justice).[29] This deficit also has serious implications for the concept of a European identity. Joseph Weiler has suggested that there cannot be affective support or trust of the European Union among the people of Europe until there is a 'transformation' of its democratic profile (Weiler, 1991, p. 2403). Ward sees this 'silence' of democracy in the post-Maastricht Europe as inevitably leading to a failure of identity (Ward, 1995, p. 22).

The European Court of Justice

Perhaps the most significant institutional aspect of the CFSP is the fact that the Court has no jurisdiction in this area – the Court's powers are limited by Art. L to Titles II to IV and VII, although it may be the case that the Court has jurisdiction over the scope of the EC's powers – Art. 164 EC requires the Court to ensure that 'in the interpretation and application of this Treaty the law is observed'. However, for the most part, the CFSP will rarely be subject to legal control by the Court. This is a striking feature of the CFSP when one considers the important role which the Court has played in furthering European integration and protecting the *acquis communautaire*. The European Court has been responsible for features which now appear to be an inherent part of the identity of European law – the concept of direct effect, the enhancement of the European Parliament's powers, the duty of loyal co-operation of the Member States (applied well beyond the obvious interpretation of Art. 5) and so on.

Although Art. C TEU requires the EU to respect and maintain the *acquis*, it is questionable whether this will be possible when, as is the case under the CFSP, institutions which are outside the EC system of law, such as the European Council, have the power to take decisions which will affect the Community legal order. In its first EEA Opinion[30] the Court stressed that the treaties are a constitutional charter based on the rule of law. However, this proto-constitutional character is endangered by the amendments of the Maastricht Treaty. Furthermore, the delicate institutional balance within the EC, which the Court was assiduous to protect in, for example, the *Chernobyl*[31] case, is threatened by the existence of the CFSP (not to mention that of the other inter-governmental pillar concerning co-operation in Justice and Home Affairs) where decision-making is governed by totally different procedures. It is true that defence matters and foreign policy are not often subject to judicial control by western courts, but the CFSP clearly encroaches on EC matters – as outlined above. Without the European Court a key feature of Europeanness is missing – although, significantly, it is a feature which some have criticized for its overt political activism (Rasmussen, 1986) or for too much attention to furthering European integration at the expense of individual rights (Coppel and O'Neill, 1992).

CONCLUSION: DEEPER PROBLEMS?

It is ironic that one of the objectives underlying the convening of the pre-Maastricht Intergovernmental Conference (IGC) on political union was the future assurance of unity and coherence in the EC's international action. Indeed, the Rome European Council in December 1990 stressed: 'the vocation of the Union to deal with aspects of foreign and security policy, in accordance with a sustained evolutive process and in a unitary manner, on the basis of general objectives laid down in the Treaty.'

This stress on unity complements the other requirements placed on the CFSP in the Maastricht Treaty – those of institutional consistency and of reinforcing of the European identity. And yet, it seems to be these very factors which the CFSP is incapable of enforcing. A unitary approach requires a single institutional framework and the uniform applicability of Community law. However there is no such coherent unitary orientation in the Maastricht Treaty.[32] The Maastricht Treaty does not create a new Union, replacing the old Communities, but rather brings certain intergovernmental activities within the general framework of the EU, producing a complex and confusing structure.

However, all this is to establish that the CFSP is at present an inadequate tool to reinforce, or even construct, a European identity. A further question remains, as to whether a possible coherent future European foreign policy is so desirable in any case. In fact, an emphasis on harmony, unity, coherence and continuity exhibits traits of 'Euro-nationalism' as suggested above, tending to repress Europe's violent past or excluding division and antagonism from the European identity. As Delanty has suggested the idea of

Europe embodies prejudices that lie deep in the history of Europe (Delanty, 1995). The irony of a European common foreign and security policy is that it emanates from a continent responsibility for some of the most violent atrocities in history. This is not to suggest that the future of the CFSP lies in war making (although the recent civil wars in former Yugoslavia are clear evidence that the European continent has not abandoned its violent past, nor should it be forgotten that the civil war in Bosnia also raises the question of European identity). It is to suggest that we should take a critical (and perhaps sceptical) look at European foreign affairs (including the CFSP) as well as this vexed notion of a European identity. We should look beyond protestations of unity and identity not just to the lack of self-confidence of the EU but also to the Other whose difference is denied by these attempts at insularity. The precedents in EC external relations are not encouraging. The 'Europe' agreements have already been criticized for placing stringent political conditions (e.g. as to the maintenance of liberal democracy, market conditions) without offering these new democracies so much in return economically, nor any firm prospect of EU membership (e.g. Batt in Miall, 1994). These agreements restrict imports such as steel as well as containing anti-dumping and safeguard clauses which are to the advantage of the EU and disadvantage of the partner countries. This subject raises the pressing issue of the less desirable aspects of an EU dominated, market-led European identity, at the expense of other competing, fragile, and even vanishing, European identities.

NOTES

1 The expression used by Judge Pescatore in 'The Doctrine of Direct Effect: an infant disease of Community law' (1983), 8 *EL Rev* where at p. 157 he observes that 'the reasoning of the Court shows that the judges had "une certaine idée de l'Europe" of their own'.
2 Burke, E. Letters on the Regicide, quoted in Burke, P. (1980, p. 21).
3 Attempted by the French historian Baptiste Duroselle in Europe: *A History of its Peoples*.
4 These collapsed in 1954, when the French National Assembly rejected the Treaty.
5 This doctrine was developed in the ERTA case, case 22/70 *Commission* v. *Council* [1971] ECR 263.
6 Subject, of course, to the operation of the Subsidiarity principle under Art. 3b EC Treaty.
7 I.e. they do not possess concurrent powers in that area. It has been clear since case 41/76 *Donckerwolcke* [1976] ECR 1921 that the EC's powers in implementing the common commercial policy are exclusive.
8 Although the Western European Union had been set up by the Brussels Treaty in 1948, this organization remained dormant until 'revived' in 1984.
9 *Bulletin of the European Commission 12/1973 118–9 Declaration of European Identity*.
10 Quoted in *RIIA Briefing Paper* on the 1996 IGC, March 1996.

11 *European Commission report for the IGC Reflection Group*, May 1995.
12 So it would seem that if a Member State enjoys special relations with certain parts of the world it may maintain its policies there. In an article in *International Affairs*, July 94 ('Developing the Common Foreign and Security Policy') Douglas Hurd suggested that the UK would be free, in this context, to pursue its own national action, e.g. re Hong Kong.
13 *A Partnership of Nations*, London: HMSO, March 1996, para. 42 and Annexe B para. 21.
14 Although the special case of the UN Security Council is dealt with separately in Art. J 5.
15 Report to the European Council in Lisbon on the likely development of the CFSP with a view to identifying areas open to joint action vis-à-vis particular countries or groups of countries. *Bull EC* 6/92 at 18–22.
16 *Commission Report*, 1995, p. 63.
17 *A Partnership of Nations*, Annex B, para. 6.
18 Note the rather tenuous distinction made by EPC between the political and economic aspects of security on the one hand and military aspects on the other (cf. A 6(a) SEA).
19 This compromise resulted from the different views on the subject of France and the UK.
20 *RIIA Briefing Paper*.
21 Furthermore, it is quite apparent from Article E TEU that the Institution will operate under different rules, viz: 'The European Parliament, the Council, the Commission and the Court of Justice shall exercise their powers under the conditions and for the purposes provided for, on the one hand by the provisions of the treaties establishing the European Communities ... and on the other hand, by the other provisions of the Treaty.'
22 The European Council is also required under Art. D to report to the European Parliament after each of it meetings as well as submitting an annual report, in order to ensure sound inter-institutional dialogue.
23 It is possible for decisions on joint action to be taken on a majority basis but only after a decision to that effect (Arts J 8(2) and J 3(2) – but not for issues with defence implications).
24 However, Association agreements require unanimity as do those areas for which unanimity is required for the adoption of internal rules.
25 Marise Cremona has written that: 'Underlying these rules is a tension between the Council of Ministers as an EEC institution and as a Council of representatives of the member states, a tension which has been responsible for many inter-institutional disputes in the EC and which is likely to be fuelled by the function given to the Council of Ministers under the CFSP.' (Marise Cremona (1994), 'The CFSP and the External relations Powers of the EC', in O'Keefe and Twomey, (eds), in *Legal Issues of the Maastricht Treaty*, Chancery Wiley.
26 TEU Arts J 5 and J 6.
27 *Commission report*, May 1995 at 66.
28 E.g. Association Agreements, and others establishing an institutional framework for co-operation.
29 Notably, matters falling within EU, rather than EC competence, are to be excluded from Art. 138d and Art. 138e regarding petitions to the European Parliament and the Ombudsman.
30 Opinion 1/91 (*re the draft treaty on a European Economic Area*) [1992] 1 CMLR 245.
31 Case C-70/88 *European Parliament* v. *Council* [1990] ECR 1-2041.

32 As is in contrast to be found in the draft treaty on European Union by the European Parliament in 1984.

REFERENCES

Adonnino, P. (1984), *Report of the ad hoc Committee on a People's Europe to the European Council*, Supplement 7/85-Bull EC.

Anderson, B. (1991), *Imagined Communities: Reflections on the Origin and Spread of Nationalism*, 2nd edn, London: Verso.

Batt, J. (1994), 'The Political Transformation of East Central Europe', in Miall (ed.), *Redefining Europe*, Pinter.

Burke, P. (1980), 'Did Europe Exist before 1700', *History of European Ideas* **1** (1).

Carlsnaes, W. and Smith, S. (1994), *European Foreign Policy*, London: Sage.

Coppel, J. and O'Neill, A. (1992), 'The European Court of Justice: Taking Rights Seriously?', *Legal Studies*, **12**.

Curtin, D. (1993), 'The Constitutional Structure of the Union: A Europe of Bits and Pieces', *CMLRev*, **1**.

Delanty, G. (1995), *Inventing Europe: Idea, Identity, Reality*, Macmillan.

Derrida, J. (1992), *The Other heading: Reflections on Today's Europe*, Bloomington: Indiana University Press.

Deutsch, K. (1953), *Nationalism and Social Communication*, New York: Wiley.

Falk, A. (1974), 'Border Symbolism', *Psycho-Analytic Quarterly*, **43**, 650.

Garton Ash, T. (1989), *The Uses of Adversity*, Cambridge.

Garton Ash, T. (1993), *In Europe's Name: Germany and the Divided Continent*, New York: Random House.

Gellner, E. (1983), *Nations and Nationalism*, Oxford: Blackwell.

Hartley, T. (1994), *The Foundations of European Community Law*, Oxford: Clarendon Press.

Ingram, A. (1993), 'The Empire Strikes Back: Liberal Solidarity in a *Europe des Patries*', in M. Karlsson (ed.), *Law, Justice and the State*, Berlin: Duncker & Humblot.

Kirchhof, P. (1993), 'Europäische Einingung und der Verfassungsstaat der Bundesrepublik Deutschland' in Isensee (ed.), *Europa als politische Idee und als rechtliche Form*, Berlin.

Kundera, M. (1984), 'The Tragedy of Central Europe', *New York Review of Books*, 26 April.

Lindberg, L. (1963), *The Political Dynamics of European Integration*, Stanford University Press.

MacCormick, N. (1993), 'Beyond the Sovereign State', *Modern Law Review*, **56**.

Miall, H. (ed.) (1994), *Redefining Europe*, Pinter.

O'Keefe, D. and Twomey, P. (1994), *Legal Issues of the Maastricht Treaty*, Chancery Wiley.

Rasmussen, H. (1986), *On Law and Policy in the European Court of Justice*, Nijhoff.

Rousseau, J.J. (1793), 'Considérations sur le gouvernement de Pologne', *Oeuvres Complètes* vol. 2, Basle.

Said, E. (1995), *Orientalism*, Harmondsworth: Penguin.

Smith, A. (1992), 'National Identity and the Idea of European Unity', *International Affairs*, **68** (1).

Von Staden, (1994), 'Towards a Common European Defence Policy', in Carlsnaes and Smith (eds), *European Foreign Policy*, London: Sage.

Ward, I. (1995), 'Identity and Difference: The European Union and Postmodernism', in J. Shaw and G. More (eds), *New Legal Dynamics of the European Union*, O.U.P.

Weiler, J. (1991), 'The Transformation of Europe', *Yale Law Journal*, **100**, 2405.

Weiler, J. (1995), 'Does Europe need a Constitution? Demos, Telos and The German Maastricht Decision', *European Law Journal*, **1** (3) November.

Wilterdinck, N. (1993), 'The European Ideal: An examination of European and National Identity', *Archives Européenes de Sociologie*, **34** (1), 119.

Wistrich, E. (1994), *The United States of Europe*, London, New York: Routledge.

8 The Politics of Alterity and Exclusion in the European Union

Carole Lyons

INTRODUCTION

The notion of the human face[1] of Europe merits evocation after almost 50 years of planned integration. What face does Europe now present or represent? A selective and inaccurate representation of the integrated European might be a white, prosperous and loyal democrat, an image often associated with the EC/EU. But Europe represents many falling outside these simplistic images, not least many non-Europeans who reside there, who are politically and economically excluded from the *nouvelle Europe*. As Walker has pointed out, it is easier to define what Europe is not rather than what it is (Walker, 1996) and arguments about integration being exclusive or elitist are not novel. But there is a renewed need to question the exclusiveness of the integration process which resides in its increasingly focused discrimination (de Búrca, 1997).

The trend since the Single European Act has observed the perpetuation of a recently invented myth of the EU serving the deity of democracy above all and consequently engaging in language of rights window-dressing and political participation fripperies (e.g. the construction of European Union citizenship).[2] These citizen-friendly initiatives are intended to give the impression of a change of register or mood. This change serves the idealism of integration since it depicts a Europe moving beyond the market-only-based phase and sighting a constitutional future on the horizon. In the cynical recognition of the realities of Treaty posturing and Intergovernmental Conference *grands projets*, some benign political duping would be supportable and indeed predictable; decorative rights provisions can be considered an inherent aspect of the early stages in most constitutional construction. But these EU initiatives have been accompanied by committed practices and policies which function within the integration framework and have very tangible effects on people who have limited access to any political or juridical means of challenge, helping to create a realm of exclusion. Exclusivity on many levels has been written into the fabric of European integration and perpetuated in myriad ways; politically, with executive élites dominating; no effective or real legitimacy (Weiler, 1996 and de Búrca, 1996) or participation; the dual dilemma of ostensible domination by large states yet in reality more 'rights' for nationals of small states; gender-based exclusions; the marginalization of the unemployed, the disabled and many more in terms of the concrete exercise of EC-derived benefits. The EC/EU's increasing attachment to the discriminatory treatment of non-Europeans is the focus of this chapter. The operation of this 'policy' can no longer be legitimately justified and sits uneasily within the current rhetoric of rights and democracy in the EU.

The concept of exclusion has become intimately linked with maintaining the perpetual motion of integration, in particular with one of its current manifestations, the identity issue. The Third Pillar, emerging immigration policy and citizenship considered together evidence the construction of a larger framework of alterity than is obvious from isolated discussion of these factors. Functioning as an inchoate whole, they ensure the effective exclusion of non-Europeans in many spheres and contribute to a negative direction for integration, one in which may be discerned the foundations of the formation of a European identity. This identity is being deliberately constructed based on opposition to an 'other' – an other readily identifiable as emerging from European history (Fitzpatrick, 1997) but who for this purpose continues to be treated collectively as a negative reference point. The joint operation of exclusionary practices coupled with the overt identity industry, and with casual and seemingly uncontrolled constitutional developments, are fundamentally at odds with the professed motivations for positive and enduring European integration.

That EU Member States demand power over immigration control and nationality is not at issue here. But what factors seduced the Member States into 'pooling' questions of inclusion and exclusion, issues which have traditionally resided at the heart of nation state sovereignty? There are undoubtedly ingrained, historically determined, race related aspects of the EU's alterity politics but this is both too simplistic and superficial an explanation. It is helpful to separate perception from reality in this sphere and to clarify some overused terminology in this context. There is a generally prevailing tendency across disciplines and discourses to speak of 'immigrants', 'migrants', Third Country Nationals etc. as if the people concerned constituted one amorphous 'other' whether they be resident within or outside the EU. When the discussion is of 'security' (Wæver, 1996) or integration imperatives this 'other' is assumed to be a threatening other, certainly of a 'different' race and class, but distinctions are rarely made and the resulting vagueness conveniently serves to make arguments for controls or restriction easier. It is a small step from perceiving all non-Europeans as 'immigrants', all immigrants as 'illegal immigrants', all 'illegal' as dangerous or as criminals. The race element of the hidden exclusion machine is often superficially suppressed but it clearly forms an integral part, and overt consciousness of this is only recently emerging.[3]

Some basic figures help to expose the realities[4] and put this discussion into perspective. There are around 18 million non-EC nationals resident in the EU. In that sense, this category of others might well be said to constitute almost a 16th Member State. However, that description serves to alienate further as it perpetuates the impression that they constitute a group apart or separate and are individually indistinguishable from each other. This is part of the exclusion ideology, the need to isolate and control an extra-European threatening force. But as the figures demonstrate there is no simplistic race dimension here. For example, compare the number of USA nationals resident in the EU (339 758) with the number of Indian nationals (210 795) and, in general, the numbers of European (non-EU) nationals (4 128 544) with African nationals (2 698 224).[5] Yet the security discourse, and its distant relation, Member State-based pockets of nationalism, sees only the foreigners who fit the stereotypical images of otherness usually on a race or religion basis. The impression of the other usually peddled creates a confusion in terms of the perception of who is 'European'; not all Europeans are uniformly of the same race or religion nor indeed 'resident' in the territory generally regarded as 'Europe'.[6] For example, a Turkish national who has lived all her life in Germany without obtaining citizenship is not only seen to be more 'foreign' than a resident of, for example, a French Departement d'Outre Mer but, more importantly, is legally treated as such.

Who is and who is not European, who decides this, how is exclusion exercised and where do these issues fit within the pattern of integration?

FREE MOVEMENT?

'A Turk ... doesn't go to the opera.'[7]

The invention of European Union citizenship involved the association of the pre-existing fundamental freedom of movement of persons as its first listed 'right' or attribute.[8] As an exercise in the conglomeration of conceptual confusions it would be difficult to better Art. 8 but it begs the question to what extent this rearrangement of the constitutional position of free movement of persons represents a change in its legal character which, in turn, directly affects the position of non-EU nationals. Whether or not free movement of persons policy in the EC/EU has undergone any transformation as a result of this reference in Art. 8 EC, its mention nonetheless affects the exclusion framework. Free movement of persons has developed around the notion that it is an 'insider' privilege and its new link with citizenship (which, as will be discussed below, evidences precisely the constitutionalization of discrimination) now renders this freedom a cornerstone of the exclusion order.

The discrimination-based history of free movement of persons is well documented; inequalities have been directly created and perpetuated by a combination of Treaty interpretation, secondary legislation, and judicial pronouncements in this field (Cholewinski, 1996; Hervey, 1996; Plender, 1990) which effectively witness the whittling down of a seemingly large expression of the 'freedom' in the Treaty to a right limited in the main to Member State nationals with an economic function. The uncertainties and lacunae produced by free movement law encompasses the situations of non-economic actors (for example, children or gypsies), non-married couples, homosexual couples and disparities between the various attendant rights contained in secondary legislation. But the position of non-EC nationals, they being effectively deprived of this so-called fundamental freedom is the most significant discrimination allowed for and engendered by free movement law. Their admittance to the club of free movers is essentially limited or exceptional, contingent upon visas, or Association Agreement rights, or derivative and dependent on an EC national's primary right.

The creation of EU citizenship has increased the exclusivity in respect of non-Europeans, creating special (albeit limited or superficial) 'new' rights for Member State nationals. In 'constitutionalizing'[9] or elevating, in an as yet undefined manner, the inequalities inherent in free movement provisions, non-Europeans have been doubly affected or excluded. Lack of thoughtful drafting of Art. 8 may partly explain this effect but the implied freezing of provisions relating to the free movement of persons at this stage of its development without regard to its discriminatory effects may entrench that discrimination.

The alterity perpetuated or caused by provisions relating to the free movement of persons operate at practical, legislative and juridical levels. In general, these effects can be regarded as the necessary and predictable consequences of a confined, functional interpretation of this fundamental freedom. If Arts 48–66 EC are narrowly interpreted as serving the demands of the reconstruction of Member State economies within the common or internal market then it is not surprising that they should function to encourage a Europe of free-moving workers and consumers. But as to why certain workers and consumers (i.e. permanently resident non-EC nationals) should be physically/territorially confined and prevented from contributing in this manner is highly questionable. Even limiting the argument within an economy-based view of integration this exclusion can be questioned on its own basis, as it effectively amounts to the exclusion of 18 million EC residents from full participation in the market and related generation of the EC economy. If a combination of inherited race and immigration issues are not to have detrimental effects there is a need to have an holistic view of integration as encompassing them. The most basic startling point is the abolition of this rather bizarre and discriminatory consequence of the process, the creation of a market for free movement which does not allow for the movement of all who find themselves within the territory of the market. This is not in any sense an abstract concept; free movement between Member States is one of the most tangible benefits of European integration and its closure to non-European residents often has very overt manifestations. Free movement of persons law has fostered a type of Euro-nimbyism which has created a living standards boundary (Smith, 1996, p. 17) between the privileged free movers and the non-movers in restricting the latter's ability to engage even in the most basic benefits of integration. Much debate on these issues necessarily acknowledges the inherent economic ideology behind Arts 48–66 EC, but the EU's *mauvaise foi* in relation to the peoples of Europe can only deepen when principles of participation are declared in the Treaties and yet not fully evidenced by 'citizens' and denied almost completely to non-citizens.

There are different levels of discrimination and inequality in terms of inequities between categories of non-Europeans seeking to move within the Union. For example, the expansive rights of non-resident EFTA nationals compared with other (resident) non-EC nationals. The tendency to evoke Asian or African non-EC nationals in this context is misleading as this contributes to perpetuation of the image of a defined and less culturally aligned category of other. There is rarely mention of injustices done to permanently resident US citizens or Australians, for example. It would be surprising indeed to read dramatic media accounts of Paris intellectuals fighting for the rights of 300 New Zealanders or Canadians taking refuge in a church[10] or indeed ECJ free movement jurisprudence involving non-nationals from countries of the North.

Limited free movement may be explicable by resorting to concepts of sovereignty and traditional state control over entry and inclusion but considering the fundamental rationale of free movement (intended to allow entry to all qualifying Member State nationals) what motivations can be found for exclusions of people legally resident here? It is difficult to deny the ethno-cultural basis for this policy; Member States are willing to honour the entry of the vast majority of those to whom other Member States have granted inclusion but not to second-class residents considered not fully part of any Member State system.

On a practical level the implications of exclusive free movement on non-Europeans are pervasive. A simple comparison with movement of goods provisions displays an irony of integration, i.e. goods produced by permanently resident non-EC nationals may freely move within the entire territory of the EC but their producers may not. The position of the non-EC national fishing boat worker must be complicated also by the fact that free movement is available to Europeans only. Equally, certain occupations and professions are presumably, by their very nature, closed to a non-European. For example, airline crew member or a long-distance lorry driver, or indeed, work for the EC institutions. ERASMUS/SOCRATES programmes, part of the European identity creation machine, are also closed to non-EC nationals. To what extent do free movement restrictions hinder political involvement of non-Europeans? For example, the attendance of a local councillor at a Committee of the Regions meeting might require a visa. These few examples serve to highlight the absurdity and injustice of selective free movement of persons.

The day-to-day discriminations are theoretically less significant than the fact that there is normative and judicial facilitation of this policy. The role of the ECJ in this regard has been important; the Court does not emerge in a totally negative light from an analysis of its position towards non-EC nationals under the free movement provision but its part in the development of the tradition of exclusion is important. In terms of the initial expansion of the concept of free movement from a narrow, EC worker only basis the ECJ played a crucial role (Craig and de Búrca, 1995, ch. 15) and its jurisprudence on aspects of the derivative rights of non-Europeans has been a positive contribution to the precarious and confused position they occupy. However, the case-law has inherently been based on the connection of the 'outsider' with a Member State national (Hervey, 1996; Schermers, 1993). For all the temporary practical benefits jurisprudence such as *Singh* or *Rush Portugesa*[11] may bring, they contribute to furthering the 'second class' position of non-EC nationals when a truly rights-based or Art. 6 EC-based line of reasoning would have ensured a different, more long-term outcome. It would not have required a massive leap of judicial imagination for arguments of the kind raised in AG Tesauro's Opinion in *P* v. *S and Cornwall County Council*[12] to have been used in respect of the permanently resident non-EC national in cases such as *Demirel, Diatta* or *Morson.*[13] This type of expansive reasoning would have taken the emphasis away from their seemingly functional only position (in the sense conveyed both by the secondary legislation (i.e. Arts 10–12 Regulation 1612/68) and the jurisprudence, as their having a role only in supporting the EC migrant worker as s/he moved or as in the case of *Rush Portugesa* serving the function only of 'cheap' labour which could be 'imported' for temporary periods only). A possibility which has not been fully exploited by the Court is the logical extension of the reasoning in *Cowan*[14] to allow for an expansion in practice of the rights of non-nationals (O'Keeffe, 1993) as wide interpretation of the decision would, in principle, cover most occasions when a person moves to another Member State. But this would have facilitated the kind of fundamental approach to the issue which is necessary. Focusing on the inertia or non-expansive approach of the ECJ in this context forces a reflection upon the overall role of law in this aspect of integration. The normative system is shown to be weak or impotent in the face of the exclusionary forces and influences (de Búrca, 1997). Further, there has been a failure to recognize the impact upon an identifiable group of persons subject, without attendant remedies, to EC law, nor has there been a realization of the full potential of the application of general principles of EC law in this context.

An image of EC free movement law emerges as operating through the combination of a less than coherent normative base coupled with an ambiguous and incoherent system of protection to create a judicially supported culture of otherness. Recent proposals[15] demonstrate institutional cognition of the effects of this background but it is arguable that, even if these proposals reach the legislative stage, the denial and limitation of this basic 'fundamental' freedom for so many years and its focused discriminatory influences will take some time to fade. Their success will be further marred if the impact of citizenship and Third Pillar measures are not acknowledged as forming part of the environment of the marginalization of the 'outsider' in the EU.

CITIZENSHIP AS DISCRIMINATION

'Le vrai sens de ce mot [citoyennété] c'est presque entièrement effacé chez les modernes.'[16]

The first part of *Du Contrat Social* was devoted to research of the means whereby man passes from a state of nature to the civic state (*'l'état civil'*); citizenship plays a primary role here. Similar reasoning applied to an analysis of European integration exposes its failure to allow Member State nationals to move from a state of low-level political participation to that even resembling a civic one. EU citizenship does not further this progression to any extent. Citizenship was one of the major discoveries to emerge from the Maastricht excavation of the large hole that constituted the lack of legitimacy and dearth of democracy in the erstwhile Communities. Despite being obvious and indeed inherent for many years these problems underwent a transformation into crisis status at the time of the TEU (de Búrca, 1996). An intrinsic aspect of this crisis was consciousness of popular lack of interest in EU integration; citizenship was conceived as one of the solutions. Criticisms of this development have been many (d'Oliviera, 1994 among others). The negative effects of the concept are immediately more important than any positive ones to the extent that it has created by default and by dual definition a selective European demos and a European 'non-demos'. Whatever the nature of its fabricated character, this *sui generis* citizenship is here to stay and it is important to prevent further discriminatory orientation and to observe its potential as an inclusionary concept (Habermas, 1992).

A brief examination of Art. 8 EC reveals it to be anything but citizenship in the accepted sense of that status, but rather a layer of Maastricht-inspired constitutionalism which can be regarded as a significant but conceptually flawed development. As a construct, historically and politically, citizenship is inherently discriminatory, the ultimate justified and accepted form of state discrimination (Brubaker, 1992). It is, therefore, not surprising that the Art. 8 definition should reflect this in being confined to EC nationals. It was, at one level, and especially in its current form, a conservative and predictable outcome of the IGC process. But that which renders this citizenship doubly discriminatory is the attachment of essentially economic rights and benefits to the new citizens, i.e. the ring fencing of free movement benefits. The second, related effect of Art. 8 is the implied legitimation of race-based nationalism and exclusion (Weiler, 1996). It does little to encourage participation of the 'peoples of Europe', it has reinforced the non-participation of permanently resident non-nationals. Sparse though the political and civil rights emanating from Art. 8 are, their selective application to a Member State-determined circle of beneficiaries emphasizes in a concrete way that the EU is making little effort to encourage a real multi-cultural or multi-racial composition of the 'European demos' or to promote the notion that the 'peoples' of Europe might encompass others than those declared to be European by EU rhetoric (a definition which, in fact, excludes both Europeans (e.g. Poles or Slovenes) and non-Europeans). There is no evidence of openness in Art. 8 and little demonstration of political maturity or sophistication.

Habermas has proposed a decoupling of citizenship from nationality as a partial panacea for the discriminations flowing from Western European definitions of citizen (Habermas, 1992). This suggestion of a post-national citizenship offers the possibility of diminishing the perpetuation of the EU self and the non-EU other as one of the attributes of integration and would allow for the separation of the EU from the Member State traditions of entrenched ethnoculturalism. Decoupling nationality at EU level would represent a threat to that over-protected virtue of integration, state sovereignty, as any notion that the definition of citizenship status might be within 'Brussels' competency would go to the root of nation-state-based definitions of sovereignty.[17] But the problem may lie partly with the use of language in Art. 8 EC; that which has been defined there cannot be properly regarded as citizenship. However, taking a positive perspective, there might be said to be the genesis of the kind of post-national status which Habermas proposes. This will not develop if Member State nationality remains as the foundation of EU citizenship but if the motivations for and purpose of the concept are seriously revised then a status which does not have to be founded in nationality can be envisaged. It would be a concrete representation of integration, detached from the Member States in terms of definition and rights, open to nationals and non-nationals with a refocusing of its benefits and rights at EU level.[18] The usual basis which is proposed for entry into this status is residence, not, however, determined by the Member States as this would simply perpetuate discrimination. It may improve the status of permanently resident non-nationals within the EU and indirectly lead to a narrowing of the chasm between both real and received impressions of European and 'outsider'. Ironically, it might allow for the possibility of eligible others to become more European than Europeans themselves as their loyalties or ties within the territory might not be split so clearly between a Member State and EU as in the case of nationals.[19]

The persistence of the connection between EU citizenship and Member State nationality will allow individual Member State law and policy to continue dictating inclusion into EU citizenship. This may take the form of individually directed decisions by national administrations[20] which directly bar European-level rights or a more generalized determining of nationality law such as the granting of Portuguese citizenship to nationals of Macao. This in fact allows a Member State individually to dictate who the 'peoples' of Europe are and consequently who the 'outsiders' are. An effect of the current confused tenor of integration is that this power, which would at any rate not be affected by the suggested development of the Habermassian notion of post-national citizenship, affects all the other Member States because of free movement provisions. Integration has promoted and encouraged free movement but left untouched Member State ability to control inclusion into each state. This trend will be reinforced with enlargement, as it will entail dealing with the effects of the discriminatory citizenship laws of some of the Member States-in-waiting (see Barrington, 1995 for discussion of the Baltic States and the treatment of their Russian populations). This will involve existing Member States taking on board further definitions of 'others' or 'outsiders', thereby demonstrating a lack of control over this basic aspect of integration.

The invention of citizenship can be seen to play an instrumental role in the perpetuation of discrimination towards both specific and wider groups of non-nationals. Conversely, it provides a potential base for addressing the nature of the EU's relationship with 'others' within. This has not gone entirely ignored by institutional actors; the Consultative Commission on Racism and Xenophobia's Report to the Council suggests that 'Consideration should be given to the possible extension of citizenship of the Union to all persons who have resided permanently in the territory of one of the Member States for five years'.[21] This would be a positive development in terms of a reorientation towards a more inclusive status. However, beneficial though this would be for resident non-nationals, the EU's nascent immigration policy would ensure that discriminations towards non-residents continues.

EU IMMIGRATION 'LAW'

'La question du droit d'asile est devenue un enjeu de la lutte révolutionnaire … "car elle a pour enjeu de determiner quels sont les droits et les devoirs reciproqués des nations"'.[22]

If free movement law can be regarded as responsible for the institutionalization and normalization of 'outsider'-directed discrimination and Art. 8 citizenship as having constitutionalized it, the introduction of Title VI (The Justice and Home Affairs Pillar or Third Pillar) TEU is intended to ensure its practical implementation. This particular outcome of the Maastricht IGC negotiations is a surprising development from the perspective of EU constitutional history. It involves a relocation of competence in the areas of immigration and asylum which are traditionally regarded as untouchable by the institutions[23] and it evidenced the inclusion at Treaty level of matters normally reserved for the sphere of administrative activity at a national level. Title VI has spawned a wealth of commentary in which its provisions are widely criticized and its lack of success highlighted (Fernhout, 1996; and Walker, 1996).

The Third Pillar's bailiwick encompasses nine areas identified as being of 'common interest' (Art. K.1 TEU) broadly encompassing asylum and immigration policy, police co-operation in the areas of drug trafficking, terrorism and international crime. There has, therefore, been a deliberate linking of traditional 'security' issues with immigration and asylum by association, thus rendering the latter also as matters of security for the Union. Thus classifying immigration and asylum lends the ultimate authority and justification to actions to prevent their increase. This ideology belies completely the reality of the numbers entering[24] as immigrants or as asylum-seekers[25] and renders mention of rights hypocritical in this context.[26]

But for whom are these security measures intended? Who or what is being protected against the 'threat' of asylum-seekers, for example. Who does the Third Pillar represent and who gives it legitimacy? If one accepts the need for security measures of this order does this imply that the Member States have insufficient power in this regard? Or is it perhaps, in fact, a question of the survival of the state or nation or integration itself that is at issue? In other words, if JHA can be accepted as having a primary role in controlling entry and exclusion, what are the motivations which underlie its operation? If it is intended that European Citizens are to protected, why is the connection between citizens and the JHA so fragile? Much of the 1996 IGC preparatory material[27] refers to the need to increase 'protection' for citizens; had the citizen not been invented under TEU from where would the authority derive? Finally, is it just the citizens who need such rights, or are the 18 million permanent resident non-citizens regarded as part of the threat?

The brief history of the Third Pillar, a story of movement from daedalic adhocery to byzantine bureaucracy, is well documented (see, among others, Korella and Twomey, 1993; Bieber and Monar, 1995; Monar and Morgan, 1994; Walker, 1996). It is an analysis which reveals the gradual removal of state activity in these areas to the safe zone of the JHA committee maze, where the state élites may practice low politics, free from the interference of either national or community institutions. The secrecy which surrounded developments during the Ad Hoc Phase and which continues under JHA, the confusion as to the status of the measures and provisions emanating from the process and the limited participation of the Community institutions (in particular the ECJ which under Art. L TEU has been refused jurisdiction in the area), are by now well rehearsed criticisms of the Third Pillar.

The pre-history of the immigration aspects of the JHA was characterized by the careful targeting of the two remaining avenues for entry into the Community states, i.e. family unification and asylum. The developments in the area of asylum can perhaps be regarded as the most significant of the Ad Hoc Phase with the emergence of the Dublin Convention[28] and also several resolutions on substantive aspects of asylum. Many of these developments were supported by a perceived mass increase in the numbers of persons seeking asylum in Member States at the end of the 1980s. It was this period which witnessed the development of the concepts of 'manifestly unfounded' asylum applications, 'safe host/third countries' and countries in which there is generally no serious risk of persecution.[29] All of these developments may be criticized on the basis of contravening the spirit, if not the letter, of the

Geneva Convention on the Protection of Refugees. As in the case of family unification, many of these innovations were 'incorporated' into national laws and there were widespread restrictive changes in asylum laws throughout the EC.[30]

In a sea of bureaucratic inventions it was easy to lose sight of the nature of asylum and its particular reference to the recent history of Europe, and indeed its intimate relationship with the development of the Communities. It says little for integrative progress to observe the treatment of asylum policy under the JHA. It is superficially perplexing as to why the EU cannot locate a common humanitarian interest in excepting this from the field of security in making an effort to develop a procedurally just system for handling the relatively small number of the world's refugees who manage to enter the EU Member States. The association of asylum with crime and terrorism artificially constructs a reality and in post-1989 Europe asylum-seekers have partially taken the place of nuclear threat and Communist influence. Mere unarmed, impoverished and generally fearful individuals[31] with the potential to harm nothing more perhaps than the Member State social security systems have been identified as threatening. Perceptions are perpetuated at many levels and it is a short route from the Treaty classification of asylum seekers as threatening to popular images of all (non-European) foreigners as threatening – the other as dangerous and therefore to be physically excluded.

JHA does not constitute the only element of emerging EU immigration law; Arts 100c and 100d EC give the EC institutions competence 'to determine the third countries whose nationals must be in possession of a visa when crossing the external borders of the Member States' (Art. 100c. EC). The confusions created by the potential clash of competencies and powers between JHA and Art. 100c have been noted (Fernhout, 1996; Muller-Graff, 1994). Policy-making in this area raises several questions. In effect it creates the category of Community immigrant without a relevant, and procedurally defined, Community immigration law. It allows for discrimination on several grounds; first, on the basis of selection of the countries on the 'blacklist' of countries whose nationals will require visas;[32] secondly in discriminating between countries which are geographically proximate but which would have different visa status and finally in re-inforcing the discrimination to which long-term resident non-EC nationals are already subject to in allowing visa entrants more freedom of movement than the former category.

If the past performance under JHA is to be repeated then the pattern will be for continued secret developments in a confused committee system. However, 1996 IGC preparations reveal the possibility of a transfer of much of the competencies in this field to the EC Pillar. While this would ensure important institutional procedures and safeguards is it appropriate for the EC institutions to determine issues of who to include and exclude, given their current state of legitimacy. What will be important for the future, and this may be facilitated by EC competence, is co-ordination of the different strands of racism and xenophobia control measures. There is clearly an important connection between the two but, that said, racism does not just apply at point of control. Equally, on the other hand, to equate too closely racism developments with immigration would reinforce the notion that the only persons who might be subjected to racism are outsiders, non-Europeans. The Member States may struggle to maintain control over their own legislation in this area[33] but if the EU is to continue to develop the mechanisms for constructing a common 'alien' it would be doubly inappropriate for discrimination to operate in terms of different race protection legislation in each Member State.

Any discussion of immigration issues in Europe inevitably becomes complicated because Member States still effectively retain the power to determine their individual immigration and asylum laws and act quite independently, if in a similarly restrictive vein, in this regard. But, as has been pointed out, the actual substance is increasingly being determined in an EU sphere, one which is closed or does not allow access in terms of examination of processes, procedures, budgets, policy objectives etc. What is confusing about the operation of immigration policy in the Member States is that any individual affected by the prevailing legislation or policy cannot easily seek judicial remedies beyond the national 'face' of that legislation (except perhaps in terms of recourse to European Convention on Human Rights institutions) in order that an EU-level inspired and negotiated instrument be examined in that context. This means that an Art. 177 EC reference, for example, might not easily be granted in respect of a question relating to national immigration or asylum laws and (ECHR input apart) this renders JHA output free from an appropriate constitutional scrutiny.

EXCLUSION AND IDENTITY

'The problem lies in the fact that, in order to be strong enough, the so-called self-identity of Europe needs to be exclusive and different.'[34]

Having examined the basic foundations of an exclusion policy in the Union the question is what objective do they serve? To what extent can it be said that the EU (in as much as that itself exists) wishes to establish an 'identity'? At one level the answers are simple; identity is referred to three times in the TEU in the Preamble,[35] in Article B [36] and in Article F.[37] What is striking about these references is, first, the intimate relationship between defence and security and identity of the Union and, secondly, the fact that it is identity of the Union (and in conflict also the identity of the Member States) which is at issue rather than any connection with a notion of fostering a sense of European identity or Europeanness among 'the peoples of Europe'.[38] This confusion as to what identity and what form of identity is being fostered is in a sense a separate issue; the point is that the constitutional forces in the EU are aware and desirous of the creation of an identity for the Union and this is formulated in the main in terms of an external identity, one which has a manifestation outside rather than inside the entity. The emphasis is less on identifying a positive source or sources for the 'European identity' to develop or be nurtured, but rather it is formulated in negative terms in the form of presenting a strong security-based identity externally.[39]

The JHA (and its control companies) is rendered more explicable in this light; common defence is identified as a major objective of the new Union. The application of this policy would have been easier in a pre-1989 past; now the defensive strategies are relocated to security against the more easy targets identified under JHA. The defence element, if it can be said to be at all present, is related to economics[40] and sense of threat to culture (a restrictively defined, Member State version) rather than defence in any real sense of the word. Integration can be perceived as useful if fulfilling this objective which is fostering the preservation of the elements conservatively identified as necessary to the Member State. Therefore, in those terms, JHA, ostensibly a reduction in Member State sovereignty, is in fact a retrenchment of its elements.

The procession of exclusion, from acceptance of discriminatory movement within the territory to the common definition of aliens and asylum control, appears less than coincidental. It has become a cliché to speak of fortress Europe and, indeed, when links are made between what might have been seen as some of the foundations of that fortress and the wider motivations of those building it, it becomes apparent that whatever edifice is being constructed it is from a position of weakness or defensiveness rather than strength. This reflects poorly on the direction for future integration. The supportive background or structure might be located in fast-moving, short-sighted integration which involves a tendency to forget the history of Europe, a history incorporating both negative (colonialism) and positive (the Islamic past of parts of Europe itself, for example) plural influences. It may be partly accounted for by what Habermas has called the chauvinism of prosperity (Habermas, 1992). In the EU, the chauvinism has become confused as, arguably, the forces of recession are even more influential than that of prosperity.

In the interplay between Member State complexes in relation to inclusion and identity and the independent drive for a continuing integration, issues of identity, otherness and exclusion have an awkward and unfortunate collision. If integration is regarded as irreversible it demands an increased consciousness of why it is happening and, moreover, whom it is serving. Implicit in that is the recognition that if we cannot identify accurately the Europeans, then it is easier and more convenient to define who we *are not* integrating. The whole complex history of the relationship between Turkey and Europe is relevant in this regard. It serves as a long-running example of the EU's inability to deal with a potential 'insider' – which it deals with by constantly redefining the meaning of 'outsider' (Robins, 1996). This can be explained by the EU's selective and flexible attitude to what European means and partly because of the hybrid insider/outsider character which Turkey presents.

The success of the internal market has fostered the increased picket-fencing of the Union, a Union which however is not closed to all elements of otherness (Korean car factories bearing gifts of employment and technological innovation will easily enter whereas the individual Korean will meet with more difficulty). But the negative aspects of the successful Delors drive has been a deliberate closure to create an illusion of isolation, of superiority within. The collaboration of identity and exclusion begin the demythologizing of the myth of neutral integration. In one sense, it is not surprising that integration should have mothered a discriminatory monster; what is less explicable is the manner in which this has occurred. The genesis may be identified in the inspired 1980s efforts to promote spontaneous integration, but much confusion now surrounds the actors (Member States and institutions) and their motives, as much of the drama now takes place in the closed boudoir of the bureaucrats.

CONCLUSION

The exclusionary trends in the integrative process which emerge are marginalization, identity manipulation, Member State domination and a lack of a moral dimension. Behind the facade of the large and open internal market resides a more exclusive boutique. The policies in the Pillars are overtaking the integrative foundations. There has been a reversal of many of the traditional concerns; problems associated with integration through law replaced by that of integration without law in the context of a reorientation towards Member State values and preferences. There, arguably, has not been progression 'beyond the sovereign state'[41] but a reassertion or redefinition of the latter determined by nationalist influences and a perpetuation of provinciality and parochialism. It calls for analysis of the EU's failures which are less likely to be located in Danish referenda results than the state of rights, discrimination and the notion of justice in the Union. *Après le marché unique le déluge*; with peace and prosperity allegedly achieved, both pro and anti-integrationists are caught, rabbit-like, in the glare of the lack of purpose. The casual constitutional developments which emerge from the IGC process seem incapable of dealing with deeper issues.[42] European integration appears to abhor a vacuum but fails to fill it with discussion and input of sophisticated theoretical analysis into the Treaty revisions.

These issues highlight the running sore of integration which is tensions on competence between Member States and the institutions they created to help achieve integration. They have parted in terms of identity; the institutions were not programmed to cover this; in principle they should be seen to protect the identity of the Member States but their wide powers and functions have naturally spawned a role for them in creating a European identity. In terms of inclusion and exclusion, the very existence of the strong centre has created the need for a unified approach, but this has in turn forced a reassertion of Member States' interests here as the state (élite) stakes its sole prerogative to uphold the values of the nation. The machinery of integration could provide the basis for an informed inclusion policy not divorced from history but decoupled from the nationalism, narrow-mindedness and other legacies of the European past. The IGC process itself is an inherent part of the dilemma; its ethos and tradition (where beef issues are bartered against Bosnia) fundamentally discourages or prevents conceptually constructive thinking.

Europe has long relied on the fiction of the barbarian other.[43] Integration offered the opportunity for an education in otherness, not a perpetuation of exclusion. Free movement of persons' provisions are inherently an important participatory force if so conceived or interpreted; Union citizenship presents a scope and mechanisms for a wider concept of inclusion that would be impossible at the nation-state level. Even within the mechanisms of the Third Pillar there is the potential to seek a highest (rather than lowest) common-denominator approach in policy and law making. More generally, the important contribution (economically, politically and culturally) of the 'other' needs to be recognized. If integration contains, as of necessity it must, an intrinsic attachment to progress, then it currently has failed in that regard. What is Europe today? It is obviously more than from 'Plato to Nato' to saying No. Identity, citizenship and co-operation on questions of inclusion are signs of a phase of integration beyond the level of institutions but they lack a positive focus.

'The petit-bourgeois man is unable to imagine the Other. If he comes face to face with him, he blinds himself, ignores and denies him.'[44] The EU and integration need to serve a purpose larger than that of reinforcing the petit-bourgeois and his need for an Other. These are eighteenth-century concerns ill suited to progression towards the twenty-first.

ACKNOWLEDGEMENT

I would like to thank Gráinne de Búrca for valuable comments on a draft and Jim Bergeron for helpful and patient editorial advice.

NOTES

1 Laffan, 1996, p. 96, referring to Willy Brandt's use of the term.
2 Art. 128 EC.
3 COM (95) 653 on racism, xenophobia and anti-semitism, Council Doc. 6906/1/95, Final Report of the Consultative Commission on Racism and Xenophobia.
4 See COM (94) 23 on Immigration and Asylum for entry and exit figures.
5 COM (94) 23 Annex I.
6 Art. 227 EC and Declarations No. 25 and No. 26 of the TEU.
7 Z. Senocak (1993), *Atlas des Tropischen Deutschlands*, Berlin: Babel Verlag, p. 22, cited in Robins, 1996. In the EU, non-EU nationals, in certain Member States may have to pay more to go to operas and museums than an EU national. Case C-45/93 *Commission* v. *Spain* [1994] ECR I-911.
8 Art. 8a. EC Treaty 'Every citizen of the Union shall have the right to move and reside freely within the territory of the Member States...'.
9 Commission of the European Communities, COM (93) 702, Report on the Citizenship of the Union, p. 2.
10 'French Celebrities support African's Paris church sit-in', *The Times*, 20 August 1996, p. 10.
11 For example *R* v. *Immigration Appeal Tribunal and Surinder Singh, ex parte Secretary of State for the Home Department* (Case C-370/90) [1992] ECR 1-4265 and *Rush Portugesa Lda* v. *Office National d'Immigration* (Case C-113/89) [1990] ECR I-1417.
12 Case C-13/94, 30 April 1996. See further de Búrca (1996b).
13 *Demirel* v. *Stadt Schwäbisch Gmünd* (Case 12/86) [1987] ECR 3719, *Diatta* v. *Land Berlin* (Case 267/83) [1986] ECR 567, *Morson and Jhanjan* v. *Netherlands* (Cases 35/82 and 36/82) [1982] ECR 3723.
14 *Cowan* v. *Trésor Public* (Case 186/87) [1989] ECR 195.
15 COM (95) 653 on racism, xenophobia and anti-semitism, Council Doc. 6906/1/95, Final Report of the Consultative Commission on Racism and Xenophobia.
16 J.J. Rousseau (1762), *Du Contrat Social*, Book I, Chap. VI.
17 See, for example Declaration No. 2 TEU and the Edinburgh Decision, 12 December 1992, Section A, Citizenship, which hint at fears of this nature.
18 Has been well commented upon (see Closa, 1992 and d'Oliviera, 1994), Art. 8 EC offers few Community or Union related rights.
19 Laffan, 1996, p. 88.
20 Some such examples would include the refusal of UK citizenship to the Al Fayed brothers (resident for 30 years) (*The Independent*, 21 February 1996), or the treatment of citizens of Mali as potentially polygamous and therefore unfit to become French citizens (Errera, 1994).
21 Council Doc. 6906/1/95. See also COM (95) 653.
22 Robespierre in the French National Assembly, 1791, cited in G. Noiriel (1991) *La Tyrannie du National*, Paris: Calman-Levy.

23 See *Germany and Others* v. *Commission* (Cases 281/85, 283-5/85, 287/85) [1987] ECR 3203, where a number of Member States objected to the Commission's attempt to propose a Decision relating to migration policies affecting workers from non-EC countries.
24 Total non-EC national immigration into the EU (1991), 1 232 636, (1992), 274 798; emigration (1991) 506 250 - COM (94) 23.
25 Total number of asylum seekers in EU (1991) 447 275, (1993) 420 718 - COM (94) 23.
26 The TEU Preamble, Art. F.2. and Art. K.2 all refer to the protection of fundamental rights by the Union.
27 See, for example, the Reflection Group's Report, SN 520/95.
28 Bulletin EC No. 6 (1990) p. 155.
29 For a full discussion see Guild (1993).
30 See for example Wisskirchen (1994).
31 The definition of 'alien' for the purposes of asylum procedure in the Dublin Convention and in derivative national legislative measures is confined to non-EU nationals and does not therefore conceive of the possibility of an EU national needing to seek asylum in another Member State.
32 Com (93) 684, COM (95) 346 and COM (95) 347.
33 See for example *The British Approach to the European Union Intergovernmental Conference 1996*, HMSO, 1996.
34 T. Ozal (1991), *Turkey in Europe and Europe in Turkey*, Nicosia: K. Rustem & Brother, cited in Robins (1996).
35 Member States 'Resolved to implement a common foreign and security policy and the eventual framing of a common defence policy, which might in time lead to a common defence, thereby reinforcing the European identity ...'.
36 Art. B TEU where, as one of the Union's objectives is listed 'to assert its identity on the international scene, in particular through common foreign and security policy ...'.
37 Art. F. 1. 'The Union shall respect the national identities of its Member States ...'.
38 See further Weiler (1996).
39 See further Laffan (1996) and Wæver (1996).
40 But see Spencer (1994a)
41 MacCormick, N. (1993), 'Beyond the Sovereign State', *Modern Law Review* **56**.
42 Art. F2 TEU as an example.
43 'What are we going to do now that the barbarians aren't there any more. They may have been the solution', Dante, *Divine Comedy*.
44 Barthes, R. (1957), *Mythologies*, (1993) (translation), London: Vintage, p. 151, where the following is footnoted: 'The petit-bourgeois is the man who prefers himself to all else' (Gorki).

REFERENCES

Barrington, L. (1995), 'The Domestic and International Consequences of Citizenship in the Soviet Successor States', *Europe–Asia Studies*, **47** (5).

Bieber, R. and Monar, J. (eds) (1995), *Justice and Home Affairs in the European Union*, Brussels: European Interuniversity Press.

Brubaker, R. (1992), *Citizenship and Nationhood in France and Germany*, Cambridge, Mass. and London: Harvard University Press.

de Búrca, G. (1995), 'The Language of Rights and European Integration', in J. Shaw and G. More (eds), *New Legal Dynamics of the European Union*, Oxford: Oxford University Press.

de Búrca, G. (1996), 'The Quest for Legitimacy in the European Union', *Modern Law Review*, **59**.

de Búrca, G. (1997), 'The Role of Equality in European Community Law', in A. Dashwood and S. O'Leary (eds), *The Principle of Equal Treatment in European Community Law*, London: Sweet and Maxwell.

Cholewinski, R. (1996), 'The Rights of Non-EC Immigrant Workers and Their Families in EC Countries of Employment', in J. Dine and B. Watt (eds), *Discrimination Law: Concepts, Limitations and Justifications*, London: Longman.

Closa, C. (1992), 'The Concept of Citizenship in the Treaty on European Union', *Common Market Law Review*, **29**.

Craig, P. and de Búrca, G. (1995), *EC Law*, Oxford: Oxford University Press.

Errera, R. (1994), 'Recent Decisions of the French Conseil d'Etat', *Public Law*, Autumn.

Fernhout, R. (1996), 'Justice and Home Affairs: Immigration and Asylum Policy, from JHA co-operation to communitarisation', paper presented to Jean Monnet Symposium on the 1996 IGC, Brussels, 5–7 May 1996.

Fitzpatrick, P. (1998), 'New Europe, Old Stories: Myths of Identity and Legality in the European Union', Chapter 2, this volume.

Guild, E. (1993), 'Towards a European Asylum Law: Developments in the European Community', *Immigration and Nationality Law and Practice*, **7** (3).

Habermas, J. (1992), 'Citizenship and National Identity: Some Reflections on the Future of Europe', *Praxis International* **12** (1).

Hervey, T. (1996), 'Migrant Workers and their Families in the European Union: The Pervasive Market Ideology of Community Law', in J. Shaw and G. More (eds), *New Legal Dynamics of the European Union*, Oxford: Oxford University Press.

Korella, G.D. and Twomey, P. (eds) (1993), *Towards a European Immigration Policy*, Brussels: European Interuniversity Press.

Laffan, B. (1996), 'The Politics of Identity and Political Order in Europe', *Journal of Common Market Studies*, **34** (1) March.

Monar, J. and Morgan, R. (eds) (1994), *The Third Pillar of the European Union*, Brussels: European Interuniversity Press.

Muller-Graff, P-C. (1994), 'The Legal Basis of the Third Pillar and its Position in the Framework of the Union Treaty', *CMLRev*, **31**.

O'Keeffe, D. (1993), 'General remarks on the free movement of various categories of persons', in H.G. Schermers *et al.* (eds), *Free Movement of Persons in Europe*, Dortrecht: Martinus Nijhoff.

d'Oliveira, H.U.J. (1994), 'European Citizenship: Its Meaning, Its Potential', in R. Dehousse, *Europe after Maastricht*, Munich: Law Books in Europe.

Plender, R. (1990), 'Competence, European Community Law and Nationals of Non-Member States', *International and Comparative Law Quarterly*, **39**.

Preuss, U. (1995), 'Citizenship and Identity: Aspects of a Political Theory of

Citizenship', in R. Bellamy, V. Bufacchi and D. Castiglione (eds), *Democracy and Constitutional Culture in the Union of Europe*, London: Lothian Foundation Press.

Robins, K. (1996), 'Interrupting Identities: Turkey/Europe', in S. Hall and P. du Gay (eds), *Questions of Cultural Identity*, London: Sage.

Schermers, H.G. *et al.* (eds.) (1993) *Free Movement of Persons in Europe*, Dortrecht: Martinus Nijhoff.

Smith, M. (1996), 'The European Union and a changing Europe: Establishing the Boundaries of Order', *Journal of Common Market Studies*, **34** (1), March.

Spencer, S. (ed.) (1994a), *Immigration as an Economic Asset*, London: IPPR/ Trentham Books.

Spencer, S. (ed.) (1994b), *Strangers and Citizens*, London: IPPR/Rivers Oram Press.

Wæver, O. (1996), 'European Security Identities', *Journal of Common Market Studies*, **34** (1) March.

Walker, N. (1996), 'Co-operation in Justice and Home Affairs: the Politics of the Third Pillar', in R. Bideleux and J. Bradbury (eds), *The Development of the European Union: Policy Integration in the 1990s*, London: Macmillan.

Weiler, J. (1996), 'European Neo-constitutionalism: In Search of Foundations for the European Constitutional Order', *Political Studies*, **44**.

Wisskirchen, C. (1994), 'Germany: Assault on the Constitutional Right to Asylum', Parts I and II, *Immigration and Nationality Law and Practice*, **8** (3) (Part I) and (4) (Part II).

PART III
EUROPEAN IDENTITY IN NATIONAL LAW AND IN THE EUROPEAN CONVENTION

9 Foucault and the 'Illegal Alien': National Identity as Focus for Distinction and Control

Sarah van Walsum

IMMIGRATION AND CONTROL IN THE NETHERLANDS TODAY

In 1987 the Dutch government tried to introduce extensive identity checks to control illegal immigration. Everyone would have to prove his or her undisputed right to residence to gain access to any payments, services, insurances, permits etc. provided by the Dutch bureaucracy.[1] By way of contrast, until then undocumented migrants could pay taxes, apply for public housing and child support, and qualify for health, disability and unemployment insurance. People whose status was still under dispute were even entitled to welfare payments.

These proposals met with strong public resistance. Such controls it was argued would institutionalize discrimination and would grant state bureaucracy too much power over the individual.[2] Now, a decade later, those same proposals have to a large extent been realized. Identification, in particular documentation concerning nationality and residence status, is now required in a large number of areas, both public and private: by applications for welfare or unemployment insurance payment; by applications for a social security and fiscal number; at registration of marriage or birth; by application for medical insurance or for a job; on boarding an aeroplane; when attending a football match – and so on. Increasingly these controls involve sexuality: immigration authorities ransack bedrooms and wardrobes to determine whether or not a couple live together 'as man and wife'; identity checks of new-born babies bring control into the site of birth itself; the controls against 'fraudulent' marriages empower immigration authorities to probe into the intimate details of lovers' lives and to veto a match they don't approve of.

The more extensive the controls become, the more pressing is the question: who, exactly, is legally resident in the Netherlands? This is more problematic than one might at first glance assume. A few examples. In 1994 less than 12 per cent of all asylum cases handled in the Netherlands actually resulted in the granting of refugee status. But in the end almost half of all the applicants were allowed, on rather vague grounds, to stay after all.[3] Women who have officially lost their right to residence because they have left their partner – or been deserted by him – before having acquired independent residence rights, are finally granted a residence permit in six out of ten cases (Van Blokland and de Vries, 1992, pp. 62–8). It is difficult to determine why some do and others do not get their permit. Recently, the Dutch government quietly carried out an amnesty for undocumented workers, while at the same time publicly and officially denying that they were doing any such thing.[4] Because the amnesty was unofficial, it was again difficult to determine who would and who would not be allowed to stay. Not surprisingly in many cases a person's status is under dispute, and what the final outcome will be is not at all certain. Those who can mobilize support for their case may succeed in reversing a negative decision, but rarely before the courts. No precedents may be established, and jurisprudence must not bear witness to the ambiguities and contradictions inherent in immigration law.[5] The clear political archetype of the 'illegal alien' must not become confused by the human dilemmas of legal practice. Significantly, the most recent proposals to date have been to expand the definition of the 'illegal alien' to include those migrants whose status is still under dispute.[6]

This indeterminate nature of illegality, together with an increasing focus on sexuality and the bureaucratic power that extensive identity checks imply, raise interesting parallels with Foucault's theories on sexuality and power. But before developing that analogy, I first want to sketch the economic and political context in which current Dutch immigration laws and policies have been developing.

MOBILITY, FLEXIBILITY AND MIGRANT LABOUR

In his book *The Condition of Postmodernity*, the geographer David Harvey describes how, as transport and communications technologies have developed, production and distribution can, and in many cases are, being organized on an international or even global scale. Capital, expertise, labour, consumer goods and the consumers themselves are all increasingly mobile.

Part of this process is the growing possibility to profit from regional and international differences in salaries, prices, taxes, available skills and infrastructure. Locally based politicians and businesses compete to attract mobile capital and to keep it in place, by reducing the costs of local labour and by improving local infrastructure. At the same time, they try to shove the risks that accompany the increasingly unpredictable movement of investments, supply and demand onto workers by introducing more flexible labour relations. Private businesses increasingly contract out to service industries, sub-contractors, employment agencies, flexible workers or home workers (Harvey, 1989). While workers are being confronted with diminishing job-security, the competition to attract mobile capital has also put pressure on social security, as indirect costs of labour in the form of taxes and social premiums are also being lowered. Those who cannot afford to compensate for cuts in social spending by buying commercialized insurances or services are forced to fall back on unpaid labour and support of family and friends (Johnson, 1987; Finch, 1989).

Under the present circumstances it is not surprising that the demand for, and the regulation of, labour from abroad has changed over the past decades. Given the growing demand for casual and unpaid labour, it is not likely that companies will systematically contract full-time workers from abroad, or make special provisions for them in terms of housing and health care, as was the case with the 'guest workers' of the 1960s and early 1970s. The introduction in 1979 of a law to regulate foreign labour did in effect reduce this form of labour migration to the Netherlands by stipulating priority for Dutch and EC labour.[7] However, this did not spell the end to the supply of labour from outside of the EC. On the contrary. In 1991, for example, the number of non-EC migrants who received a permanent work permit exceeded the total number of foreigners who were granted a residence permit in 1967, when little or no restrictions were imposed on hiring labour from abroad (Groenendijk and Minderhoud, 1992, pp. 23, 60). The difference is that now the successful applicants have entered the Netherlands as the partner or dependent child of a Dutch citizen or of a landed immigrant, in which case they are entitled to a work permit, regardless of the availability of Dutch or EC labour.[8]

These foreign workers, recruited not directly but via family reunification, seem better adapted to the present demands of the labour market than the 'guest workers' of the 1960s and early 1970s. An established migrant family can be a good source of temporary, part-time or flexible labour and can offer mutual support in dealing with the insecurities that such work implies, thus sparing the state and the employers the costs of covering those risks. Dutch immigration law which, as I shall discuss below, places these migrants in a very dependent position via-à-vis their settled family members, reinforces these advantages.

Undocumented workers – unorganized, extremely dependent on their employer and increasingly excluded from social insurances and services – offer similar advantages and also meet the demands of the present-day labour market. We can seriously question whether in a context of increasing mobility and deregulation the new proposals to increase the scope of identity checks can bring a halt to the employment of undocumented workers. To this day, the government has been unsuccessful in its attempts to do so. The recent unofficial amnesty for undocumented migrant workers was a silent witness to that fact.

WHY THE OBSESSION WITH CONTROL?

In October 1992, an aeroplane crashed onto an apartment building in the densely populated Bijlmermeer, on the outskirts of Amsterdam. As Dutch civil servants tried to take stock of the resulting deaths and casualties, a bureaucrat's nightmare emerged. The city registrars proved useless. Many, many people had not been living at the addresses where they had been registered. In fact, many victims of the crash proved to be undocumented migrants, who were not registered at all.

It was after this tragic incident that the issue of illegal migration left the extremist margins of Dutch politics to take centre stage, engaging all parties, from left to right. Undocumented residence in itself is nothing new. In fact it was the norm in the Netherlands rather than the exception from the moment the first Dutch immigration law was introduced in 1848, up until the introduction of a new immigration law in 1965 (Swart, 1978, pp. 11–14). Why has it now become such a pressing political issue? Again, I think we should take into consideration the international context in which present-day migration takes place.

As companies transcend national boundaries, divide their productive activities over various places and regularly shift the locus of those activities, the role that the nation-state can play in the organization and control of economic activities changes. In trying to attract and hold down increasingly mobile capital, governments tend to give more priority to the demands of internationally operating businesses than to national social issues. In many countries including the Netherlands we see governments renouncing much of their authority over local investments and claims on locally made profits, on labour relations and social policies. The new dominant ideology is that of neo-liberalism. The state must no longer pamper its citizens.

But the presently popular neo-liberal rhetoric should not be mistaken for a call for less state. It is a call for a different state (Hirsch, 1991, p. 73). As governments have been retracting their redistributive policies of wage controls, progressive income tax and collectively financed social security and services, while at the same time favouring internationally operating capital, the gap between rich and poor has rapidly increased (Wilterdink, 1993, pp. 3–42). The need to exert control over those most strongly affected by the casualization of labour relationships and the dismantling of the welfare state – mostly women, blacks and members of ethnic minorities – has grown accordingly. Recent technological developments have provided the automatic data-systems and communicating networks necessary to conduct such controls. This technological infrastructure in turn has extended the already existing bureaucratic infrastructure of city registrars, police and welfare bureaucracy. During the past century, as the Dutch welfare-state came to maturity, people have been enabled and/or obliged to deal with state and semi-state institutions on more and more occasions for services, permits and payments, which were only granted if applicants met certain requirements. These requirements often involved the personal circumstances and behaviour of the person involved. Thus many state and semi-state institutions, who had to confirm whether or not applicants qualified for help or support, became not only agents of welfare, but also of control. Equipped with the new information technology, institutions originally designed to protect the 'worthy poor' against the powerful can now be reconstituted to protect the 'worthy Dutch citizen' against crime, social fraud and illegal migration. Typically the discussions over illegal migration triggered by the plane-crash in the Bijlmer merged with debates over the growing discontent in the inner cities. Controlling illegality, it was suggested, would help resolve tensions caused by unemployment, poor housing and violence in the streets (Rodrigues and Tazelaar, 1993, pp. 15–23).

FOUCAULT

In his book *La volonté de savoir*,[9] Foucault explores the paradox surrounding the repression of what was construed to be perverse sexual behaviour, particularly in the course of the nineteenth century. He notes that the stronger the taboo surrounding sexuality became, the greater the pressure to give it expression – in the first instance through the Catholic confession, but later through the secular inquests conducted by medical doctors, psychiatrists, social workers and criminal courts. While norms regarding sexuality seem to be more relaxed now than a century ago, the taboo against illegal residence has increased considerably. But, like 'perverse sexual behaviour', 'illegal residence' is proving difficult to discern and define. Again the desire of certain powerful groups, in this case politicians and bureaucrats, to fathom and control what they see to be an undesirable social aberration, has paradoxically increased the scope of that aberration, making it reach and involve more and more aspects of more and more peoples' lives. Finally the rather schizophrenic immigration policies remind one of Victorian sexual hypocrisy. One doesn't admit publicly to that which one secretly condones.

CONTROLLING BEHAVIOUR BY CONTROLLING ILLEGALITY

According to Foucault the ubiquitous system of power engendered by the obsession with sexuality made its influence felt in a number of ways. First, sexual behaviour became a distinguishing characteristic that set off bourgeois virtues against the unruliness of the working masses and aristocratic decadence. Secondly, the preoccupation with sexuality fed into a preoccupation with human improvement. It inspired norms for behaviour considered to guarantee offspring who were healthy and well-bred, in both the pedagogical and the biological sense: sex bounded by and limited to heterosexual and monogamous marriage between 'compatible partners': caring, virtuous mothers and hard-working, responsible fathers. How men and women were implicated in this normative programme depended on their circumstances. Construed differences in sexual behaviour served, in turn, to legitimate social differences and inequalities (Foucault, 1984, pp. 118–29; 137–48).

Again we can draw parallels between policies to control illegality and Foucault's theories on power and sexuality. Studies carried out among undocumented workers in the Netherlands indicate how fear of discovery influences their behaviour. They do all they can to avoid notice, toeing the line, jealousy guarding their health, taking on any paying job to support themselves (Glerum and Glerum, 1995, pp. 151–8). But the shadow of illegality also reaches beyond the undocumented themselves to taint the existence of legal migrants, their partners and colleagues. Anyone who wishes to live together in the Netherlands with a partner from abroad, must – aside from some exceptions – earn at least 70% of the Dutch minimum wage. Many students, unemployed, divorced women, single mothers, freelancers, temporary or part-time workers and people employed in the informal sector are unable to meet this requirement (LAWINE, 1995). Moreover, since 1 November 1994, all marriages involving a non-Dutch partner are subject to control in order to prevent 'fraudulent marriages'. The immigration authorities must issue a declaration regarding the status of the foreign partner, and both immigration authorities and the authorities at City Hall who conduct the civil marriage ceremony must interrogate the couple to determine whether or not the marriage is 'genuine'.

These two new restrictions on family reunification affect women differently than they do men. Most women in the Netherlands cannot meet the new income requirements, while most men can (Hooghiemstra and Niphuis-Nell, 1995, pp. 244, 251). Relationships between Dutch women and men from abroad are treated with more suspicion and hostility than relationships between Dutch men and foreign women (Kaminga, 1993). As a result, it has become more difficult for men to gain access to legal residence and work in the Netherlands via a relationship, than for women. Often the only way for men to extend their stay is as an undocumented migrant. But while it is easier for women than men to acquire status via a relationship, the price they must pay to keep that status is complete subjection to their partner. A women must stay with him for at least three years before she can acquire independent status. She need not be formally divorced to lose her status. The simple fact that she and her partner no longer share the same roof is enough to render her illegal.[10] A study conducted among women with a dependent status concludes that the most important effect of this 'three-year-rule' is not that it prevents 'fraudulent marriages', which was the ostensible reason for establishing this rule. Nor do women leave troubled or violent homes to return to their country of origin. Instead, they try to cope and survive as best they can until the three-year term is finally over (Van Blokland and de Vries, 1992, p. 68). But even then, their position remains precarious. Once they acquire independent status, women must find and keep work that pays enough to qualify for the extension of their permit. Although officially mothers with young children are exempt, in practice they too are often put under pressure to take on a full-time paying job.

Because paid labour is so important, both to gain permission for family reunification and to extend an independent residence permit, not only undocumented but also many documented and Dutch workers are forced to accept whatever work they can find, and to avoid losing their job at all costs. For those who risk losing a residence permit and for those whose partner and/or children have applied for a residence permit, the insecurity which increasingly characterizes Dutch labour relations is compounded. Their bargaining position is weaker than that of colleagues who do not have to fear for their own or their family's right to reside in the Netherlands.

The focus on illegality has broadened the scope of control in three loci: the family, the bureaucracy and the workplace. These in turn interconnect and reinforce each other. Thus a woman with a dependent status, who wishes to leave her husband, can be thwarted by bureaucrats who refuse to provide welfare or permission to work legally until her papers are in order. Her only options are then to return to her husband, submit herself to the care of relatives, or accept the risks of undocumented employment.

CONCLUSIONS

Current economic, technological and political developments have stimulated a growing preoccupation with illegality and an increase in control which has resulted among other things in the further marginalization of undocumented migrants. While the undocumented disappear farther and farther into a clandestine existence, the archetype of the 'illegal alien' is evoked more and more insistently, forcing more and more people to profess their right to reside, and to give proof of their proper conduct. The messy dilemmas of legal practice show how construed and convoluted the concept of illegality is. Still the fiction is kept alive that there is an *essential* difference between those on the one side and those on the other side of the distinguishing criterion of legality.

The perceived distinction between legality and illegality, like the perceived distinction between 'perverse' and 'normal' sexual behaviour, legitimates the powers that explore and maintain it, and the social inequalities that it delineates. This system of control with its focus on illegality not so much parallels, but actually extends the complex of power relationships engendered by an older obsession with sexuality, as described by Foucault. Increasingly, the pursuit of the 'illegal alien' involves probing into sexual attachments, family relationships and the site of birth itself. As a result, immigration law has become even more strongly gendered than it already was.

NOTES

1 Voorontwerp herziening van de Vreemdelingenwet (Preliminary Proposal to Change the Law on Immigration), presented by the Dutch Minister of Justice to the Dutch parliament in 1987.

2 Examples are: De herziening van de vreemdelingenwet (3), in: *Migrantenrecht* 1987, no. 9, pp. 231–6; Advies Herziening Vreemdelingenwet, advies Emancipatieraad, no. 11/42/87; and Legebeke, 1987, pp. 9–12.

3 According to statistics provided by Vluchtelingenwerk (Dutch organizations for refugees) in 1995.

4 The Nederlands Centrum Buitenlanders (Dutch Centre for Foreigners) first signalled that amnesty was being granted according to a pattern of criteria in May of 1992. This was subsequently denied by the Dutch Ministry of Justice when the question was raised that August by Dutch members of parliament (Tweede Kamer 1991/92, Aanhansel 760). Finally, in November 1994, the Ministry admitted they had been granting amnesty, in a letter later published in *Migrantenrecht* 1995/1, pp. 20–1.

5 In 1994 for instance, according to statistics provided by Vluchtelingenwerk, the Ministry of Justice pulled back in more than half the cases in which migrants had sued for suspension of deportation, pending appeal. Further, for a rather cynical description of Dutch procedure in immigration law, see Hamerslag, 1993, pp. 57–60.

6 Tweede Kamer, 1993/94, 23715.
7 Wet Arbeid Buitenlandse Werknemers, 1–11–1979. For an analysis of the effects of this law for the Dutch labour market, see: A. Böcker and L. Clermonts, 1995.
8 According to E. Naborn (1991, p. 13) roughly 70% of the migrants coming to the Netherlands in 1989, entered on the basis of family reunification. Since recent restrictive measures have been imposed, this percentage has dropped. However according to statistics from the Centraal Bureau Statistiek (Central Bureau for Statistics), family reunification still accounted for 50 per cent of all immigrants from outside of the EU who legally entered the Netherlands in 1994 (Volkskrant, 18 March, 1995).
9 I used the Dutch translation *De wil tot weten*, translated by Peter Klinkenberg *et al.*, Nijmegen: SUN, 1984.
10 Vreemdelingencirculaire (circular on immigration law), January 1994, B 1/2.2.

REFERENCES

Böcker, A. and L. Clermonts (1995), *Poortwachters van de Nederlandse arbeidsmarkt*, Nijmegen: Instituut voor Rechtssociologie.

Finch, J. (1989), *Family Obligations and Social Change*, Cambridge: Policy Press.

Foucault, M. (1984), *De wil tot weten* (translated from the original text, *La volonté de savoir* by Peter Klinkenburg), Nijmegen: SUN.

Glerum, E. and K. Glerum (1995), 'Wie naar Nederland komt moet sterk zijn. Overleven in de marge van de Nederlandse samenleving', *Migrantenstudies*, 1995/2.

Groenendijk, K. and P. Minderhoud (1992), 'Sturing van migratie in Nederland en Europa na 1992. Effecten en dillemma's', in Sociaal Economische Raad, *Migratie, arbeidsmarkt en sociale zekerheid*, The Hague: Sociaal Economische Raad.

Hamerslag, R. (1993), 'Een middagje kort gedingen', *Rechtshulp*, 1993/11.

Harvey, D. (1989), *The Condition of Postmodernity: An Enquiry into the Origins of Cultural Change*, Oxford: Basil Blackwell.

Hirsch, J. (1991), 'From the Fordist to the Post-Fordist State', in B. Jessop, H. Kastendiek *et al.* (eds), *The politics of flexibility*, Hants: Edward Elgar Publishing.

Hooghiemstra, E. and M. Niphuis-Nell (1995), *Sociale atlas van de vrouw, deel 3: allochtone vrouwen*, The Hague: Vuga.

Johnson, N. (1987), *The Welfare State in Transition: Theory and Practice of Welfare Pluralism*, Sussex: Wheatsheaf Books.

Kaminga, M. (1993), *Grensoverschrijders*, Amsterdam: Wetenschapswinkel.

LAWINE (an organization of Dutch women with a foreign partner) (1995), *Kostokindjes en caissieres. De problemen van de inkomenseis bij gezinshereniging/gezinsvorming*. Amsterdam: LAWINE.

Legebeke, G. (1987), 'Nieuwe pasjeswet. Nauwelijks een verbetering', *KRI*, October.

Naborn, E. (1991), *Gezinshereniging: de overkomst van gezinsleden van migranten en Nederlanders*, The Hague: Ministry of Justice.

Rodrigues, R. and K. Tazelaar (1993), 'Ongegronde angst voor illegalen leidt tot discriminatie', *Rechtshulp*, 1993/11.

Swart, A.H.J. (1978), *De toelating en uitzetting van vreemdelingen*, Alphen aan de Rhijn: Kluwer.

Van Blokland, E. and M. de Vries (1992), *De afhankelijke verblijfstitel van migrantenvrouwen*, Nijmegen: Wetenschapswinkel.

Wilterdink, N. (1993), 'Ongelijkheid en interdependentie. Ontwikkelingen in welstandsverhoudingen', *Amsterdams Sociologisch Tijdschrift*, **20** (2).

10 Querelle Asks for Asylum[1]

Thomas Spijkerboer[2]

This one is for Zoran – but for which one?

It must have been in the fall of 1982 (I was in my second year of studying law) that I was early for a party. No music and no alcohol yet. But I was not alone; H. and M. were early also. We decided to go and see a movie. Fassbinder's posthumous film, *Querelle*, had just opened in Amsterdam. We went to one of the biggest cinemas in town, got in, and were only a few minutes late. I missed the – crucial – first scene, yet the film made a great impression. I still vividly remember the blue and yellow light. I had to go to the toilet, and remember thinking that others must think I went to masturbate. I don't remember the party afterwards. The film stayed with me, and I saw it at least three more times before starting to work on this chapter.

On 13 August 1981, the Judicial Department of the Council of State, then the highest Dutch court in asylum cases, decided that persecution on the grounds of sexual orientation should be considered as persecution that can lead to refugee status (Afdeling rechtspraak van de Raad van State [Judicial Department of the Council of State] 13 August 1981, *Rechtspraak Vreemdelingenrecht* [Jurisprudence Immigration Law] 1981, 5, *Gids Vreemdelingenrecht (oud)* [Guide on Immigration Law (old edition)] D12–51). And let's be precise about things. At that time, Rainer Werner Fassbinder was in Berlin, acting the main role in Wolf Gremm's film *Kamikaze* '89 – an adaptation of Per Wahloo's detective novel *Murder on the Thirty-first Floor* (Katz, 1987, p. 176). Dutch jurisprudence was ahead of legal developments in other countries. In Germany, for example, homosexuality was recognized as a relevant persecution ground only in 1986, while it is accepted by some courts that a particularly stringent burden of proof can be put on the asylum-seeker in these cases, as homosexuality is despised in all cultures and states to some degree (Marx, 1991, p. 847–8). In Canada persecution on the grounds of sexual orientation was recognized as persecution in the sense of refugee law in 1986 (Hathaway, 1991, p. 163; comp. the Canadian Supreme

Court decision in *Canada (Attorney General)* v. *Ward* [1993], 103 D.L.R. (4th), 1, at 34). In the US, the first reported decision granting asylum to a persecuted homosexual dates from 1990 (Decision of the Board of Immigration Appeals *In re Fidel Armando Toboso-Alfonso* A23-220-664 Int. Dec. 3222 (12 March 1990), abstracted in *International Journal of Refugee Law*, 1994, pp. 475–6 as IJRL/0201; see on this decision Goldberg, 1993, p. 617, Grider 1994, p. 221). The Attorney General in 1994 designated that decision as precedent in all proceedings involving the same issue (Order of 16 June 1994, of Janet Reno, US Attorney General). In the United Kingdom, the first decision that allowed for the possibility of persecuted homosexuals to be recognized as refugees dates from November 1994 (in the case of *Vraciu*, unreported, Immigration Appeal Tribunal No. 11559). However, in a case heard the day after this one the same court (in a different composition) decided that homosexuals do not constitute a social group and therefore cannot be refugees (in the case of *Jacques*, unreported, Immigration Appeal Tribunal No. 11580. See on these cases Haran, 1995).

The refugee definition requires not only that a person fears persecution, but also that the fact that persecution may occur is linked to one of the five persecution grounds, being race, religion, nationality, membership of a particular social group or political opinion. At stake in case-law is whether or not there is a persecution ground if gays and lesbians are persecuted. The 1981 Council of State decision provided the first affirmative answer, by deciding that 'a reasonable interpretation of persecution for reasons of membership of a particular social group can include persecution for reason of sexual nature'.[3] As a result, persecuted gays and lesbians could be recognized as refugees. However, this was to be one of the last Dutch asylum decisions that gay rights activists could welcome. The problem since 1981 was not the persecution ground. Somehow what had happened to the applicants (or what they had good reasons to fear) was never sufficiently serious to amount to persecution. The long series of negative decisions has given rise to rather sharp accusations (e.g. *Nieuwsbrief Asiel- en Vluchtelingenrecht* [Newsletter Asylum and Refugee Law] **8** 1992, pp. 230–3; Bos, Pot and Willems (1992)). I have some problems with this line of criticism. The fact that homosexual asylum-seekers are turned down is no conclusive proof of homophobia. *Prima facie*, there is no reason to believe that gays and lesbians are even less welcome than straight men and women who claim asylum. And in some cases, gays and lesbians have been recognized as refugees by the administration (e.g. decision of the State-Secretary of Justice of 16 November 1993, No. 9110.09.0034 (Russian gay man); refugee status for a lesbian woman from Iran, reported in *Nieuwsbrief Asiel- en Vluchtelingenrecht* [Newsletter Asylum and Refugee Law] **8** (1992), p. 327). The administration wants to admit as few refugees as possible; I see no reason why it would be especially restrictive when it comes to gays and lesbians.

But things are more interesting than that. What concerns me in this chapter is not the equality principle, but how gay and lesbian asylum-seekers are treated. When one thinks of how one is treated in, say, a restaurant, one doesn't think of whether one gets food, yes or no. Treatment in this context refers to the attitude of the waiter, the interactions between customers and personnel. It is this treatment I want to investigate. The result of the treatment may be negative for the asylum-seeker; but how was the treatment itself? My argument will be that, although it is hardly possible to argue that the outcome of the procedures in themselves show homophobia, the treatment of homosexual asylum-seekers is queer. That queerness, I will argue, does have something to do with homosexuality. It is only then that the question whether or not this could have influenced the outcome of the procedure resurfaces.

I will first explain why Fassbinder's *Querelle* is important to me, and how. I will then give an interpretation of one court decision concerning a gay asylum-seeker from Russia, which, as I will argue on the way in the footnotes, is representative for Dutch case law. I will do so in the light of *Querelle*. My line of argument will be that the problem with Dutch case-law on homosexual asylum-seekers is *not* that it is homophobic, as has been argued up to now (e.g. *Nieuwsbrief Asiel- en Vluchtelingenrecht* [Newsletter Asylum and Refugee Law] **8** (1992), pp. 230–3; Bos, Pot and Willems (1992)). Quite the reverse: it is exemplary of the laid back liberalism that is characteristic of Dutch mainstream thinking on *any* form of otherness or deviance. What is problematic is the idea that straights and non-straights are two clearly distinct groups of people. This presumption plays an implicit, but all the more central, role in both Dutch case-law and in writings of gay and lesbian refugee advocates. In *Querelle*, Fassbinder shows that such dichotomic thinking is extremely violent and even celebrates violence. Furthermore, because of the triangular structure of the film, *Querelle* is particularly useful in analysing how, in the court decision that I will analyse, the judge, the applicant and his lawyer are brought to re-enact this celebration of violence. The last section of this chapter will enquire whether refugee law doctrine allows for the possibility to advocate cases of gay and lesbian asylum-seekers while at the same time undermining the straight/non-straight distinction.

One caveat seems opportune. This chapter interprets a decision on a gay man by looking closely at a film with lots of male characters and just one woman. This analysis is written from and about a man's world. I am sure that female sexualities are constructed in a different way. I think however that the theoretical and doctrinal points that I will try to make are relevant for cases of lesbian asylum-seekers as well.

*

In La Feria, a brothel in Brest, Lysiane, who together with her (black) husband Nono owns the brothel, lays cards for her lover, Robert. Looking up from her cards to Robert, she asks him:[4]

> LYSIANE: You have a brother?
> ROBERT: So what if I do?
> LYSIANE: You've never even mentioned him? You're quite alike, aren't you?
> ROBERT: Well, that's what people say. But it's not true. Querelle is a sailor.
> LYSIANE: Maybe they are right, after all. And … uh, you two love each other, more, uh, more than you'd really like to.
> ROBERT: Don't be crazy! We're just brothers, that's all. Why are you shaking your head? What do you see now?
> LYSIANE: I don't know exactly, but your brother is in great danger.
> ROBERT: Danger? What kind of danger?
> LYSIANE: He's … he's in danger of finding out who he really is.

In the screenplay, Lysiane says: 'He's in danger of committing a murder.'

The ship of Querelle, a sailor in the Merchant Marine, arrives in Brest. Querelle heads for La Feria, and Robert introduces him to Nono. They make a business deal concerning opium. Querelle returns to the ship, where he gets another sailor, Vic, to help him smuggle the opium past customs. They meet again in a park, where Querelle slashes the throat of the sailor. Querelle goes to La Feria. In order to sleep with Lysiane, he has to gamble with Nono. If he wins, he can have her; if he loses, Nono can have him. Querelle loses, but as Nono says, he probably cheated in order to lose. Querelle denies this. It is, he adds, the first time he will have been fucked.

After Nono has told Robert that he has fucked his brother, Robert takes Querelle out for a fight. The screenplay describes the battle as 'brutal and strangely erotic'.

> ROBERT: You goddamn fucking asshole! Let yourself get fucked by some nigger, will you! You're some swell brother, getting fucked by a nigger!
> NARRATOR: The resemblance between the two brothers grew greater and greater. Their fight was more like a battle between two lovers.
> QUERELLE: Say it again! Say I'm a fucking asshole! Say it! Say it again!
> ROBERT: I've got nothing to say.
> QUERELLE: I am wading across the river filled with clutching seaweed. Help me to reach your bank.
> ROBERT: That will be hard, brother. I can feel you resisting.
> QUERELLE: What did you say? I can hardly hear you. Leap up into my laughter. Hold fast to it. Don't be afraid that it might hurt me. Leap! come on, leap!
> ROBERT: Be yourself!
> QUERELLE: I am becoming myself, I can feel it!
> ROBERT: Not so loud. Speak softer now. I am already near you.

QUERELLE: I love you more than I love myself. My hate was only an illusion. Dangerous melancholy draws me to you, but my struggling keeps me away. My smiles are sunshine and drive away the shadows you cast on me. I was the one to seek out the night of daggers. I put up the barricades. My laughter cuts me off, it separates me from you. You're so exciting and so beautiful.
ROBERT: You're just as beautiful.
QUERELLE: Don't talk. Be still. Be careful that we don't lose ourselves in a union that is too complete. Set your hounds and wolves on me!
ROBERT: It's hopeless. Every battle crowns you with a radiance that wounds me.
QUERELLE: Don't be discouraged. Try hard!

During the fight, a religious procession crosses the street and walks through the battle scene. A Christ is carrying his Cross, accompanied by familiar figures who follow Him on the way to the Crucifixion. Most notably, Seblon (the captain of Querelle's ship) in a white toga and Lysiane recalling Mary walk right next to the Christ.

Meanwhile, on the ship, Seblon – whom we have seen earlier speaking into a tape recorder on his fascination for sailors in general and for Querelle, who serves him, in particular – records that he is in love with Querelle.

SEBLON: (…) The more I love Querelle, the more defined the woman in me becomes, and the more sensitive, delicate, and sad, because she cannot be fulfilled. (…)

Back in La Feria, Lysiane is tending Robert after the fight. They dance. Nono invites Mario – who has been constantly present in La Feria and is said to be a policeman, but looks like a gay leather freak – to throw dice. Querelle is also willing to play. Then Robert suddenly attacks him. Mario and Nono keep the two apart.

Mario and Querelle take a walk. Mario suggests that if Querelle lets Nono fuck him, he might let him as well. Querelle says, 'That's no reason for you to get any funny ideas. I'm not a faggot'. Mario worms the admission out of Querelle that he liked being fucked by Nono. Mario says he gets a hard-on from talking about this and invites Querelle, who says he doesn't believe this, to feel whether it is true. Querelle, encouraged by Mario, starts to masturbate Mario, and ends up being fucked by him.

Gil Turko, a Polish worker, is accused by his colleague Theo of being gay, and in revenge slashes his throat with a broken bottle. He hides in a deserted bagno, suspected of both the murder of Theo and of the sailor who was killed by Querelle. His friend Roger asks Querelle for help. Querelle is fascinated by Gil, as he is meeting another person who has killed. He gives Gil a pistol, and tells him he can rob Seblon when he is in the pissoir where Seblon 'gets himself all horny and worked up from the junk scribbled on the walls'. He gives Gil a false moustache – and at that moment the spectator sees that Gil and Robert are played by the same actor. Gil robs Seblon (and wounds him while doing so), after Seblon has resisted and has been able to recognize him. Gil returns to the bagno, and there Querelle fully realizes he is in love with him. However, as he was the passive partner up to now, it seems impossible to fuck Gil. Gil (still wearing the moustache) and Querelle tell each other they want to live together always, and kiss. The screenplay says that Gil fellates Querelle, but this scene was cut in order to appease the American distributor of the film (Lardeau, 1990, p. 74).

Querelle then informs the police that Gil will be on the 4.20 train for Bordeaux. Querelle himself has urged Gil to leave Brest and has bought the ticket.

Querelle returns to the ship, and goes into Seblon's cabin. Seblon is absent. Querelle pushes the button of the tape recorder and hears Seblon's voice pronounce an ode on himself. Seblon walks in, Querelle draws his knife.

SEBLON: I've always known you were a common murderer, Querelle. Come on then, stab me, kill me!

Then Mario and another policeman come on board and take Seblon with them to identify the suspect of the attack on him. At the police station Seblon declares that he is absolutely sure that he doesn't know Gil (now again without moustache).

Querelle, who has become the lover of Lysiane, is in Lysiane's bedroom. Earlier, we have seen a similar scene with Lysiane and Robert, where it is suggested that Robert is impotent. Lysiane has expressed the fear that in between Robert and Querelle, there is no room for her.

Lysiane asks Querelle why he rejected her for so long. Querelle says that was because she was his brother's woman.

LYSIANE: And what about now?
QUERELLE: Now I'm taking revenge on my brother.
LYSIANE: That's the reason? And what about me? What about me??
QUERELLE: What about you? You're just a woman, that's all.

In a final scene, Lysiane tells Querelle that he is nothing more than a fairy, a faggot. Querelle laughs, and says that that makes Nono a faggot too.

LYSIANE: And Robert?
QUERELLE: Robert? What do I care about Robert? I'm *me*!
LYSIANE: You're disgusting. You're my enemy! You're destroying me! You've got some secret kind of power; some power that goes multiplying forever. Querelle, you're not human; you don't come from this world.

Seblon enters, and recognizes Robert as the man who attacked him. Querelle, who has declared his dedication to Seblon in the scene before, follows him to the ship. He says to Seblon:

> QUERELLE: I am very close to that point of disgrace from which there is no return; but I think that it is also a place where I shall find eternal peace. I am so weak; I am subdued, completely subdued. And my thoughts are sad – sad because of the premonitions of autumn and filth and delicate mortal wounds I feel inside myself. I shall not find this peace until you have taken me. But you must do it in such a way that afterwards I may rest across your thighs, as in a pieta, and you will watch over me as Mary watches over the dead Jesus.

Lysiane joins Robert, who is totally drunk, at his table. She again lays cards and looks at them.

> LYSIANE: I was wrong all along. You don't have a brother. Can you understand? I made a mistake. Did you hear me, Robert? I made a mistake; you haven't got any brother! He hasn't got any brother. Did you hear me, everybody?

*

It is not a coincidence that the first words that are spoken in *Querelle* are about murder:

> NARRATOR: The thought of murder often awakens in us thoughts of the sea and sailors. Thoughts of the sea and thoughts of murder are then usually followed by thoughts of love or sexuality.

Querelle murders the sailor, Vic. Gil murders Theo. But the theme of murder is even more prominent than that if we include the metaphorical killings that occur in the movie. In the brothel, Lysiane several times sings

> Each man kills the thing he loves
> Each man kills the thing he loves
> Some when young
> Some when old
> Some with passion
> Some with gold
> Each man kills the thing he loves.

It doesn't go too far, then, to consider the moment when Lysiane declares Querelle has never existed as a murderous act, in which Robert participates. Robert also kills Querelle by denying they are very much like each other, by fighting with him and by not being Gil. On the other hand, when Querelle says he is not interested in Robert and leaves him, this can be seen as murder. In the same scene, Lysiane is not wrong when she says that Querelle is destroying her. And finally, when Querelle betrays Gil he murders him. Furthermore, Seblon encourages Querelle to kill him, and Querelle wants to lie dead on Seblon's lap. They have a mirrored wish to be dead to the other.

The murders mirror each other in a complex way. But first, let us remark that only Querelle and Gil, two gay characters, commit literal murders. They commit visible murders that we immediately recognize for what they are. The murder of Vic by Querelle is filmed as a liturgy, and contains many visual references to Christian imagery; e.g. when he is killed Vic only wears briefs that remind one of the loincloth Christ wears on the cross; and after the murder Querelle washes his hands. The scene is accompanied by organ music. Also, the scene is very sexually charged. Querelle and Vic slowly undress just before the murder and one expects a sexual scene; which in fact, the murder turns out to be as well. This murder is the more shocking as an opening scene because it is perfect. And by murdering the sailor, Querelle begins to discover who he himself is.

Gil's murder is almost accidental. In a fit of rage, provoked by Theo's insinuations that he is gay, he kills him with a broken bottle and runs away. In a way, by this murder Gil becomes who he is not: he is charged with the murder of Vic as well, and will masquerade as Robert when he robs Seblon. But it is this murder which causes the meeting between Querelle and Gil, which makes Gil into 'another criminal, a brother, a murderer of his own class, someone with whom he could discuss business'. Querelle realizes that Gil is just an 'awkward youth' who has committed an imperfect crime, but Gil's 'reputation had now been crowned with a true murder', i.e. Querelle's. But because Gil has committed this murder Querelle considers him as a brother; Gil in a way will become Robert: and, as the narrator says, Gil becomes

> … a little Querelle for whom Querelle cherished a strange feeling of admiration mixed with curiosity. He wanted to make love to Gil, for then he would be even more intimately united with him. But he did not know what he had to do. Until now, he had always been the passive partner, and it seemed impossible for him to fuck another guy. […] Querelle sensed that love was something voluntary. One must want to love. Even if one is not in love with another man, it can still be fun to get fucked by him. But to be able to fuck someone else, one must love him even only for a split second. And so, if he wanted to love Gil, he had to relinquish his passivity. Querelle made that effort.

The love scene between Querelle and Gil is tender and romantic – the only one in the entire film. It is followed immediately by Querelle's betrayal. It is through murder that Querelle begins to gain the dangerous knowledge of who he is; it is through murder that Querelle discovers the will to love and the accompanying desire of being active sexually. As if this is not perverse enough, it seems as if this love cannot exist and has to be betrayed. In this act of betrayal, Querelle not only betrays Gil; he also betrays Robert (his older brother, played by the same actor), and himself (Gil is 'a little Querelle'). The betrayal is Querelle's way of doing what he told Gil he would like: to live together always.

We should not forget that when Gil kills Theo, this might also be seen as Robert killing Querelle. Gil says he wanted to be Theo's friend at some moment, but that now he wants to smash him in the mouth and to fuck him, in order to make clear that he himself is a man. He goes as far as saying that Theo is not a man, but a whore. This combination of repulsion and attraction, of masculinity that is both threatened and acted out, is characteristic of the relation between Robert and Querelle as well. As we saw, Querelle at some moment finds Gil his brother. Gil and Robert are played by the same actor, so in this act Robert kills the man he desires and fears: Querelle. But the parallel works the other way round as well. Theo and Robert both are queer-bashers. Gil is 'a little Querelle'. When Gil kills his queer-basher, this is also Querelle killing his.

The central relation in *Querelle* is the one between the two brothers. Querelle and Robert are the same person. We have already seen this in the killing of Theo by Gil. Also, Lysiane says to Robert:

> The two of you are close in this world, and night is stretched over the loneliness of an endless plateau. Your double statue is reflected in each of its two halves. You are lonely, living within your double loneliness. [...] You live only within your brother – in his eyes. Only in your own brother. And he – he lives in you. You know that.

The narrator then says about Lysiane: 'She saw the inexorable, precise, and yet indefinable fusion of the two muscular, sinewy bodies.' Apart from being the same person, they are also brothers; they are lovers (via Gil, but also during the fight); they fight each other; and they kill each other. It is during the fight – caused by Robert's anger at Querelle's sexual behaviour – that they are closest, but they seem to be unable to reach each other. The fight is about whether they will be the same person or not; it is also a way of being close yet distant. It is the only physical contact in the film that is represented as involving 'true' feelings apart from the love scene between Querelle and Gil, and thus is the counterpart of that scene (that significantly involves the same actors). It is this scene that sets off the process in which the worlds of Robert and Querelle will be totally segregated. Robert will end up in Lysiane's arms, drunk and impotent, as Querelle will end up in Seblon's arms, equally drunk but not impotent, I think. Robert in La Feria, on land, law abiding; Querelle on the sea, surrounded only by gorgeous men, an outlaw.

At the origin of everything is Lysiane, who imagines Querelle and thus gives birth to him. Querelle initially is just a fantasy of Lysiane, who is joined in it by Robert. Querelle becomes an outlaw by killing the sailor, but nobody knows that. He then becomes an outlaw because Robert outlaws Querelle's sexual behaviour. Subsequently he is seduced into having outlawed sex by and with the law, personified by the cop Mario. Only after that does Querelle become gay, loving Gil and entering into a relationship with Seblon. Initially Querelle denies being gay, although he admits he enjoys being fucked. Querelle becomes gay and an outlaw during the movie, because that is where the violent vectors from outside direct his desire. For Robert in particular it is unacceptable that Querelle's sexual orientation is unclear; he has to be able to tell the difference between gay and straight, between himself and Querelle. It is made clear to Querelle that he is gay and an outlaw, and therefore he becomes one. But he is not a passive victim of this process. By taking on the role that is given him, he can become sexually active. Initially, he is passive, being hardly more than the embodiment of the repressed side of the straight world. But being forced to live up to other people's fantasies, he becomes fantastic.

Having seen murder as ritual (Querelle), murder as powerlessness (Gil) and murder as denial of the self (Robert, Lysiane, Querelle), we can end with love taking the form of – minimally fantasized – murder in the relationship between Seblon and Querelle. Seblon wants to be killed by Querelle because he knows that Querelle is a common murderer; that is precisely what he is in love with. And Querelle wants to rest dead over Seblon's thighs, impersonating Christ on Mary's lap. Querelle and Seblon act out an S/M fantasy, with Querelle polishing Seblon's boots and getting himself dirty and sweaty by doing heavy work. In a way, Seblon (played by 'the virile Italian star' (White, 1994, p. 615) Franco Nero) is very masculine: he is powerful, in control, wears a uniform. On the other hand he is totally dependent on Querelle; he is passive, waits for his chance, and is obsessed with the strength and hardness of Querelle's body. 'The more I love Querelle, the more defined the women in me becomes,' says Seblon. But he also says that he is increasingly filled with a sense of absolute power. One might see Seblon as the sum of Mario and Nono – Mario, the powerful man, and Nono with, in Lysiane's words, 'something feminine that oozes out of him'. This does make some sense, as long as it is recognized that Seblon's character, like the others in the film, is not a stable one but constantly shifting. But in the relation with Seblon, Querelle also moves. As we saw, during the film

Querelle becomes sexually active, masculine in a sense. In his relationship with Seblon he is passive, dependent, and in the final scenes totally drunk. The film culminates in utter melodrama. Seblon more or less carries Querelle to the ship; they are exiled to a men's world that consists of hierarchy. Robert is totally drunk as well, and Lysiane denies that she ever gave birth to Querelle; to have thought so is a mistake.

In this reading, *Querelle* is a mirror palace. It is impossible to tell where things begin and end; there is no original, only representations exist. Everyone is everyone and as such betrays everyone. The characters are imagined by each other, but are far from imaginary. They hurt each other in a lethal way. Power, in the form of the male body, does not have one source, but is all around, goes all ways and hurts. Mirrors are an important and very frequent image in Fassbinder's work. On this, he said that 'it makes the whole thing even stranger and more distant. But it also has something to do with the actors, who get closer to their own identity in contact with mirrors' (Fassbinder, 1992, p. 151). At the end of the film, the narrator says

> Querelle had arrived at the point of inner harmony, and this harmony was indestructible – for he was now on that lofty region where mirror images converge and are united.

It is significant that it is not Querelle's 'real' identity and his image that converge, but 'only' the mirror images. There is no original; at the core of identity, there is a void. The convergence is twofold: first, the image that Querelle has of himself and the image that the others have of him converge – he is a fairy, a faggot. But there is also a convergence, be it mirrored, of Robert and Querelle. They are both subjected to the roles that they participated in creating, but that violate them and leave them powerless, out of control. The fact that Querelle's identity is imagined and artificial does not mean that it is unreal. If nothing else, the fact that it is not only a product of violence, but also a cause for violence makes it real.

Thus, Fassbinder blows up the concept of identity and authenticity. It is fantasy to think that we can be liberated by living up to our true identity; also, it is fantasy that we can be free from power and thus be authentic (this is the analysis that makes Richard Dyer so hostile to *Querelle* (Dyer, 1990, p. 96). Identities and authenticities are constructed in violent struggle and thus fraught with violence. But that there is no beyond does not mean that people are puppets. Querelle actively takes on the role of the gay outlaw, and subverts its meaning. He 'slips out from under the phallic sign' (Silverman, 1992, p. 155), in a move that might be labelled as 'subversive repetition' (the term is taken from Butler, 1990). This leads to intense suffering, but also to intense joy; the joy is present in the film in the form of the excessive aesthetics that drip from every image (cf. Shaviro, 1991, pp. 171–2). As Fassbinder wrote in the Introductory Notes to the screenplay of Querelle, 'every action that takes place in this world, every gesture, every glance, contains some added signification; in each case it is something else, something greater, generally something sacred'.

Querelle's identity is a product of violence and thus is violent. Instead of being a passive object of violence, Querelle refracts the violence directed at him, thus becoming its subject. As he chooses not to be an oppressed gay man, he has to find another way of giving meaning to violence. He does so by valuing it. This aesthetics of violence reflects, mirrors the violence directed at Querelle. The violence that makes him gay is lawful and invisible, and has a noble purpose: creating stable identities. Querelle's violence is visible and outlawed, and has a perverted noble purpose: beauty. It is his way of rejecting victimization, of shifting the meaning of the identity forced upon him.

Of course, Fassbinder has been bitterly attacked for his exuberant political incorrectness. At its kindness, his position is seen as 'politically dangerous' (Silverman, 1992, p. 155). To be sure, *Querelle* is one of Fassbinder's most disturbing films. It is also a central work in his oeuvre, as it picks up and combines many themes. That he was conscious of this may be concluded from the fact that all his three great loves have a role in this movie. Günther Kaufmann, the first one, plays Nono. The film is dedicated to El Hedi ben Salem M'Barek Mohamed Mustafa, the second. And in an interview from 1982, he linked Armin Meyer, his last great love who committed suicide in 1978, with *Querelle*, anticipating the criticism mentioned here.

> *You're very cautious when it comes to love affairs?*
>
> I wasn't always, which was stupid of me, and that's why I had the experience two or three times that relationships I'd entered into euphorically ended in disaster. [...]
>
> *The next film will be based on Genet's* Querelle ...
>
> That's really a difficult story; it can so easily turn out corny or fascistoid; I hope I can keep to the fine line where it's neither.
>
> *Fascistoid– what do you mean by that?*
>
> When you read it, it reads like a glorification of violence, of murder, of betrayal, simply because Genet says human existence is actually consummated only when you've descended to the worst, the lowest level possible in society. But, it has to be absolutely clear that this pertains only to this particular society. If you don't function perfectly in this society, you have to become a traitor, a murderer, you have to become violent. (Fassbinder, 1992, p. 71)

As Shaviro puts it, 'By aestheticizing violence, and providing such beautiful images of domination and submission, Fassbinder self-consciously locates himself within the very formations of social oppression which are the objects of his own radical critique' (Shaviro, 1991, p. 171).

Let us return once more to the two literal murders in the film. The murder of Theo by Gil we can understand, we can sympathize with Gil. The murder of Vic by Querelle is hardly bearable because it has no reason and is aestheticized. Couldn't we decide that the unbearable murder is not a real murder, but a metaphorical one? This would mirror the numerous unreal murders that have to be read as real murders. Surely, Querelle's murder is surreal and can be interpreted as such. One of the values of such an interpretation would be that thus we are confronted with an uneasy fact. We insist on metaphorizing the aesthetic, motiveless murder. But Gil's murder does have a motive: he wants to re-establish his masculinity. This motive makes it even more an act of powerlessness. No need for metaphors, here. A powerless gay man who, in this futile gesture, wants to prove his masculinity: that is murder as we like to see it.

*

By the decision of 31 August 1994, the President of the District Court in Zwolle dismissed the request of the Russian national Mikhail K. to grant suspensive effect to the appeal in his asylum case, i.e. that he could await the result of that appeal in the Netherlands (Pres. Rb. Den Haag (Zwolle) 31 August 1994, *Rechtshulp* [Legal Aid] 1995, no. 5, pp. 22–9). The criterion for this procedure is not whether or not the complainant has made plausible that he is a refugee; that is the criterion in the appeal concerning refugee status. The criterion for this interim injunction procedure is whether there can be doubt as to whether or not he is a refugee; this is called the Mosa-criterion, after the name of the complainant in the case where it was first confirmed. When doubt is possible, the President has to grant suspensive effect (Hoge Raad [Supreme Court 22 June 1984, *Nederlandse Jurisprudentie* [Netherlands Jurisprudence] 1985, 82, *Rechtspraak Vreemdelingenrecht* [Jurisprudence Immigration Law] 1984, 11, *Gids Vreemdelingenrecht (oud)* [Guide on Immigration Law (old edition)] F-131, *Administratiefrechtelijke Beslissingen* [Administrative Law Decisions] 1985, 40. The criterion is presently laid down in Article 32, first paragraph sub a of the Aliens Act).

The statements of Mikhail K. are rendered as follows.

> (...) the complainant has stated that he has left Russia because of problems he has encountered in his country on account of his homosexual nature. As a result of his homosexuality he could not finish his studies. For a short time he has worked as a manager at a trade firm. In December 1993 he has been dismissed, officially on the ground of an 'immoral attitude'. At the end of November 1993

> the police raided his apartment, where he lived together with his friend X. Five homophile couples were present in the apartment. At the police station a verbatim report was made after a four-hour interrogation. The police informed the complainant's employer, after which he was dismissed. About December 1993 the complainant received a call-up from the police. He didn't comply with it. Two friends who had done that before are still being detained, probably on the ground of their nature. His friend received a call-up as well two days later, but didn't comply either. On December 20 he went to the travelling agency together with his friend, where they booked a three-day journey to the Netherlands. On January 23 they left Moscow by bus. He travelled on his own passport and has not encountered difficulties at the border. On January 25, 1994, he arrived in the Netherlands.

The President first expresses doubts about the credibility of this flight story. One might consider it characteristic that the flight story of a homosexual is doubted, but that would be too easy a conclusion. It is a very common part of asylum decisions to express doubts about credibility (Spijkerboer and Vermeulen, 1995, pp. 54–62). This is not specific for gay asylum-seekers. Also, the decision contains an 'even so' version, which presumes the credibility of the flight story – which also is not exceptional.

A second preliminary remark is that, as we will see, the President does not use the Mosa-criterion, but the (substantially more stringent) criterion that should be used in the procedure on refugee status. However, any relation with the sexual orientation of the complainant cannot be laid. Strange as this may sound, application of the incorrect criterion is a routine affair (Spijkerboer and Vermeulen, 1995, pp. 430–5).

On the claim to asylum the President writes the following.

> Whatever may be of the credibility of the flight story of the complainant, and assuming first of all that the position of a homosexual man in Russia might not be simple, this is not sufficient to consider the complainant a refugee. There is no systematic persecution of homosexuals in Russia, the less so as since May 27, 1993, Article 121 Paragraph 1 of the Penal Code[5] has been withdrawn. [...]
>
> Subsequently it has to be established whether the personal experience of the complainant makes him a refugee. The flight story of the complainant gives insufficient clues to regard him as a refugee. The fact that he has been dismissed on the ground of his sexual nature is not decisive. The complainant also states that he has been arrested once. That also does not make him a refugee, as he has been released immediately. The penal investigation advanced by the complainant doesn't make this different. An offence against Article 121 second paragraph of the Penal Code[6] is a common law offence, for which the protection of the Refugee Convention cannot be invoked.
>
> In this case there is no violation of Article 3 of the European Convention on Human Rights.[7] The complainant has stated that there is no issue of qualified

> homosexuality, so one cannot see on which ground the applicant has to fear a prison sentence. The penalization of the civil offence of Article 121 paragraph 2 also is not of a scale that this would mean violation of Article 3 of the European Convention on Human Rights.

It is rare that courts which dismiss an asylum claim express their empathy with the complainant, as the judge does by first of all showing that he realizes that life may not be easy for Russian gays. This happens predominantly, if not solely, in cases concerning raped women (Spijkerboer, 1994a) and gay men.[8] Statements of this kind may be considered as efforts by the President to show to the broader public that, although he is dismissing a claim of a homosexual, he is not homophobic. Thus, it can be seen as an expression that the President is aware of the possibility that his personal views on homosexuality might influence the decision. He indicates that his views on harassed homosexuals are sympathetic. There is no reason whatsoever to doubt this self-image of the President. Dutch law is very liberal in sexual matters; penalization of homosexuality as occurs in some American states look pretty much like the Stone Ages. The President here genuinely expresses a commonality he feels with the complainant.

We can see a parallel with the battle scene between Robert and Querelle. This is the moment of the most genuine communication between the two. The resemblance between them grows greater and greater. When Querelle challenges his brother to say he is a fucking asshole, Robert says that he has nothing to say.

The process at work in the battle between the brothers has been reversed, however. In the film, it is Querelle who is trying to reach his brother's bank. Mikhail K. has expressed his wish to reach the judge's bank by asking for asylum, and for an interim injunction. This happened before the decision was given. In the decision itself, it is the judge who tries to reach Mikhail K. Before explaining why he doesn't think Mikhail K. can reach his bank, the President expresses his sympathy. Implied in this is the judge's power over Mikhail K. Compassion in this sense of the word can only be given by someone in whose power it is to give or withhold it. By empathizing and thereby articulating his more powerful position, the judge also separates himself from Mikhail K. (comp. Halley, 1995). In this short sentence, thrown in between the real legal arguments, the judge precisely re-enacts the wish to be one, and the denial of the oneness that form the core of *Querelle*. The President and Mikhail K. together are in a river filled with clutching seaweed.

The judge then proceeds to state there is no systematic persecution of homosexuals in Russia. This should be understood as meaning that the sole fact that Mikhail K. is a Russian gay in itself does not make him a refugee;

this rejection of a possible appeal to the concept of group persecution is by now a standard passage in Dutch case-law (Spijkerboer and Vermeulen, 1995, pp. 82–97). The judge's position seems to be a legitimate one (comp. Gessen, 1994; Amnesty International, 1994, pp. 27–32).

The judge further finds that neither the dismissal, nor the single arrest, nor the criminal procedure constitute persecution. In themselves, these are correct statements. A single dismissal, a single arrest, and a single criminal procedure are insufficient for refugee status. However, these things didn't happen separately, but form one string of events that are related in a causal way. The police raid led to the arrest, which led to the dismissal; the raid also led to the criminal procedure. By chopping the flight story in pieces, the judge significantly weakens Mikhail K.'s claim to asylum. However, as before, concluding that this is homophobic would be too easy. It is again standard not to see the interconnection in flight stories of asylum-seekers, and this phenomenon is not unique to gay asylum-seekers.

Nevertheless, there is an observation to be made. The judge refuses to see the connection between the things that happened to Mikhail K. The fact that the police is behind the arrest and the dismissal and behind the criminal procedures suggests that, taken together, this might be persecution (see on this so-called persecution on 'cumulative grounds' UNHCR *Handbook*, para. 53). Whether or not that would be so in this case is open to debate. In *Querelle* we have seen the relevance of looking. When Lysiane and Robert cease to see Querelle at the end of the movie, this is a violent and murderous act. But also outside the cinematographic realm, not noticing gay-bashing is making it possible, is in a way joining in doing this to people. Not seeing, ignoring, is not an innocent thing.[9]

Again, I stress that this is not specific for asylum cases concerning gay men. But the judge, even when dismissing Mikhail K.'s claim, could have done what was in his power to do. He could at least have noticed (comp. Lahey, 1991).

Art. 121, Paragraph 2 of the Russian Criminal Code penalizes sexual conduct that in many jurisdictions is considered abusive. But the decision goes further. Mikhail K. is on the run. The judge concludes that the only thing he can be on the run for is a criminal procedure concerning unacceptable conduct. If, as one must conclude, Mikhail K. is not guilty of such conduct, he could as well have awaited his acquittal in Russia. If the judge really trusts the Russian legal system as he seems to do, his conclusion must be that it is well possible that Mikhail K. is guilty of something or other. Mikhail K. is thus pushed into the world of crime, in a way that parallels the script of *Querelle*.[10]

Isn't this an over-interpretation? Imagine the judge was conscious of the possibility that the legal system in Russia is well capable of criminalizing gays for being gay, and not for committing criminal offences (see Gessen, 1994). Then he wouldn't have expressed the unwavering trust he places in the Russian judiciary. He does trust it however, and by implication he does not trust Mikhail K.

Although the judge at the beginning has expressed his sympathy for Mikhail K. that I take to be honest, he gives something away by using the term 'qualified homosexuality'. A qualified robbery is a robbery with violence, or with another aggravating circumstance. The term the word qualified is about, indicates something unacceptable and criminal. Did one ever hear of a qualified purchase, or of qualified heterosexuality? No. What one might call qualified purchase we call fraud, and what could have been called qualified heterosexuality in fact is called rape or incest. The judge expresses the view that homosexuality may not be criminal, but is unacceptable. Mikhail K. in other words is a fairy – a faggot.

It is the structure of the legal procedure that thrusts upon the judge the obligation to be impartial and objective. This requires having access to a universal sphere. No one has such access. But by taking on that position, one does choose a position in which one cannot but silence the people one has to decide about. It is the judge who writes the decision; a legal decision cannot be a conversation. The judge tries to reach the other bank, but is caught in the clutching seaweed. He drowns in the connections made by other people, to use a related Fassbinderian metaphor (Fassbinder, 1992, pp. 43–4). The decision – clearly involuntarily – reflects homophobia, and to a certain extent the decision has been influenced by it, especially in the closing remarks. If without it, the outcome would have been different is impossible to tell. But by its impartial voice it strengthens the homophobia it reflects, again explicitly against the wishes of the judge. At the basis of this inconsistency is the clash between the wish of the judge to be like Mikhail K., to be his brother, and his denial of their resemblance. It is the neurotic urge to tell apart gay and straight. This decision is *not* an illustration of homophobia. It is an illustration of heterosexuality.

Of course, the striking difference between this court decision and *Querelle* is that in the film Querelle is the hero and Robert is not. Here the judge is not a hero, but still definitely better off. Mikhail K. is not a refugee, but the victim beyond doubt. This is not caused by the wickedness or homophobia of the judge, I would maintain. It is caused by the fact that Mikhail K. cannot act, cannot speak. If Robert had been the only actor in *Querelle*, Querelle would have been the total victim. Robert is ready to victimize Querelle, but doesn't succeed. Mikhail K. is totally passive in this decision.

He has a lawyer, but this representative speaks *for* him; he is safe in the knowledge that he cannot be interrupted by his client, by no fault of his own. I think the structure of the legal procedure implicates the lawyer in the legal structure. Like the characters in *Querelle*, s/he becomes entangled in a structure that s/he re-creates at the same time. It is only by defying the unspoken presumptions of the legal process, while at the same time taking part in it, that a lawyer could escape being a legitimizing part of a structure that as such leads to a negative decision for his client (Spijkerboer, 1993). It seems that in this case the lawyer did not succeed in this task – that, by the way, is impossible by definition. Thus, the lawyer is more the brother of the judge than of Mikhail K.

What is hidden from view in this way is what Fassbinder declared to be one of his central concerns in making *Querelle*: showing that what happens 'pertains only to this particular society'. The judge to the contrary does not take a position, but speaks the truth – in a sympathetic way. The judge honestly disclaims that he is biased. And that is the most powerful bias imaginable.

Thus, both the judge and the lawyer have been seduced by the legal aesthetics of violence. The legal system is fair, everyone can have his say, it is an objective and non-violent way of resolving conflict. *Querelle* however shows us that this view is a position. The invisible murders are disastrous and lead to visible murder. Admittedly, Mikhail K.'s invasion of Dutch territory was a violation of the norms, as the judge makes out. When, after dutiful deliberation, he decides against Mikhail K., he establishes on behalf of Dutch society that Mikhail K. should not be here. Echoing Lysiane's words, he discovers that he does not have a brother. Thus Mikhail K. (and his partner, whose case was dismissed on the same day) is banished from his refuge; he is not from this world. But his partner is not a captain; they cannot sail the seas on a ship called *Le Vengeur* [The Revenger]. The Court's decision is legitimized violence, but violence none the less. As Foucault wrote,

> ... the law is a calculated and relentless pleasure, delight in promised blood, which permits the perpetual instigation of new dominations and the staging of meticulously repeated scenes of violence. [...] Humanity does not gradually progress from combat to combat until it arrives at universal reciprocity, when the rule of law finally replaces warfare; humanity installs each of its violences in a system of rules and thus proceeds from domination to domination. (Foucault, 1977, p. 151)

In this analysis, the decision on Mikhail K. reflects the heterosexual matrix. At the same time, it strengthens it, because it represents heterosexuality not as a position among many others, but as the valid, objective, unqualified one.

What happens pertains not only to this particular society; it pertains to the universal community of mankind. Bias is represented as truth, thereby reinforcing bias. And yes, seen this way it is true that the decision on Mikhail K. depends on bias. But, contrary to the criticism I shortly sketched at the beginning of this essay, this bias is not something the judge simply should get rid of. It is not the judge's prejudice that leads to the negative decision; it is the heterosexual matrix that we (straights, gays, lesbians, bisexuals, non-straight heterosexuals and other queers) are all part of, and that we re-enact every day.

However, as *Querelle* points out, there is more than one way to re-enact it. The judge in Mikhail K.'s case presumes that universality means homogeneity. As his decision and its wording make clear, he has a homogenized view of identity: there are people, and queers; people who belong, and foreigners. Robert and Querelle have separate identities. This homogeneity does not deny the existence of others, but can only perceive them as deviants, exceptions, or, liberally, as minorities. That is why the judge subtly but unmistakably places himself in a group of straights, and separates it from sexual minorities. As Mikhail K. deviates from the judge's homogeneity, he is cast out of the brotherhood of men.

Refugee law, I think, requires an experience of universality. We are willing to give protection to persecuted creatures like ourselves, not to persecuted trees or animals – assuming first of all that their position in many countries is not simple. But universality cannot only be imagined as homogeneity. At some level we all feel the necessity to believe we are different from everybody else; then why couldn't everybody else have the same wish to be different from us? To be sure: this experienced necessity of difference is just as artificial as the identities of the characters in *Querelle*. There is no difference with a capital D. But if we admit that it is central to (believe) our identities to be unique, then couldn't a basis for universality be that we assume that everyone wants to be that as well? Passion for fellow human beings, I believe, cannot be based on sameness; that leads to compassion, which is condescending, as we have seen. It can be based on the idea that this other person is taking part in the project we also take part in: that of making a difference.

*

In this analysis, the early victory in Dutch refugee law, consisting of the recognition of homosexuals as a social group and persecution on account of homosexuality as a ground for asylum, was a Pyrrhic victory. We thought we were there when legal doctrine had done its thing. Since then, we have been complaining that jurisprudence doesn't live up to its promises – which, to be sure, it doesn't. Maybe the dogmatic neatness of Dutch jurisprudence has blinded us to the fact that special rights and special rules for minorities do not win the battle (comp. e.g. Spijkerboer, 1994b; Macklin, 1995; Danielsen, 1995).

The most elaborate plea for considering homosexuals as a social group (and therefore eligible for refugee status) is Goldberg's article. Arguing along the lines of US case-law, she finds homosexuals are a minority group (Goldberg, 1993, pp. 613, 615), who share a common central feature of their individual identities (Goldberg, 1993, p. 609), and argues that 'sexual orientation – whether heterosexual, lesbian or gay – is fundamental to human identity and highly resistant to change. [...] In addition, like race, ethnicity, religion, and political opinion, sexual orientation cannot be altered or renounced according to the dictates of the government in power. Regardless of whether sexual orientation has a generic origin, lesbian women and gay men cannot dissociate themselves from the basis of their persecution. To that extent, sexual orientation is indeed immutable' (Goldberg, 1993, pp. 613–14, footnote omitted). She also finds that lesbian women and gay men form a close and voluntary association (Goldberg, 1993, p. 612). On these grounds, she finds lesbian women and gay men a social group.

Grider has criticized such an approach. He finds that immigration law is not the proper arena in which to debate whether or not sexual orientation is immutable, and whether or not sexual orientation is fundamental or incidental to identity (Grider, 1994, p. 220). He proposes as an argument for recognizing homosexuals as a social group that in situations where they are persecuted on the ground of their sexual orientation, they are considered as a social group by their persecutors or the society at large (Grider, 1994, pp. 221, 224). I fully share Grider's criticism of the approach advocated by Goldberg. Apart from the inconsistency in the simultaneous claims that sexual orientation is *immutable* and that there is a close and *voluntary* association of gay men and lesbian women, the debate on the nature or whatever of sexual orientation is a hopeless one. In this debate, Goldberg takes positions on homosexuality which are extremely simplistic. Would anyone, straight or queer, agree that sexual orientation is 'the shared fundamental characteristic' (Goldberg, 1993, p. 610); that there is a close and voluntary association among homosexuals as a group (Goldberg, 1993, p. 612); that one can make an opposition between popular confusion on the nature and origins of sexual orientation on the one hand, and apparently more enlightened social scientists and psychologists on the other, whose findings can be summarized in a few sentences (Goldberg, 1993, p. 613); that sexual orientation is immutable (Goldberg, 1993, p. 612)? Or even that it makes sense to put things this way? How intensely does one have to ignore Foucault and the popularized version thereof in order to be able to claim that 'Greeks and Romans had relatively free attitudes regarding sexuality', and that in the eighteenth century homosexuality came to be viewed as pathological (Goldberg, 1993, p. 615, note 63)?

Is it really a requirement for being homosexual (or, if I understand Goldberg correctly, for being sexually oriented at all) to always experience sexual orientation as a fundamental characteristic? Are queers allowed to be as frivolous as to have as a dominant experience that they are eating a sandwich, enjoying a book, or swimming? Should we feel weird, oppressed or proud all the time because we don't share everybody else's preferences; can we never take a holiday from our sexualities? Do I really have to associate closely and voluntarily with the people with whom according to some I share one or more sexual orientations? About such identities Stephan Sanders wrote: 'Strongholds they are of liberation. It's just that there is no exit. The bridge has been drawn, the circuit is closed. Inside, the silence of unanimity reigns. And only who stands outside sees that it is a prison' (Sanders, 1989, p. 36).

Apart from this (but is it apart, really?), it seems that at one point Goldberg sets the standard for recognition as a refugee too high. If consensual same-sex sexual behaviour is criminalized, she finds that persons guilty of this are refugees only 'when the penalties imposed are extremely disproportionate to the putative statutory goal, or administered without due process' (Goldberg, 1993, p. 620, footnote omitted). It is however incorrect to require more intense persecution when sexual orientation is the persecution ground than when other grounds are at stake.[11]

The problem is not, as one might think after my summary of her argument, that Goldberg is berserk. The problem is that she argues that her position is confirmed by US case-law. Therefore, she has to deal with a decision such as *Bowers* v. *Hardwick* (478 US 186 (1986); see for an analysis of this decision Thomas, 1995); and she has to act as if she totally agrees with judges who are at great pains to decide (as Grider points out, not on the basis of social science but on the basis of legal precedent!) whether sexual orientation is immutable, and whether homosexuals are a group voluntarily and closely. In this respect, Goldberg's argument is a remarkable tight-rope act. But, indeed, as Grider remarks: what is to be done if scientists discover that sexual orientation is, for example, not immutable (Grider, 1994, p. 220)? Would we find then that persecuted homosexuals are not refugees? Grider allows himself more liberties, and without directly attacking precedent argues that a better foundation for the decisions taken would be the one he proposes. However, what do we care? Since the US Attorney General has designated a positive decision as precedent, everything is fine. Presecuted homosexual are refugees, who cares about the details?

I'm afraid that I do, and I'm afraid that 15 years of Dutch experience give cause for that. In the Netherlands, as in other countries, the social group category has been used successfully to raise the issue of the persecution of homosexuals (and women). It is important that this happens. However, I think this popularity has more to do with the fact that the concept of the social group fits with a crude version of identity politics than with virtues inherent to the concept itself. It is possible to raise the issue without invoking the social group category. In as far as it is used (and when it works, why shouldn't one use it), its success just leads to the next problem. Far from being opposed to recognizing persecuted homosexuals as refugees, I think the doctrinal shift towards considering homosexuals as a social group both makes it possible to recognize persecuted gays and lesbians as refugees, and by the same gesture prevents that this possibility comes true (some extreme exceptions that prove the rule left aside). The claim that homosexuals form a social group has to presume that gays and lesbians exist as a group out there. As I have argued earlier, precisely this presumption, that separates straight and gay, is at the heart of the heterosexual matrix, of which homophobia (or at best finding all that a bit weird and ever so slightly disgusting[12]) is a part. The argument that homosexuals form a particular social group fits very well with this way of thinking. I have argued that its results are visible in Dutch case-law.

In *Querelle*, Fassbinder both denies and confirms that gays and straights exist. He acknowledges that gays are oppressed, but refuses to see gays as victims. And, most importantly, he refuses to leave the straight majority alone. Straights might not be that straight; and far from finding homosexuality alien, they might themselves participate in producing it. Straightness might be a way of dealing with same sex-eroticism. Is it possible to argue for recognition of persecuted gays and lesbians in a comparable way? Might that be done without getting stuck in the heterosexual matrix, as happened to Mikhail K.'s judge?

I think Grider sets a first step. He argues that it is the persecution in the country of origin that makes persecuted homosexuals a social group. This recognizes that sexual identities exist in interaction and do not exist out there (comp. Fernhout, 1990, p. 99). However, for the purposes of the asylum procedure in the country of refuge, homosexuality is something out there, even in Grider's approach. Therefore, I propose to pursue an idea that Goldberg once hints at in passing (Goldberg, 1993, p. 614): not to invoke a special persecution ground at all when arguing for recognizing persecuted homosexuals as refugees.

It is seductive to argue that sexual behaviour is something that occurs in the private sphere; that the boundaries of the private sphere are a matter of political contest; that doing something forbidden in the private sphere (e.g. engaging in sexual activities with persons of the wrong sex and/or gender) means at least implicitly making a statement on the boundaries of the private sphere, and therefore is an expression of a political opinion; and that, in conclusion, persecution because of homosexuality is persecution on account of (minimally an attributed) political opinion. On this point, one might follow the very elaborate theory of Heinze. He argues that the right to privacy has a decisional and a spatial aspect. The decisional aspect of the right to privacy boils down to 'a right to choose the way in which, and the people with whom, one seeks to pursue intimacy'. The spatial aspect is exemplified by, but not limited to, the home (Heinze, 1994, p. 173). In the footsteps of Blackmun in his dissent to *Hardwick*, Heinze argues that the decisional aspect of the right to privacy itself contains two aspects. First, it includes the 'ability independently to *define one's identity* that is central to any concept of liberty'. Second, encompassing a 'right of *intimate association*', which 'does not depend in any way on ... sexual orientation', privacy includes the right to choose how and with whom one is to express one's affection (Heinze, 1994, p. 183, italics in original). 'The four brick walls of a "home" materially exemplify the private sphere. Yet, here again, it is not *per se* the material manifestation of that sphere, but rather [...] it is above all the quality of seclusion which characterizes the spatial aspect of the right to privacy' (Heinze, 1994, pp. 184–5, italics in original).

However, this approach has the same defects as the ones rejected earlier. Sexual acts and identity are still inseparable, and still certain acts have to be central to the identity. Second, central to the concept of privacy is the idea that the state shouldn't intervene in certain spheres; and that this increases the amount of liberty people enjoy in the private sphere. However, as has been argued extensively in feminist literature, non-intervention means liberty for some (people with more power, e.g. the husband), and less liberty for others (people with less power, e.g. the wife). Thus, non-intervention enhances the liberty of the powerful, and is not non-intervention but a form of intervention. Finally, this would mean just another ghetto for non-straights. There is nothing private about heterosexuality. As *Querelle* shows, we simply are confronted with normative heterosexuality and this has intense consequences for our lives. If the judge's sexuality is so blatantly public, why should Mikhail K.'s sexuality be referred to the liberal version of the closet called privacy (see Califia, 1994, esp. pp. 71–82)?

Let us step back, and wonder what is the reason that refugee status may be granted to someone who has engaged in, say, royalist activities in Iran. The reason is not that the legal order in the country of asylum is so fond of what the Shah used to do – or so I hope, as his regime used to violate the human rights of its citizens on a routine basis. The reason is that according to the legal order of the country of asylum the persecution is illegitimate – regardless of whether the particular political opinion is a valid or laudable one. The legitimacy or validity of political opinions is precisely the thing that is not the affair of the state, neither of the country of origin nor of the country of asylum. In the same way, it is irrelevant what we think of homosexual behaviour, how we conceptualize it, whether we think it is central or immutable, or whether we think homosexuals characteristically form voluntary associations. It is essential whether or not we think penalizing homosexuality, or torturing people on account of same sex acts, is legitimate (or at least within the margin of appreciation of states).

What, then, would the persecution ground be? Grahl-Madsen in his classical work on refugee law wrote:

> Any real, alleged or implied opinion which leads to persecution in violation of the Universal Declaration of Human Rights, may qualify as a 'political opinion' in the sense of the Refugee Convention. Thus, if a person is threatened with persecution merely because he prefers a blue flag to a green flag, or because he favours the construction of a road on the right bank of a river and not on the left bank, or because he wants to vote for candidate A and not for candidate B in a municipal or general election, or because he holds another opinion which is not in conformity with that of the authorities, he may claim fear of persecution 'for reasons of political opinion' because of the fact that the persons in power consider his opinion 'political' in the existing circumstances. This is but another facet of what we have pointed out in another connexion, namely that the behaviour of the persecutor determines what persons shall be considered refugees. (Grahl-Madsen, 1966, p. 250 (reference omitted)

Hathaway in this respect uses the term 'political opinion implicit in conduct' (Hathaway, 1991, pp. 152–7; the Canadian Supreme Court likewise finds that a political opinion may be manifested through other conduct than speech, in *Canada (Attorney General)* v. *Ward* [1993], 103 D.L.R. (4th), 1, at 40–1).

Clearly, opinions on the punishability of same sex sexual acts are of a political nature. They involve the contents of penal law and the activities of state authorities, such as police officers, public prosecutors etc. Engaging in homosexual conduct will normally be accompanied by the opinion that people should not be prosecuted because of that. Prosecution of homosexual acts occurs because those acts are seen as morally/politically undesirable. People engaging in same sex activities take liberties in this political context. Persecution on account of that is persecution on account of a (minimally attributed) political opinion. I do not say that asylum should be granted because the country of origin finds sexuality a political issue while it shouldn't. That would be an implicit appeal to the privacy principle. The country of origin is completely right to consider sexuality as political. It is because of the political reaction to same-sex acts, because the persecution is illegitimate in absolute terms,[13] that asylum has to be granted.

However, this does not mean that every homosexual asylum-seeker has to be recognized as a refugee. It is simply incorrect to state that lesbian women and gay men are persecuted *globally* (Goldberg, 1993), at least if one uses the word persecution in the refugee law-sense. There should be a well-founded fear of being persecuted, and this is a standard that requires more than unpleasant or even extremely unpleasant experiences. There are however no special requirements for homosexuals on this point. But there are hosts of hard questions. When exactly does discrimination of homosexuals, when exactly does a danger of gay bashing while the police looks the other way, become persecution? As we have seen in Mikhail K.'s case, this is not an easy question. And it certainly isn't answered by facile criticism that sees a homophobic decision-maker around every corner. That doesn't mean, on the other hand, that dominant views on sexual orientations do not play a role.

In this way, I would hope, an argument for recognizing persecuted gays and lesbians would at the same time deny the importance of sexual orientation, and at least not reinforce the idea that sexual orientations are clear and separate things (or that there are just these boring two, for that matter). It is only when the majority ceases to exist, when its coherence is being exposed as a fragile construction, that 'the people who react a little different to reality' (Fassbinder, 1992, p. 16) will get some more space. Or as Mary Joe Frug wrote in respect to women and men: 'Only when sex means more than male or female, only when the word "woman" cannot be coherently understood, will oppression by sex be fatally undermined' (Frug, 1992, p. 153). So, when Querelle asks for asylum, at issue is not his 'minority' status, but the status of the 'majority'.

NOTES

1 This is a revised version of a paper originally written for the third Damwoude Conference, held at Bergen aan Zee, the Netherlands, 9–11 June 1995, presented in revised versions at the Critical Legal Conference in Edinburgh (UK), 8–10 September 1995, and at the Conference on New Approaches to International Law, Madison (Wisconsin), 14–16 June 1996. I thank Robert Barsky, José Bolten, Roel Fernhout, Dennis de Jong, Karl Klare and Audrey Macklin for their (rather diverse) comments on the earlier versions. I greatly thank Frans Lankers for allowing me to use his work in progress on homosexuality and asylum in Dutch case-law; and Chris Randall for information on homosexuality and asylum in British case-law.

2 Thomas Spijkerboer is Lecturer of Migration Law at Centre for Migration Law of the University of Nijmegen, the Netherlands, Address: Faculty of Law, PO Box 9049, 6500 KK Nijmegen, Netherlands. Tel + 31 - 24 - 36 123 07, fax +31 - 24 - 36 16 145. E-mail address: thomass@jur.kun.nl.

3 I use the word nature as a translation of the Dutch word *geaardheid*, which suggests that sexual orientation is innate.

4 Quotes conform to Fassbinder (1982). This contains the dialogues as spoken in the filmed version of *Querelle*, from which I will normally quote. Sometimes, I will quote the screenplay, also printed in this book. If so, this will be mentioned explicitly.

5 Penalizing 'sodomy', i.e. homosexual contacts between men, see Gessen 1994.

6 Arts 121, Paragraph 2 reads: Sexual relations between men committed with the use of force or in relationship to a minor or through taking advantage of the victim's dependent position shall be punishable by incarceration for a term up to seven years. See Gessen, 1994, p. 26.

7 Art. 3 ECHR, which forbids cruel or inhuman treatment, can be violated by deporting someone to a country where s/he can be treated in a way that is contrary to the standard laid down in that article, see European Court of Human Rights, 7 July 1989 (Soering), *Publications of the European Court of Human Rights*, Series A, vol. 161; European Court of Human Rights, 20 March 1991 (Cruz Varas), *Publications of the European Court of Human Rights*, Series A, vol. 201; European Court of Human Rights, 30 October 1991 (Vilvarajah), *Publications of the European Court of Human Rights*, Series A, vol. 215.

8 Compare the following examples on gay men. 'The fact that homosexuals have to live under difficult circumstances because homosexuality [...] is met with hostility in all of Latin America does not compel the conclusion that the complainant is a refugee', Afdeling rechtspraak van de Raad van State [Judicial Department of the Council of State] 28 July 1983, *Gids Vreemdelingenrecht (oud)* [Guide on Immigration Law (old edition)] D12-85; '[...] these incidents (gay bashing, TS), regrettable as they are in themselves, are insufficient [...]', Pres. Rb. Den Haag (Zwolle) 4 August 1994, no. VI 93/3/1457 (Ukraine). '[...] although present legislation in Rumania concerning homosexuals cannot stand close scrutiny [...]', Pres. Rb. Den Haag (Zwolle) 18 November 1994, no. AWB 94/6637.

9 Comp. Afdeling rechtspraak van de Raad van State [Judicial Department of the Council of State] 17 June 1992, *Rechtspraak Vreemdelingenrecht* [Jurisprudence Immigration Law] 1992, 9 in a Czechoslovakian case that is comparable to Mikhail K.'s; and Afdeling rechtspraak van de Raad van State [Judicial Department of the Council of State] 26 May 1993, *Rechtspraak Vreemdelingenrecht* [Jurisprudence Immigration Law] 1993, 4, *Gids Vreemdelingenrecht (oud)* [Guide on Immigration Law (old edition)] D12-230: a Russian case in which the complainant had been forcibly hospitalized in a psychiatric institution; the court finds that the complainant has not made plausible that his forced hospitalization occurred *on account of* his being gay.

10 Comp. Afdeling rechtspraak van de Raad van State [Judicial Department of the Council of State] 2 February 1987, *Gids Vreemdelingenrecht (oud)* [Guide on Immigration Law (old edition)] D12-139: an Austrian man had been sentenced twice (once to ten months conditionally and once to ten months unconditionally) for sexual contacts with 17-year-old men; under Dutch law these acts would not have been illegal, and under Austrian law this would not have been illegal if the partner would have been female. The court decides: 'Under these circumstances the fact of the criminal convictions of the complainant is no reason to conclude there is persecution as stated by the applicant. Also, in the light of the fact that the offence against Article 209 of the Austrian Penal Code is threatened with prison terms ranging from six months to five years, the punishment cannot be considered excessive, the less so as the Landesgericht für Strafsachen G., as is clear from the verdict of September 18, 1979, in its decision on the character of the punishment has taken into account on the one hand an earlier condemnation for the same offence and on the other hand that the acts have been repeated three times and that two minors were involved.' See for a comparable case of

a British man who, on account of sexual contacts with young men that under Dutch law would be legal, and in the UK were only illegal because of the sex of the persons involved, had served three prison terms (of 18 months, 28 months and 28 months respectively) and against whom again a criminal procedure had been started: Advisory Commission on Aliens Affairs, 12 November 1990, *Nieuwsbrief Asiel- en Vluchtelingenrecht* [Newsletter Asylum and Refugee Law] 8 (1992), pp. 283–5; the applicant nevertheless received a residence permit on humanitarian grounds, decision of 14 April 1992, o.c. p. 286.

11 Goldberg in fact deals with penalization of same-sex sex as if this were legitimate prosecution; only in cases where prosecution in itself may be legitimate the issues of disproportionality comes into view. It may be that Goldberg's position is influenced by her effort to deal with US case-law refusing to find criminalization of consensual same-sex sexual acts between adults unconstitutional, see Goldberg, 1993, p. 621. However, once one concedes that homosexual behaviour can be criminalized, pleas to find exactly that a ground for asylum become implausible.

12 In some decisions this disgust seeps through. We already noted the 'qualified homosexuality' thing. Comp. Afdeling rechtspraak van de Raad van State [Judicial Department of the Council of State] 17 June 1992, *Rechtspraak Vreemdelingenrecht* [Jurisprudence Immigration Law] 1992, 9, in which the court notes with badly concealed shudders that in Czechoslovakia in 1988 'so-called *gay bars*' (gay bars in Dutch original) were opened. Also, the word 'homophile' (according to Dyer, 1990, p. 74, it is of Dutch origin and was first used in 1949) in Dutch has a condescending tone. The word usually used in court decisions to refer to homosexuality, 'geaardheid' (translated here with nature) has biologistic, 'these poor guys can't help it' – connotations and, although less outdated, is part of the same vocabulary as 'homophile'.

13 As the European Court of Human Rights has decided in several of its decisions in resolute terms; see most recently European Court of Human Rights, 22 April 1993 (Modinos), *Publications of the European Court of Human Rights*, Series A, vol. 259.

REFERENCES

Amnesty International (1994), *Violations of the Human Rights of Homosexuals*, January (AI Index: POL 30/01/94).

Bos, Marten, Margot Pot and Erwin Willems (1992), 'Grensverlegging of grensversperring? Vreemdelingenrecht en homoseksualiteit [Shifting the border or blocking the border? Immigration law and homosexuality]', in M. Moerings and A. Mattijssen: *Homoseksualiteit en recht* [Homosexuality and law], Arnhem: Gouda Quint, pp. 163–84.

Butler, Judith (1990), *Gender Trouble. Feminism and the Subversion of Identity*, New York and London: Routledge.

Califia, Pat (1994), *Public Sex. The Culture of Radical Sex*, Pittsburgh and San Francisco: Cleis Press.

Danielsen, Dan (1995), 'Identity Strategies. Representing Pregnancy and Homosexuality', in Dan Danielsen and Karen Engle (eds), *After Identity. A Reader in Law and Culture*, New York and London: Routledge, pp. 24–38.

Dyer, Richard (1990), *Now You See It. Studies on Lesbian and Gay Film*, London and New York: Routledge.

Fassbinder, Rainer Werner (1982), *Querelle. The Film*, trans. Arthur S. Wensinger and Richard H. Wood, London: Schirmer Art Books.

Fassbinder, Rainer Werner (1992), *The Anarchy of the Imagination. Interviews, Essays, Notes*, edited by Michael Töteberg and Leo A. Lensing, trans. Krishna Winston, Baltimore and London: John Hopkins University Press.

Fernhout R. (1990), *Erkenning en toelating als vluchteling in Nederland* [Recognition and admission as a refugee in the Netherlands], Deventer: Kluwer.

Foucault, Michel (1977), *Language, Counter-Memory, Practice, Selected Essays and Interviews*, transl. Donald F. Bouchard and Sherry Simon, Ithaca, New York: Cornell University Press.

Frug, Mary Joe (1992), *Postmodern Legal Feminism*, New York and London: Routledge.

Gessen, Masha (1994), *The Rights of Lesbians and Gay Men in the Russian Federation*, San Francisco: Gay and Lesbian Human Rights Commission.

Goldberg, Suzanne B. (1993), 'Give Me Liberty or Give Me Death: Political Asylum and the Global Persecution of Lesbians and Gay Men', *Cornell International Law Journal*, **26**, pp. 605–23.

Grahl-Madsen, Atle (1966), *The Status of Refugees in International Law*, Volume I, Leyden: A.W. Sijthoff.

Grider, Stuart (1994), 'Sexual Orientation as Grounds for Asylum in the United States', *Harvard International Law Journal*, **35**, pp. 213–24.

Halley, Janet E. (1995), 'The Politics of the Closet. Legal Articulation of Sexual Orientation Identity', in Dan Danielsen and Karen Engle (eds) (1995), *After Identity: A Reader in Law and Culture*, New York and London: Routledge, pp. 24–38.

Haran, Michael (1995), '"Social Group" for the Purposes of Asylum Claims', *Immigration and Nationality Law and Practice*, **9**, pp. 64–6.

Hathaway, James (1991), *The Law of Refugee Status*, Toronto/Vancouver: Butterworths.

Heinze, Eric (1994), *Sexual Orientation: A Human Right*, Dordrecht/Boston/London: Martinus Nijhoff Publishers, (diss).

Katz, Robert (1987), *Love is Colder than Death. The Life and Times of Rainer Werner Fassbinder*, New York: Random House.

Lahey, Kathleen A. (1991), 'Reasonable Women and the Law', in Martha Albertson Fineman and Nancy Sweet Thomadsen (eds), *At the Boundaries of Law. Feminism and Legal Theory*, New York and London: Routledge, pp. 3–21.

Lardeau, Yann (1990), *Rainer Werner Fassbinder*, Paris: Éditions de l'Étoile/Cahiers du cinéma.

Macklin, Audrey (1995), 'Refugee Women and the Imperative of Categories', *Human Rights Quarterly*, **17**, pp. 213–77.

Marx, Reinhard (1991), *Asylrecht, Band 2: Rechtsprechungssammlung mit Erläuterungen* [Asylum Law, Volume 2: Collection of Jurisprudence with Commentary], 5th edn, Baden-Baden: Nomos Verlagsgesellschaft.

Sanders, Stephan (1989), *Gemengde ervaring, gemengde gevoelens. De Rushdie-affaire; een besluit tot inmenging* [Mixed experience, mixed feelings. The Rushdie-affair; a decision to intervene], Amsterdam: De Balie.

Shaviro, Steven (1991), 'Masculinity, Spectacle, and the Body of "Querelle"', *Discours Social/Social Discourse*, nos 3 & 4, pp. 171–7.
Silverman, Kaja (1992), *Male Subjectivity at the Margins*, New York and London: Routledge.
Spijkerboer, Thomas (1993), 'A Vow to Defend. De crisis van de sociale advocatuur - III [A vow to defend. The crisis of public interest advocacy - III', *Advocatenblad* [Dutch Bar Association Journal] **73**, pp. 98–100.
Spijkerboer, Thomas (1994a), 'Sheherazade en haar zusters. Sexueel geweld en vluchtelingenrecht [Scheherazade and her sisters. Sexual violence and refugee law]', *Nemesis*, **10**, pp. 95–106.
Spijkerboer, Thomas (1994b), *Women and Refugee Status. Beyond the Public/Private Distinction*, The Hague: Emancipation Council.
Spijkerboer, T.P. and Vermeulen, B.P. (1995), *Vluchtelingenrecht* [Refugee Law], Utrecht: Nederlands Centrum Buitenlanders.
Thomas, Kendall (1995), 'Beyond the Privacy Principle', in Dan Danielsen and Karen Engle (eds), *After Identity. A Reader in Law and Culture*, New York and London: Routledge, pp. 277–93.
White, Edmund (1993), *Genet. A Biography*, New York: Vintage Books.

11 Legal Pluralism in Britain: The Rights of Muslims after the Rushdie Affair

Kathleen M. Moore

We are here to change things ... we shall ourselves be changed ... We are other than what we would have been if we had not crossed the oceans, if our mothers and fathers had not crossed the skies ... We have been made again, but I say that we shall also be the ones to remake this society, to shape it from the bottom to the top. We shall be the hewers of the dead wood and the gardeners of the new. It is our turn now ... . (Salman Rushdie, *The Satanic Verses*, 1988)

INTRODUCTION

The words in the epigraph, spoken by a character in *The Satanic Verses*, at one and the same time express a sense of hope – for readers who identify as the subjective 'we' who 'have been made again' and are 'the gardeners of the new' – and an ominous note of warning hinted at another audience, the dominant (British) society. The warning is contained in the subject's intentions to 'remake society ... from the bottom to the top', and the declaration that 'it is our turn now'. Change is happening, both in the status quo and in the agents of change themselves who, at least in this fictional account, experience themselves as being cut off and alien from the dominant tradition.

The theme of post-colonial migration runs throughout Salman Rushdie's novel, *The Satanic Verses*. In an earlier article commenting on Britain's race relations, Rushdie had suggested that there was a 'new empire' in Britain defined by race: 'Britain is now two entirely different worlds and the one you inherit is determined by the colour of your skin' (Rushdie, 1982, cited in Modood, 1994). Ironically, perhaps, the problems in the publication of *The Satanic Verses* were the volatility of this new imperialism, the hidden injury it inflicts, and the contestation (by Muslims and non-Muslims alike) over the issues of authenticity and alienation which rest at the heart of the post-colonial migration experience. Far from having a monopoly on the struggle to define and defend cultural authenticity, immigrant communities have provoked a resistance of equal force.[1] The presence of communities from the 'New' Commonwealth in Britain in the face of imperial decline has contributed to the persistence of the myth of a singular national culture in which racist stereotypes and imperialist forms of self-understanding remain. For instance, during the 1980s Margaret Thatcher's public rhetoric of western power and idealism was massively loaded, uttered in terms of an imperial British national culture which she alone could defend from a series of threats, whether external or from within (Wright, 1985, pp. 2–3, 25). This national culture could not exist, let alone prosper, without containing the people and things to which it describes itself in opposition. Without acknowledging the 'alien' within, yet at a distance, there would be a crisis of identity. In the discursive production of this national culture, what it means to be 'British' is antithetically related to the image of the 'alien' within and, for its 'essence' is dependent upon it. As Homi Bhabha puts it, 'paradoxically ... cultural otherness functions as the moment of *presence* in theory of *différance* ... The place of otherness is fixed in the west as a subversion of western metaphysics and is finally appropriated by the west as its limit-text, anti-west' (1990a, p. 73).[2] Thus actions surrounding the publication of Rushdie's novel – book burnings, the *fatwa* – jar with the living memory of a national past in the UK and elicit responses which disclose the 'question of *historicity*, of cultural authenticity and security in the face of change' (Wright, 1985, pp. 25–6).[3]

The events following on the publication of *The Satanic Verses* accentuated the polarity operative in the phenomenon labeled Orientalism in Edward Said's analysis of 'otherness'. The production of knowledge about Islam and the Muslim world historically differentiates and devalues the Muslim Other from Europeans (Said, 1979, 1993). Much has been written on this subject and others have pursued this analysis expertly (for instance, Anon., 1994). Suffice it, for our purposes, to say that the dichotomy between the west and the Muslim world, the celebration of the west as the universal and the displacement of the colonial subject as inferior, have been identified (and reinforced) in many accounts of the protests surrounding *The Satanic Verses*. For instance the Africanist scholar Ali Mazrui points out: 'In North-South relations, sometimes simple things, like a book, can shake relations between the Muslim world and the West. One sees the West bewildered by the intensity of Muslim reaction [to *The Satanic Verses*]. On the other hand, we see Islam absolutely appalled by Western insensitivity' (Mazrui, 1990, p. 222).[4] Homi Bhabha puts it:

> *We are embattled in the war between the cultural imperatives of Western liberalism, and the fundamental interpretations of Islam, both of which seem to claim an abstract and universal authority.* What results is an implacable antagonism that is continually rehearsed in the media, sometimes by journalistic reportage, at other times as informed opinion or intellectual debate (emphasis in original; cited in Alibhai, 1989, p. 34).

The polarity made evident (and plausible) in many accounts – which themselves in a sense collude with the Orientalist production of the colonial subject by focusing on that seemingly primary, irreducible division between the west and Islam – affects how Islam is represented and understood in non-Islamic societies. The distinction is important because it poses a central problematic in which the source of the 'problem' (that is, the 'clash of civilizations' à la Huntington's thesis[5]) is located in one of two camps: the west, in western constructions of colonial discourse; or in Islam, understood as a monolithic, monocultural, and anachronistic entity.[6] Rather than view this in terms of opposition, as a stand-off between two mutually exclusionary worldviews, I claim that it is necessary to restore to our attention the polymorphous, cross-cutting factors – the 'pushes' and 'pulls' of cultural differentiation – which produce not simply two, but a range of differences among colonial subjects (the colonizer and the colonized). As legal scholar Martha Minow points out, the problem of dualism in attempts to understand the complexities of domination requires that we expose the

> ... rigidity and limitations of patterns of thought that force perceptions into dualities: good/bad, same/different, white/black, male/female. Becoming adept at recognizing how each half of a given duality depends upon the other half in self-definition, and how crudely each duality divides varieties and ranges of perception and experience, can help people challenge the seeming inevitability of dualisms in social practice. (1990, p. 236)

Borrowing from Bhabha again, this suggests that 'the point of intervention [in reading colonial discourse] should shift from the *identification* of images as positive or negative, to an understanding of the *process of subjectification* made possible ... through stereotypical discourse' (1990a, p. 71), and provides a useful framework for the analysis of the circulation of 'otherness'. My argument is that the problem lies not in western prejudices nor in the so-called 'clash' between civilizations, fundamentalist, secularist or otherwise. Rather the difficulty in understanding the significance of such events as the protests over *The Satanic Verses* lies in the absence of what Bhabha refers to as a theoretical third space (1990b) in which novel political and legal forms and identities can develop, and dissent by a fledgling community from the prevailing norms of the 'hegemon' (both the western individualistic and the

Muslim communitarian models) can be allowed to flourish. One wonders what the effects of this absence of a third space are for the Muslim communities living in the UK and for pluralism in general, for, as Talal Asad notes, the discursive devices of inclusion/exclusion and the ways in which their effects become socially constituted through various traditions (including law) are always integral to the concept of 'the whole form of our common life' (1990, p. 473).

It is the object of this chapter to explore efforts to claim and expand a third space out of the Rushdie Affair, and how the effects of discursive devices of inclusion/exclusion, embedded in the law, have furthered the development of the legal and political consciousness of Muslim communities in Britain. More specifically the aim is to see the struggles over the meaning and representation of identities in the law, and how *new* forms, and challenges to *older* or conventional forms, of identity are implicated in the complexities of the legal process. Here the focus is on how those Muslims who raised legal challenges think about and understand the law, as well as how a range of Muslim individuals collaborate with or challenge the dominant legal discourse as it structures their rights and identities in British society. The argument relies on the notion that law is pluralistic, and will develop the hypothesis that 'multiple spheres of law' (Merry, 1988), from Islamic[7] to the Western juristic model, have been central to the constitution of the personal and group identity of Muslims living in dispersed communities at the end of the twentieth century. However this is *not* to claim simplistically that both Islamic law and British law have been factors in shaping that identity; instead the point is to demonstrate that legal discourse and the selective use of laws are historically contingent (that is, they have to do with the social conditions of the times), that the intersubjectivity of Muslim life is socially formed, and that the outcome (the shifting and heterogeneous personal and group identities) can indicate a new 'space' or third ground (Bhabha, 1990b) which has been uncharted or, to use Peter Fitzpatrick's term, mute (Fitzpatrick, 1992).

Secondly, I hope to show that, as Sally Engle Merry points out, legal *centralism* – 'the predisposition to think of all legal ordering as rooted in state law' (1988, p. 889) – fails to capture the pluralistic character of law and the full scope of legal activity in a given society in its transnational-national-local dimensions (Santos, 1995). Articulating Muslim experiences helps to show not only the legal complexity of British society but also the salience of legal pluralism[8] by indicating the points of interaction between a significant religious minority – having its own normative code (Islamic) as a potential alternative to official law – and the legal institutions of the state.

This chapter examines the mobilization of Muslim constituencies around legal norms and formal legal initiatives which were introduced in the wake of the initial whirlwind of the Rushdie Affair. I argue that this mobilization has resulted in: (1) demands to extend blasphemy and race relations laws to include Muslims under their protection, which were a plea for equal treatment in a pluralist nation-state; and (2) a proposal for Muslim legal sovereignty requesting official recognition of and freedom for Muslim *shari'a* courts to operate in Britain as an alternative to state law. Further, the proposal for *shari'a* courts in the UK illustrates both: (1) the intersubjectivity of legal forms – that the legal forms of distant localities (for instance, courts) have been cultivated and have interpenetrated the ex-colonizer as well as the ex-colonized (see Asad, 1990); and (2) the development of a uniquely 'minoritarian' or 'diasporic' legal culture, characterized by contemporary challenges and solutions, but traceable to certain historical social relations as well. This legal culture is complicit with emergent forms of identity in Britain.

RESPONSES TO *THE SATANIC VERSES*

The turmoil sparked by the novel beginning in 1988 is of course well-known. Not unlike the 'Dreyfus Affair' of the last century in France, this controversy, dubbed the 'Rushdie Affair', aroused visceral reactions in the United Kingdom and beyond. Scores of tabloid headlines and 'mainstream' news accounts appeared with titles such as 'Why I'm Outraged', 'Blasphemers Must Die', 'A Satanic Uproar' and so on, reflecting the fury unleashed by the controversy. In its reductive powers the typical media representation of the Rushdie Affair has described it in binary terms, as a battle between the forces of secular liberalism and religious obscurantism. Similarly book-length treatises attempted to capture the high emotions of the controversy and their titles often reinforce the impression of battle lines being drawn: *Be Careful With Muhammad; The Kiss of Judas, Affairs of a Brown Sahib; The Satanic Conspiracy; A Satanic Affair, Salman Rushdie and the Wrath of Islam; Sacrilege vs. Civility*, and so on.[9] Seemingly long-held antagonisms surfaced between Islam and the west, and the tendency has been to conceal the significant pluralities of each side, thereby displacing internal political tensions with the unifying perspectives of a dominant culture.

Of course the reality is more complex. Rather than being monolithic, the affected community – UK Muslims – is a highly differentiated and heterogeneous population, and their responses to the publication of the novel cannot be understood accurately to emanate simply from one reactionary point of view. The controversy elicited a variety of responses, and attempts to identify a single response have elided over substantial differences in perspective and have described the subjects' positions as unitary and static, as if all consciousness had frozen into an 'arresting display of the past' (Wright, 1985, p. 3). What is left out of most accounts is any recognition of the dynamism of the social and political processes in which communities define and defend their identities and conditions of existence. To lose sight of that dynamism is to misunderstand the complex social relations of late-twentieth-century Britain and the circumstances in which UK Muslims, not to mention the broader Asian community, now find themselves.[10]

And yet in certain respects the impact of the Rushdie Affair *has* had a homogenizing effect, 'brought about both by external agencies, like the press, and by self-definition' (Sahgal and Yuval-Davis, 1992, p. 15). The risk of the vision conveyed in *The Satanic Verses*, perched between cultures, is the possibility of mistranslation and the tendency to resort to the hammer and anvil approach when staking out a social location. Communities previously known in Britain by national origin or ethnic affiliation (Pakistani, Bengali, Sylheti, Punjabi etc.) thanks to policies of multiculturalism, or which were internally differentiated by kinship, clan or sectarian networks, are now primarily identified with a larger, if diverse, Muslim community. One observer of Muslim immigrants in Britain has argued that the effect of such pressures on Muslims in the UK has been 'to provoke a degree of cooperation among Muslim groups previously unknown' (Nielsen, 1995, p. 157). For its part the British press defined *The Satanic Verses* controversy in terms of 'culturally resonate' stereotypes and, however unintentionally, 'united the Muslim community, created a new orthodoxy, and made every Muslim who wished no harm to Rushdie feel "inauthentic" and not a "true Muslim"' (Parekh, cited in Cottle, 1991, p. 46). At the same time the rise of Muslim fundamentalist movements transnationally has provided an 'aggressive Muslim[11] identity' for Muslim youth in particular living in Britain, where asserting a Muslim identity now has become an integral part of maintaining a presence in a society where they are under constant attack for being Muslims (Sahgal and Yuval-Davis, 1992, p. 16). Ayatollah Khomeini's *fatwa*, although repudiated by almost all UK Muslim organizations, nevertheless heightened local concerns about the potency of a unified Islam and created the impression that a city such as Bradford, for instance, where copies of *The Satanic Verses* were ceremoniously burned in January 1989, would become 'a bridgehead in the West for the establishment of separatist, Islamic enclaves' in the centre of the UK (Lewis, 1994, p. 4).

This suggests that, in terms of identity politics, Muslims often are caught by a false essentialism: that, as Steven Vertovec suggests, '[p]opulations and population segments ... [can be] categorized ... according to cultural essences which are presumed to be imparted at birth' (1996, p. 51). This essentialist conception places Muslims in a double-bind, subject to the (mis)perceptions and political agenda of both Orientalism and Islamism. It obscures the distinctive concerns and self-expression of various communities and different generations.[12]

While neither of these two perspectives of Orientalism or Islamism is complete, both are present in the Law. Whether and how UK Muslims will be changed by these essentializing pressures is contingent upon the social relations[13] in which they find themselves in late-twentieth-century Britain. Such change is highly dependent upon the degree to which opportunities exist in Britain for creative challenge of both the stereotypes about Islam and Muslims and, more generally, the dominant legal order. The transnationalization of the legal field (attendant to such phenomena as the global migration of people and the integration of Europe) that Boaventura de Sousa Santos describes is being promoted, among other things, by popular movements. The contribution that UK Muslims are providing in this direction, as a movement making certain claims for protection by the European Court of Justice and other transnational tribunals once their efforts on the domestic front fail, is one example. As Santos puts it:

> Far from being a monolithic phenomenon, [the transnationalization of the legal field] is extremely diverse, combining uniformity with local differentiation, top-down imposition with bottom-up creation, formal declaration with interstitial emergence, boundary-maintaining orientation with boundary-transcending orientation. (1995, p. 252)

MUSLIMS IN BRITAIN: UNITY OUT OF ADVERSITY?

Two factors are especially formative of Muslim life in diaspora in the late twentieth century and contribute to the dynamics of identity politics. These factors require attention here in order to situate the primary thesis of this chapter. First, UK Muslims of various national and cultural origins and perspectives are subject to the constraints imposed by two contradictory and reductionist understandings in Britain that are constituted by the Orientalist and Islamist productions of knowledge about Islam and Muslims.[14] The Orientalist construct, based on 'a particular closeness between Britain and France and the Orient' from the beginning of the nineteenth century to the end of the Second World War (Said, 1979, p. 4), tells us that Islam is necessarily reactionary, misogynistic, despotic, censorious (in both moral and legal understandings), cruel and sensuous. The Islamist[15] construct – which resists European imperialism, Western intervention, and the Orientalist construct – positions Islam as an anti-colonial and anti-Western ideology and, significantly, as the true source of cultural authenticity. It propagates the notion of a (re)Islamization of society, a 'return' to religious law and the creation of a contemporary religiously-based order replicating the 'pure' Islam of the days of the Prophet Mohammed. It makes central the importance of *shari'a*, or Islamic law, in governing all aspects of society, despite the fact that in its contemporary forms *shari'a* governs only personal status laws, including gender relations (Khan, 1993; Ali, 1992).[16] The aim of the Islamist construct is to retrieve and retain the culture, rituals, and values associated with a divinely ordered society (Roberson, 1994, p. 293) and, as a result, places great emphasis on what it means to be an observant Muslim.

The second factor that characterizes the social relations examined here is that, within the constraints imposed by the Orientalist and Islamist productions of knowledge, the role of law and legal mobilization can be seen to have both direct and indirect effects on social struggles such as those encompassed by the Rushdie Affair. Within the framework of multiculturalism in Britain, where non-Christian religious affiliation has come to signify collective identity and a central model of inclusion and exclusion among minority communities, Muslim leaders are now pressing certain demands upon the British state, specifically for the reform of blasphemy and race relations laws and the introduction of *shari'a* courts. The direct and indirect effects of this can be seen in the following areas: how individuals who are identified with a diasporic community constitute themselves around legal concepts and what happens to divergent views *within* that community; how law is authoritative in constructing expectations and ways of thinking about rights; and how relations of domination and resistance are revealed in legal discourse. In some respects there appears to be a certain reliance, even in resistance, on what John Brigham refers to as 'governmentally promulgated rules' (1987b, p. 307), a factor which can 'infuse and inform' Muslims' consciences 'by becoming an essential part of their thought, their identity, and their social boundaries' (ibid., p. 304). For decades multiculturalist policies have encouraged the separate development of ethnic identities and state-sponsored essentialist categories can be seen to have conditioned responses to the political pressures of the Rushdie Affair.

Migration and the demographics of Muslim presence in Europe

Due to population shifts over the second half of the twentieth century, a significant portion of the global Muslim population now lives in minority status in non-Islamic countries (see Shahid and van Koingsveld, 1991; Haddad *et al.*, 1991; Khalidi, 1989; Kettani, 1986; and Roberson, 1994). With between five and six million Muslims now in Europe, of which roughly one and one-half million are in Britain,[17] the renewed salience of Islamic law[18] in the lives of Muslims in 'lasting exile' (Leveau, 1992, p. 170) is essential to understand when analysing the sociolegal implications of global migration. Muslims are not only the largest minority religious group in Britain but in the whole of Europe (Anwar, 1990; Solomos and Wrench, 1993). Since the 1950s and 1960s Europe has witnessed the movement of former colonial subjects into the metropoles of Britain, France and the Netherlands (el-Manssoury, 1989; Roberson, 1994). Many of the Muslims in Britain have arrived during the last four decades. In several respects they do not comprise a homogeneous population; these migrants came from various regions and countries, and speak several different languages. About two-thirds are of South Asian origin (Pakistani, Indian, Sri Lankan and Bangladeshi), but there are also sizeable groups from Arab countries, Cyprus, Malaysia, and some parts of Africa. Most are British citizens and about 50 per cent were born in Britain. There are also a small number of converts. Settlement is concentrated in the geographic and industrial centre of Britain, in manufacturing, industrial and textile cities of the middle of the country (Anwar, 1990; Lewis, 1994; Nielson, 1995, p. 42).

The Muslim population of South Asian origin in Britain is very youthful. According to the 1985–87 statistics provided by the Labour Force Survey, 46 per cent of the Pakistani population and 50 per cent of the Bangladeshi population are under the age of 16, compared to 20 per cent of the so-called 'white' population of Britain. Yet it is precisely this segment of the population whose interests have been poorly represented by the current 'community relations' leadership, fostered by Britain's official policies of multiculturalism. Young people particularly have felt alienated from the strong ethnic identity of their parents' generation, and criticism has arisen of a system that marginalizes and depoliticizes their existence in Britain. In comparison, the appeal of an Islamic internationalism seems to be making some headway in eroding the constricting bonds of state-sponsored ethnicity categories. Hence the discourses and public policies of multiculturalism appear at present to be under assault from various forms of Islamism as general frustration with the wider society has led to 'a resort to religion as a solace' (Shah, 1994, p. 19) and the younger generation shows a revived interest in Islam. In this context, Islam seems to be offering 'the possibility of a wider world in which to live' (ibid., p. 113). Because the multicultural system is perceived and experienced by the younger generation as a fine-tuned system which exoticizes the communities in Britain of non-European origins, its leadership has had only a limited degree of authority. Community formation and the collective and individual identities of Muslim Britons are shifting, heterogeneous and diverse. A number of representative Muslim British organizations have appeared on the scene, reflecting various perspectives.

Local associations, often organized around mosques, proliferated to satisfy the demands of cultural politics.

Demographics should not be overlooked because they have consequences; namely, in this instance the growing presence of British Muslims is experienced by society at large as provoking tension and anxiety, evident in some (alarmist) accounts in the media regarding the threat to the national culture and cultural authenticity of Britain as well as the future of Europe.[19] However, this brief overview having been provided, it is important to emphasize that like John Brigham in his study of the legal discourses of American political movements, I am writing of persons and groups who identify themselves *conceptually* rather than demographically. Discourse and chosen strategies become the organizing frame in community formation, as groups coalesce 'in the way they articulate demands and constitute their own identity' (Brigham, 1987b, p. 315). Some observers of Muslim migration assert that the current trend is 'not a process of acculturation but of cultural syncretism' – that Muslim settlers are 'carving out a hybrid cultural space' (Gross *et al.*, 1994, p. 5; see also Gilroy, 1987; Leveau, 1992) in Europe and the rest of the west. The recent appearance of Islam 'as an instrument for building new identities and transnational solidarities' (Leveau, 1992, p. 170) in order to negotiate with states and societies of settlement has raised unwelcome challenges in the so-called 'secular' societies of the European Union. Muslims who assert cultural and religious rights in secular contexts in France (schoolgirls wearing headscarves), Germany (Turkish guest workers), and Britain (the Rushdie Affair) find that the host societies 'are no longer used to dealing with religious values as a way of collective self-assertion' (ibid.). This means that the emergence of a group rights consciousness and a movement among British Muslims to reform British law to protect their rights in the wake of the Rushdie Affair have taken place within the limitations set by British cultural and legal norms and is highly contingent upon these factors. The specificity of UK Muslims' experiences is inserted into very specific economic, political and ideological conditions, and is historically and politically determined by both the domestic (multiculturalism and race relations) and international (post-colonial migration and rising Islamism) arenas.

Multiculturalism

Multiculturalist policy in Britain grew from the state's response to the arrival of immigrants from the former colonies of the British Empire from the late 1950s and 1960s. Inaugurated in the context of the first Race Relations Act (1965) and Local Government Act (1966), multiculturalism targeted certain (dark-skinned) minorities and new immigrants as the beneficiaries of a social policy that granted what Yasmin Ali has called limited autonomy over internal, non-political community affairs – for instance, cultural observances – as long as 'their presence offer [ed no] major challenges to the basic framework of social, economic, and political relations in society' (1992, p. 103). Drawing on the British experience with colonial administration, the British state in an era of decolonization constructed a layer of minority or 'ethnic' leaders who, as members of Community Relations Councils, were appointed to represent their communities to the state and interpret the state to their communities. Through Community Relations Councils the British state 'could liaise directly with an unelected community leadership' (ibid., p. 104) to secure the social and political quiescence of a growing non-white population. This depoliticized the presence of New Commonwealth 'cultural communities' that included Muslims as well as other communities from the New Commonwealth, and thwarted the development of autonomous political positions. Poorly conceived ideas and implicit understandings of 'cultural communities' at one and the same time have served to integrate minorities into the majority public domain while legitimating various forms of social and political exclusion (Vertovec, 1996). These contradictory tendencies conditioned a heavy reliance on the state without establishing a reciprocal relationship or a need on the part of the state to gain these communities' electoral support. This perpetuated the unequal relations between cultures and subgroups co-existing on the British scene. The effect of the political discourses surrounding multiculturalism tends to conflate ethnicity and religion where Muslims are concerned, confusing the basis upon which these communities were recognized as subject to multiculturalist policies in the first place. Communities formerly viewed as being divided into Pakistani or Bangladeshi, for instance, are now united in the public mind by an essentialist understanding of 'culture', defined as a cohesive and single-minded mass associated primarily with a particular religious affiliation, despite the foundation laid by almost three decades of multicultural politics which conditioned the relations between these minorities and the state.[20]

Some of the voices now audible from within the British Asian and African communities have been critical of multiculturalist policies that they claim have isolated and marginalized, rather than integrated, minorities and new immigrants (for instance, see Sahgal and Yuval-Davis, 1992). This is not a matter of race alone, but a reflection of a widespread disregard for non-European cultures and non-Christian religious and cultural norms. Further, multicultural policies are said to have benefited a certain organized element within British Muslim society – largely an upper-middle class, educated, patriarchal elite of South Asian origins. These self-selected leaders of 'community relations' have been recognized by the British state to represent this community to the state regardless of significant social, class and gender divisions within. However, because of patterns of mass migration from the Indian subcontinent, many of those whom the 'community relations' leadership claims to represent come from rural backgrounds and are working class and of a different ethnic (although not necessarily national) profile. The common link has been defined by the British state via multiculturalism as being simply the 'cultures' they supposedly inhabit (Ali, 1992, p. 102). This official practice has restricted the emergence of multiple positions expressed by individuals who are considered to be 'minorities' and their own critiques of the condition they are in.

By the mid-1980s the 'community relations' leadership and other leaders of Muslim associations alike were engaged in debates over educational reform, arguing over legislation of the Education Reform Act 1988 that required Christian worship and religious education in schools (Sarwar, 1989), and putting forward unsuccessful demands for state funding for Muslim schools. However the level of activism on this issue within the Muslim population was low and limited to a small percentage who felt their needs were being marginalized and that Muslims were being singled out for unfair treatment. Within this context of limited community mobilization the publication of *The Satanic Verses* proved to be a catalyst for more effective organizing around notions of legal rights and the exposure of the flaws of multiculturalism.

MOVEMENT PRACTICES IN MAKING A CLAIM FOR RIGHTS

The Satanic Verses epigraph at the beginning of this chapter suggests that the process of uprooting oneself and moving across continents has a transformative impact. In Yasmin Ali's words, '[a]s communities have experienced the trauma of their creation in the process of migration, so forms of politics have developed within them which have looked … for more powerful allies or patrons (real or imagined) in the country of origin, in Britain, or both' (1992, p. 102). What British Muslims experienced in the events encompassed by the Rushdie Affair illustrates that point, as well as the existence of a transnational-national-local axis (Santos, 1995). Existing organizations – councils such as the United Muslim Organization (UMO), funded in part by Saudi Arabia – and organizations created in the wake of the Rushdie Affair – for instance, the Muslim Parliament, an offshoot of the existing Muslim Institute – traditionally depended for their existence not only on foreign patronage but also local support. Externally provided resources are simply *one*, albeit an important, factor in the emergence of a Muslim identity as a self-conscious social category and basis for political action.

The mobilization of law on the part of British Muslim activists to protest the publication of *The Satanic Verses* began early in the Rushdie Affair with an appeal to ban the novel under Britain's laws on blasphemy. In street demonstrations in Bradford, Birmingham and London protesters rallied around slogans calling for the author's prosecution as a blasphemer. Blasphemy laws were not invoked frequently in Britain, but they had been recently in Mary Whitehouse's 1978 successful prosecution of *The Gay News* for blasphemous libel over the publication of a homoerotic poem about Jesus.[21] Thus their importance was more than just symbolic. Simon Lee, Professor of Jurisprudence at Queens University in Belfast, puts it, 'even where the law is rarely used, it has a ... role in shaping our arguments' (Lee, 1990).

The Satanic Verses, released in September 1988, was immediately shortlisted for the prestigious Booker Prize but much of the British public, including British Muslims, remained unaware of it. Ironically, Rushdie's novel initially received more attention in his country of origin, India, than in Britain, his adopted home. Soon after the book was released the Indian government banned its importation and distribution under the Indian Customs Act and various penal codes. Within weeks the novel was also banned in Pakistan, Saudi Arabia, Egypt, Somalia, Bangladesh, the Sudan, Malaysia, Indonesia, Qatar and South Africa. News of the Indian ban travelled quickly through the British Asian communities, bringing significant public attention to the novel in Britain for the first time. In November the Grand Sheikh of Al-Azhar University in Cairo, Egypt, perhaps the most influential religious leader in the Sunni Muslim world, called on Islamic organizations in Britain to join in taking legal steps to prevent the novel's distribution there.[22]

In London Dr Syed Pasha – the Secretary of the Union of Muslim Organizations (UMO), an umbrella organization of over 180 Muslim groups in Britain which had been in existence for more than 20 years – called an emergency session on 15 October 1988 to determine what action the UMO would take regarding *The Satanic Verses*.[23] Shortly thereafter he wrote to the publisher, Viking Penguin, but received no reply. He also wrote to the Prime Minister Margaret Thatcher and British Attorney General Sir Patrick Mayhew to ask that Rushdie and Viking Penguin be prosecuted under the Public Order Act (1986) and the Race Relations Act (1976). In November Thatcher responded at length in a public letter, making it clear that the government would not consider banning the book. Mayhew announced that the book constituted no civil offence and therefore could not be prosecuted under race relations laws. Receiving no satisfaction on these two fronts, Pasha then wrote to the Lord Chancellor, Lord MacKay, and the British Home Office in charge of community relations to request a ban on the book under the blasphemy laws of Britain. The response from this direction was also a denial of the request, and the Home Office added that it did not intend to introduce legislation in Parliament to change the blasphemy laws in order to protect Islam (Bradney, 1993, p. 87). According to the Home Office blasphemy laws protect only Christianity, the established religion, and none of the other religions in Britain. This led Muslims to begin to ask whether the laws should be expanded to protect Islam (Levy, 1993, p. 558).

Although the statutory offence of blasphemy was abolished in 1967, the British common law on blasphemy still exists (Bradney, 1993, p. 82). Several attempts were made to prosecute the author and publisher of *The Satanic Verses* in the courts. In March 1989, Abdul Hussain Choudhury filed papers with the Chief Metropolitan Magistrate of London at Bow Street Magistrates Court petitioning for the criminal prosecution of Rushdie and Viking Penguin for blasphemous libel and seditious libel. However, the magistrate Sir David Hopkin ruled that the common law protected only Christianity, and so refused to issue summonses against the defendants named in the complaint. This ruling was contested and taken to the Divisional Court of the High Court for judicial review. In four days of hearings the British Muslim Action Front, an organization created to protest *The Satanic Verses* and to use legal means to censor it, testified that 'many law-abiding Muslims who are United Kingdom citizens' are deeply offended by the book (cited in *R. v. Chief Metropolitan Stipendiary Magistrate ex parte Choudhury*) and that the protections against blasphemy ought to extend to Islam and the Qur'an. In April 1990 the High Court affirmed the magistrate's decision and later (July) refused leave to appeal to the House of Lords. Choudhury then brought his case before the European Commission of Human Rights, claiming that the UK was in violation of Article 9 of the European Convention of Human Rights since the government 'has not given the Muslim religion protection against abuse or scurrilous attacks, and that without that protection there will inevitably be a limited enjoyment of the right to freedom of religion' (*Choudhury v. U.K.*, ECHR decision of 5 March 1991). However this appeal was also turned down. Meanwhile, back in the United Kingdom, an attempt to prosecute Viking Penguin under the Public Order Act (1986), the racial hatred law, also failed because the court ruled that Muslims are not a racial or ethnic group according to this law, and thus have no legal standing (*R. v. Horseferry Road Metropolitan Magistrate ex parte Siadatan* [1990] 3 WLR 1006, QBD).[24]

As Muslim criticism grew in Britain, the UMO convened a conference on 'the law of blasphemy – an Islamic perspective' in February, 1990. Britain is unique among countries in having blasphemy laws that were invoked by citizens with regard to Rushdie and *The Satanic Verses*. In some (but by no means all) Muslim countries and in India Rushdie's fate was considered in the light of the Islamic legal category of apostasy[25] – abandonment of religious faith – and, in India, in terms of incitement to religious hatred, which is prohibited by Indian law.[26] But blasphemy *per se* is not an offence under Islamic law, while it is under British common law. Thus it was invoked and explored by Muslims in Britain because the common law provided for its punishment, and the provisions of British statutory and common law set the terms for the debate about *The Satanic Verses*. This illustrates that consciousness corresponds to the provisions of law or, in other words, to what law makes possible (Merry, 1990; Brigham, 1987a). British Muslims raise certain claims – and their legal consciousness has developed as it has – precisely because they are in Britain.

Criticism of the current status of blasphemy law in Britain developed from other quarters as well. That the dominant law was perceived to discriminate against Muslims by protecting Christianity but not Islam gave rise to some unusual political alliances. The Labour Party, the traditional ally of minority and new immigrant communities and the main proponent of multiculturalism, was quite mixed about its reaction to the mounting protests over Rushdie's novel. Commitments to civil liberties mitigated the left's sympathies for the plight of a 'racialized' group claiming to be oppressed. In the House of Commons pressures were put to Labour MPs who counted on the South Asian/Muslim vote to take sides with the cause of free expression as opposed to the demands of Muslim constituents to reform the laws of blasphemy and race relations. Khomeini's *fatwa* issued in February 1989 alienated Labour sympathies in particular, even though the Shi'a cleric's religious/legal decree was an isolated act that had very limited support among the Muslim communities in Britain. In fact many Muslim associations distanced themselves from the *fatwa* because it was considered by them to be 'unlawful'. The chair of the UK Action Committee on Islamic Affairs (UKACIA), Dr Mughram Ali al-Ghamdi, said in response to the announcement of the *fatwa*:

> [We] are a minority living in this country and we do intend to fully abide by the law. We are not above the law. We do not condone violence of any kind by anybody under any pretext.
>
> This book caused real, genuine, and universal hurt. We are doing all we can within the legal framework of this country to get it banned and the author punished for blaspheming Islam. But Britain is not a Muslim country. Islamic laws do not apply here and even in Islamic countries, it is not for individuals to take the law in their hands. (Cited in *New Life*, 17 February 1989)

In this statement al-Ghamdi indicates his attachment to British, rather than any other, law.

Some Muslims made common cause with groups on the right rather than the left of British politics. Aziz al-Azmeh, Professor of Islamic Studies at the University of Exeter, noted that 'a symbiosis [developed] between a section of Britain's Muslims and extreme right-wing caucuses within the Tory party over social and moral issues' (*New Statesman and Society*, 20 January 1989). Joining with groups that had protested Martin Scorsese's film, *The Last Temptation of Christ*, some Muslims lobbied elements of the Conservative Party to amend the British blasphemy law to cover all religions. In the debates that followed in the House of Commons and beyond, opponents of this proposal argued to repeal blasphemy laws altogether.

Efforts were made to lobby for legislation to change not only blasphemy laws but race relations laws as well in order to remedy discrimination on religious grounds. The point was to criminalize incitement to religious hatred in the same manner that incitement to racial hatred is now a crime, so that the legal provisions offering protection against incitement to racial and religious hatred will be parallel (see Ahsan and Kidwai, 1991; Poulter, 1991). Particular rights claims in this context are being associated with race relations laws because the opportunity to claim these rights exists at least in principle in the law. The demand for the protection of the law is based on the belief that the state will eventually have to recognize the legitimacy of the Muslims' argument – that protection from one form of bigotry ought to extend to victims of all forms of bigotry. By using these laws to advance their case, Muslims were constituting themselves around legal concepts that had originally been formulated to combat colour racism in the context of urban race riots. The promises of justice and equality offered by these laws were constituted around racial identity. By casting their lot with race relations laws, and making religion an analogue of race before the law, British Muslims who took this legal action indicated that they were viewing themselves through the prism of British legal categories, and that existing law to protect racial minorities was legitimate and would be an acceptable means to redress their grievance. Thus as Tariq Modood argues, while most Muslims 'do not see themselves in terms of colour and do not want a public identity that emphasizes colour', it was understood that the way to combat discrimination was to embrace 'a concept of race that not only allows minorities a purchase upon their mode of being but, equally importantly, also upon how white British society defines them – that is to say upon their mode of oppression' (1990, p. 159). These appeals to the law were unsuccessful in British courts, where the author's and publisher's right to freedom of expression was held to outweigh the Muslims' interest. The indirect effect, though, helped to generate support across various constituencies for a new rights claim being articulated by Muslims protesting the novel and bolstered the movement for legal reform of blasphemy and race relations laws.

INITIATIVE FOR INTRODUCTION OF *SHARI'A* COURTS

Out of the failure to gain the protection they sought under the law, some Muslims activists constructed an initiative to introduce *shari'a* (Islamic legal) courts in Britain, which was presented to John Patten, the Home Office Minister in charge of community relations. This initiative was based on the historical experience of British colonial rule in India, where the British allowed the development of Muslim family law with its own separate courts and the Muslim minority was subject to *shari'a* rather than British colonial law in certain matters (Hardy, 1972, p. 224; Sahgal, 1992, p. 168). In the summer of 1989 a delegation representing various Muslim groups presented a proposal for a similar practice of local autonomy for Muslims living in the 'mother country' of the former British Empire (Modood, 1990, p. 159). Within the structure of existing legal arrangements this action suggests that the ethic of pluralism allow an alternative jurisprudence (Muslim family law) to exist alongside the dominant jurisprudence (British) within the same nation-state. This contributes to the normative discourse in British society and proposes to alter both the dominant legal order and the Muslim legal culture under domination. Confronting the 'powers that be', this proposal is a form of recontextualizing, a strategy that attempts to change the perceptions and frames of reference of the legal and judicial power elite. Although the proposal was dismissed by the Home Office, the debates about assimilation as a one-way process of 'them' adjusting to 'us' cannot continue to ignore the pressures for pluralism. A shift in our attention to include in our line of vision alternative forms of normative ordering (for instance, forms introduced by acculturating groups, such as *shari'a*) helps to reveal the emergent forms of identity and connection, as well as disjuncture, between people that are implicated in the current processes of global migration.

FUTURE DIRECTIONS

A growing body of literature has been developing over the past decade concerning various models for Muslim acculturation in secular societies. Two international organizations, the Muslim World League and the Organization of Islamic Conference, have advocated the development of what is being called *fiqh al-aqalliyah* (jurisprudence of minority) and *fiqh al-darurah* (jurisprudence of necessity) to address issues related to Muslim minority life (Moore, 1994, p. 240). Although 'most of the available resources are written from the perspective of [male] Muslim jurists' (Abou al-Fadl, 1994, p. 182) residing in majoritarian Muslim societies, an increase in the literature written by Muslims who have settled permanently in a non-Muslim setting has been noticeable (Moore, 1994).[27] Much of the literature on *shari'a* courts in non-Muslim countries suggests that the 'traditional criteria worked out by earlier generations of Muslim jurists pose difficult questions for the modern age, when the application of Muslim personal or family law in a secular state has become a difficult matter' (Abou al-Fadl, 1994, p. 186). Thus responses to the recent proposal for *shari'a* courts as an alternative juridical mechanism in Britain need to be studied. Similar proposals made in Canada (Khan, 1993) and Australia, and the operation of a *fiqh* council in the United States (De Lorenzo, 1994), have provoked opposition within Muslim communities, particularly among Muslim feminists. One of the most unsettling features of the proposal for adoption of *shari'a* courts is the ease with which the courts could be used to reinforce and normalize patrilineality and male authority, replicating patriarchal forms of law and society associated with 'conventional' forms of Islamic jurisprudence. Similarly the idea of *shari'a* courts may reinforce the reductive, polarized stereotypes of Muslims, and thereby perpetuate a falsely coherent narrative about Muslim life in which oppressive patriarchal social and legal forms are 'essentialized'. Divergent views within Muslim communities about this proposal indicate the possibilities for the discovery of a 'third ground', or the expansion of interstices between the totalizing conceptions offered on the one hand by western discourse (the devaluation of Islam by Orientalism) and, on the other, by the Islamist approach (the rejection of secularism and the concomitant valorization of traditional Islamic law courts). One indication appeared recently in *al-Mujtama'*, an Arabic-language magazine published in Kuwait for a global readership. Arguing that the 'Islamist intellectual output' has produced a contextual explanation of historical social relations and the impact of imperialism, appropriate only in countries 'where Muslims constitute the majority population', the author of a recent article asserts that the needs of Muslims in diaspora are different. 'We the Muslims in the west are in need of new ideas, of a creative jurisprudence which takes into account the new realities' (al-Tamimi, 1996, p. 44; translation mine) of migration and settlement in non-Muslim societies. Further, he asserts that '[j]urisprudence is the mirror that reflects the conditions to realize the greatest good and impede corruption' (ibid.).[28]

Further attention to such calls for a 'new' jurisprudence would contribute to our understanding of the pluralistic character of law and how this pluralism contributes to the discursive production of personal and group identities in diaspora. The exclusion of Muslims from the protection of British law, by narrowly interpreting the common law on blasphemy and denying legal standing under existing racial hatred statutes, has implicated new ways of representing identities under the law and, ultimately, new ways of thinking about law. The perception of *The Satanic Verses* as an attack on the integrity of Muslims led to the use of law by some Muslims in Britain in defence of minority rights. In proposing to alter the laws on blasphemy, or to introduce *shari'a* courts, Muslim activists attempted to generate law as they critiqued the legal system and transformed a defensive mobilization into an affirmation of identity. Such actions allow us, as Santos argues, to appreciate the distinction between the uniformity of law and local differentiation, and to understand the combination of 'top-down imposition' of jurisprudence with 'bottom-up creation' (1995, p. 252). It illustrates the development of a uniquely 'minoritarian' version of Islamic law, characterized by domestic challenges and solutions, as well as the temperance of international factors which have provided the ideological ballast and direction for Muslim discontent (Sahgal and Yuval-Davis, 1992, p. 181).

In terms of European integration, an analysis of legal pluralism is needed. As Merry points out, legal centralism is inadequate to capture the full scope of legal forms and activity in a given society, and Brigham supplements this by observing that the state does not have a monopoly on the production of law; rather, social movements generate law as they advocate change. Santos suggests that the constitutive effect of the state and 'other law-generating forms', such as popular movements or minority/immigrant communities, is reciprocal, that relations are 'multi-directional' (1995, p. 250). The mass translocation of people over the last 40 years poses a particular set of questions for the ways we study globalizing processes. We are poised to engage in what Santos calls a diatopical hermeneutics, a cross-cultural dialogue 'with one foot in one culture and the other in another' (ibid., p. 340). The particular challenge of European integration is to integrate the contending pressures which pull in many different directions at the same time. The state will continue to need, as it has in the past, to interact with other state legal orders, with local legal orders within it, and with transnational normative orders such as Islamic organizations and the European Courts of Justice and Human Rights. These interactions will help to constitute shifting European legal identities as social relations within Europe change.

In the newly integrated European Union the issue of religious communal relations will become very important in sustaining pluralistic societies into the next century. The critical issue will be what kinds of plural pressures the dominant legal order will grant recognition. My intent is to continue to examine the role of law in mediating relations between a significant religious minority and the institutions of the state. As Abdullahi Ahmed An-na'im notes, 'unless one is advocating the abandonment of Islam itself, *shari'a* will continue to be extremely important in shaping the attitudes and behavior of Muslims even if it is not the public law of the land' (cited in Santos, p. 343).

NOTES

1 As Talal Asad writes: 'The political mobilization of Muslim immigrants in Britain to get *The Satanic Verses* banned produced an emotional reaction on the part of the liberal elite that was out of all proportion to what actually happened' (1990, p. 462).

2 Homi Bhabha explains the theory of *différance* as an ambivalence in constitutive discourse about representing the British nation as a tolerant liberal society, the pinnacle of civilization, while at the same time exercising the power to subjugate and/or exclude the devalued Other. In the discourse of colonialism the process of *différance* leads the 'west – here we are talking specifically of the UK – to the colonial margin 'where the west must face a peculiarly displaced and decentered image of itself "in double duty bound," at once a civilizing mission and a violent subjugating force' (1990a, p. 71).

3 As Peter Fitzpatrick notes critically about the mythology of the west and infinite progression, and conformist pressures associated with western idealism: 'Universal becoming is the prerogative of the west. It is "enacted in the destiny of sedentary peoples" [citation omitted]. Non-western "others" came to be known and possessed within that universality, the knowledge of which can only be acquired by those others if and to the extent that they can enter positively into this universality' (1992, p. 41). This requires abandonment of particularism, or 'otherness'.

4 See also Mazrui's thought-provoking essay, '*The Satanic Verses* or a Satanic Novel? The Moral Dilemmas of the Rushdie Affair', based on a lecture given at Cornell University on 1 March 1989.

5 See Samuel P. Huntington, 'The Clash of Civilizations?' *Foreign Affairs* 72 (Summer 1993).

6 For a discussion of the binary opposition between the Islamic world and western civilizations propagated in classical Islamic jurisprudence and in modern Islamic thought, see Moore (1995), Abou al-Fadl (1994), and el-Manssoury (1989).

7 I hasten to add that there are numerous variations in Islamic schools of law and widely divergent legal discourses. Thus I do not refer to Islamic law in any single of unitary sense, but suggest that there is a varied pluralism evident in Islamic jurisprudence.

8 Legal pluralism is generally defined as 'a situation in which two or more legal systems coexist in the same social field' (Merry, 1988, p. 870). Sally Engle Merry argues that 'virtually every society is legally plural, whether or not it has a colonial past' (ibid., p. 869). We can imagine that Britain, a former empire, is all the more so given its imperial past and post-colonial demographics.

9 See generally Steven Vertovic (1993), *Annotated Bibliography of Academic Publications Regarding Islam and Muslims in the United Kingdom, 1985–1992*. Bibliographies in Ethnic Relations 11, Coventry: Centre for Research in Ethnic Relations, University of Warwick.

10 These social relations should not be viewed as ahistorical. British colonialism in the Indian subcontinent has conditioned these social relations. In terms of the complex experiences of migrant and diasporic peoples, South Asians in Britain in particular, see Marie Gillespie's study of London Punjabi teenagers, living in 'The largest "Asian community" outside the Indian subcontinent [including Hindus and Sikhs as well as Muslims]' (Gillespie, 1995, p. 2). This study is attentive to 'the tension between global diasporic, national and local perceptions of "shared identity"' (ibid.).

11 This assertion by the younger generation is of a putatively universalistic Muslim identity, opposed to the hegemony of ethnic absolutism (Gilroy, 1987; Ali, 1992) supported by UK multiculturalist policies. See discussion of multiculturalism below.

12 There are of course differences of opinion among persons and groups of the different

generations and sexes concerning a broad range of issues including education, employment, religion, politics, and public incorporation. See especially Vertovec (1996).

13 Social relations are understood here at determining who is 'in', who is 'out', and how we define something as 'political' (see Brigham, 1987b).

14 I am grateful to Shahnaz Khan for this analytical point, which is contained in her doctoral thesis (1995).

15 For a definition of Islamists see Bobby Sayyid, where he describes Islamists as: 'People who use Islamic metaphors to convey their hopes, to think their political utopias, and to narrate a story of their destiny ...' (1994, p. 268). They are not, strictly speaking, fundamentalists, interpreting literally the canonical texts, because their interpretations 'are imaginative re-descriptions of the canon' (ibid.). Philip Lewis offers another description: Islamism is a totalizing world view which insists 'that the Qur'an, traditions, and Islamic law, properly understood and interpreted, should be the basis of the state and society in all its dimensions' (1994, p. 5).

16 Present forms of Islamic law are the result of colonialist rule which, in countries such as India, confined the scope of *shari'a* courts to personal status laws, which grant unequal status to women in divorce, child custody, inheritance, and testimony in court (Khan, 1993, p. 54). See also Hardy (1972) and Note (1994).

17 No accurate statistics of the Muslim population are available because 'the census does not collect information according to the religious affiliation of persons in the UK although in 1991 an "ethnic origins" questions was included' (Shah, 1994, p. 18). Estimates of the size of the Muslim population in Britain vary. One source (Modood, 1990), estimating there are over one million UK Muslims, relies on Labour Force Survey data of 1985–87. Another source (Peach, 1990a and 1990b) claims that the Muslim population is between 550 000 and 750 000, much lower than the widely cited estimates of between 1.5 million and 2 million currently in circulation (representing about 2 per cent of the total UK population). See also Poulter, 1991; Lewis, 1994, pp. 13–16.

18 The diversity of the multiple understandings among Islam's branches and sects about what Islamic law is makes it impossible to say that there is presently, or has been in the past, one uniform Islamic law. See Khaled Abou al-Fadl (1994, p. 186), De Lorenzo (1994); Roberson (1994, p. 292), and Khan (1993, p. 57), where the legal pluralism within Islamic jurisprudence, giving rise to divergent interpretations, is emphasized. These interpretations have made the question of application of *shari'a* requirements in dispersed communities especially problematic.

19 See newspaper headlines and captions and book titles referred to above, indicating the depth of feeling expressed in reactions to *The Satanic Verses*.

20 'Culture' in this sense is understood as a set of essentialist practices, a 'kind of package ... of collective behavioural-moral-aesthetic traits and "customs", rather mysteriously transmitted between generations, best suited to a particular geographical origins yet largely unaffected by history or a change of context ...' (Vertovec, 1996, p. 51). The vocabulary of multiculturalist policies in Britain conflates 'culture' and national origins, and creates categories based on national origins, investing particular categories with consequences that affect the positionality and social relations of minority communities. Through multiculturalism we focus on persons' traits rather than conduct, and on the effect of the absence or presence of the traits we designate to be significant.

21 The case was *R. v. Lemon* 1 All ER 898 (1979).

22 For reference to the Egyptian religious leader's statement, see *The Times*, 22 November 1988, cited in Lisa Appignanesi and Sara Maitland (eds) (1989), *The Rushdie File*, London: Fourth Estate, p. 53.

23 At roughly the same time the UK Action Committee on Islamic Affairs (UKACIA) was created to lobby and litigate against the distribution of *The Satanic Verses*. The UKACIA is a non-partisan vehicle for lobbying the government to reform laws and legislate penalties for incitement to religious hatred. Several similar groups appeared in the first months of the Rushdie Affair presenting demands to the publisher to withdraw the book. Not succeeding in this endeavour, most of these groups made protests to the British government.

24 In a 1988 ruling (*Nyazi* v. *Rymans Ltd.* [E.A.T., 10 May 1988, unreported]), an industrial tribunal held that in the case of Muslims several characteristics of ethnicity, previously identified in *Mandla* v. *Dowell Lee*, were missing: 'Muslims include people of many nations and colours, who speak many languages and whose only common denominator is religion and religious culture.' This essentialist notion of what constitutes ethnicity serves here as a legal device of exclusion, denying protection of the law to Muslims. See Poulter, 1991, p. 373, n. 17.

25 The Ayatollah Khomeini's *fatwa* against Rushdie sentenced the author to death for the crime of apostasy.

26 Art. 295A of the Indian Penal Code reads: 'Whoever, with deliberate and malicious intention of outraging the religious feelings of any class of citizens of India by words either spoken or written ... shall be punished with imprisonment ... or with fine ... or with both' (*Times of India*, cited in Appignanesi and Maitland, 1989, p. 38). Some Indian MPs proposed to try Rushdie for violation of this and other laws in absentia.

27 Articles can be found in the British *Journal of the Institute of Muslim Minority Affairs* and *Islamic Law and Society* and in daily periodicals written for a Muslim diasporic audience.

28 The final clause of this statement, 'to realize the greatest good and impede corruption', bears a resemblance to the Qur'anic injunction, widely cited in contemporary times with respect to the duties and coherence of a diasporic, 'global' Muslim community (called the *ummah*), that: 'You are the best of peoples, evolved for mankind, enjoining what is right and forbidding what is wrong, and believing in Allah' (see Qur'an 3:110). I wish to thank Dr Yvonne Yazbeck Haddad for bringing the article in *al-Mujtama'* to my attention.

REFERENCES

Abou al-Fadl, Khaled (1994), 'Islamic Law and Muslim Minorities: The Juristic Discourse on Muslim Minorities from the Second/Eighth to the Eleventh/Seventeenth Centuries', in *Islamic Law and Society*, **1**, 141–87.

Ahsan, M.M. and A.R. Kidwai (1991), *Sacrilege vs. Civility: Muslim Perspectives on The Satanic Verses*, Leicester: The Islamic Foundation.

Ali, Yasmin (1990), 'Many Muslim Truths', *Marxism Today*, Feb.

Ali, Yasmin (1992), 'Muslim Women and the Politics of Ethnicity and Culture in Northern England,' in Gita Sahgal and Nira Yuval-Davis (eds), *Refusing Holy Orders: Women and Fundamentalism in Britain*, London: Virago Press.

Alibhai, Yasmin (1989), 'Beyond Fundamentalism and Liberalism', *New Statesman and Society*, 3 March, 34–5.

Anon. (1994), 'Interpreting Oriental Cases: The Law of Alterity in the Colonial Courtroom', *Harvard Law Review*, 1711–28.

Anwar, Muhammad (1990), 'Muslims in Britain, Some Recent Developments,' in *Journal Institute of Muslim Minority Affairs*, **11**, 347–61.

Appignanesi, Lisa and Sara Maitland (eds) (1989), *The Rushdie File*, London: Fourth Estate.

Asad, Talal (1990), 'Multiculturalism and British Identity in the Wake of the Rushdie Affair,' *Politics and Society*, **18**, 455–80.

Bhabha, Homi K. (1990a), 'The Other Question: Difference, Discrimination, and the Discourse of Colonialism', in R. Ferguson, M. Gever, Trinh T. minh-ha, C. West (eds), *Out There: Marginalization and Contemporary Cultures*, Cambridge, MA: MIT Press.

Bhabha, Homi K. (1990b), 'The Third Space', in J. Rutherford (ed.), *Identity Community Culture Difference*, London: Lawrence & Wishart.

Bradney, A. (1993), *Religions, Rights and Laws*, Leicester: Leicester University Press.

Brigham, John (1987a), *The Cult of the Court*, Philadelphia: Temple University Press.

Brigham, John (1987b), 'Right, Rage and Remedy: Forms of Law in Political Discourse', *Studies in American Political Development*, **2**, 303–16.

Cottle, Simon (1991), 'Reporting the Rushdie Affair: a Case Study in the Orchestration of Public Opinion,' *Race and Class*, **32**, 45–64.

De Lorenzo, Yusef Talal (1994), 'Islamic Law, American Civil Law, and the Role of the *Fiqh* Councilor', unpublished paper presented at the SWANA Program Annual Conference, SUNY Binghamton, New York, 30–31 October.

Fitzpatrick, P. (1992), *The Mythology of Modern Law*, London and New York: Routledge.

Gillespie, Marie (1995), *Television, Ethnicity and Cultural Change*, London and New York: Routledge.

Gilroy, Paul (1987), *'There Ain't No Black in the Union Jack': The Cultural Politics of 'Race' and Nation*, London: Unwin Hyman.

Gross, Joan, David McMurray and Ted Swedenburg (1994), 'Arab Noise and Ramadan Nights: Rai, Rap, and Franco-Maghrebi Identity,' in *Diaspora*, **3**, 1–39.

Haddad, Yvonne Y., John O. Voll and John Esposito with Kathleen Moore and David Sawan (1991), *The Contemporary Islamic Revival: A Critical Survey and Bibliography*. Westport, CT: Greenwood Press.

Hardy, Peter (1972), *The Muslims of British India*, Cambridge: Cambridge University Press.

Kettani, M. Ali (1986), *Muslim Minorities in the World Today*, London: Mansell Publishing.

Khalidi, Omar (1989), 'Muslim Minorities: Theory and Experience of Muslim Interaction in Non-Muslim Societies', in *Journal Institute of Muslim Minority Affairs*, **10**, 425–37.

Khan, Shahnaz 91993), 'Canadian Muslim Women and *Shari'a* Law: A Feminist Response to "Oh! Canada"', *Canadian Journal of Women and the Law*, **6**, 52–65.

Khan, Shahnaz (1995), 'Muslim Woman: Interrogating the Construct in Canada,' PhD thesis, University of Toronto.

Lee, Simon (1990), 'Protecting Both Gods and Books: Abolish Blasphemy Laws and Make Incitement to Religious Hatred a Crime', *The Independent*, 9 March, 17.

Leveau, Remy (1992), 'Magrebi Immigration to Europe: Double Insertion or Double Exclusion?', *Annals of the American Academy of Political and Social Science*, **524**, 170–80.

Levy, Leonard (1993), *Blasphemy: Verbal Offense Against the Sacred, From Moses to Salman Rushdie*, New York: Alfred Knopf.

Lewis, Philip (1994), *Islamic Britain: Religion, Politics and Identity Among British Muslims*, London: I.B. Tauris.

Manssoury, F. el- (1989), 'Muslims in Europe: The Lost Tribe of Islam?', *Journal Institute of Muslim Minority Affairs*, **10**, 63–84.

Mazrui, Ali F. (1989), '*The Satanic Verses* or a Satanic Novel? The Moral Dilemmas of the Rushdie Affair', essay published by the Committee of Muslim Scholars and Leaders of North America, New York.

Mazrui, Ali (1990), 'The World of Islam: A Political Overview', *Journal Institute of Muslim Minority Affairs*, **11**, 218–25.

Merry, Sally Engle (1990), *Getting Justice and Getting Even: Legal Consciousness Among Working-Class Americans*, Chicago: University of Chicago Press.

Merry, Sally Engle (1988), 'Legal Pluralism: A Review Essay', *Law and Society Review*, **22**, 869–96.

Minow, Martha (1990), *Making All the Difference: Inclusion, Exclusion, and American Law*, Ithaca, NY: Cornell University Press.

Modood, Tariq (1990), 'British Asian Muslims and the Rushdie Affair', *Political Quarterly*, April/June; 143–60.

Modood, Tariq (1994), 'Political Blackness and British Asians', *Sociology*, **28**, 859–76.

Moore, Kathleen (1994), 'Muslim Commitment in North America: Assimilation or Transformation?', *American Journal of Islamic Social Sciences*, **11**; 223–44.

Moore, Kathleen M. (1995), *Al-Mughtaribūh: American Law and the Transformation of Muslim Life in the United States*, Albany, NY: University of New York Press.

Nielson, Jorgen (1995), *Muslims in Western Europe*, 2nd edn, Edinburgh: Edinburgh University Press.

Parekh, Bhikhu (1989), 'The Rushdie Affair and the British Press', *Social Studies Review*, November.

Peach, Ceri (1990a), 'Letter: Estimating the Number of British Muslims', *The Independent*, 16 January, 18.

Peach, Ceri (1990b), 'The Muslim Population of Great Britain', *Ethnic and Racial Studies*, **13**, 413–19.

Poulter, Sebastian (1991), 'Towards Legislative Reform of the Blasphemy and Racial Hatred Laws', *Public Law*; 371–85.

Roberson, B.A. (1994), 'Islam and Europe: An Enigma or Myth?', *Middle East Journal* **48**; 288–308.

Rushdie, Salman (1982), 'The New Empire Within Britain', *New Society*, 9 December.

Sahgal, Gita and Nira Yuval-Davis (1992), *Refusing Holy Orders: Women and Fundamentalism in Britain*, London: Virago Press.

Said, Edward W. (1979), *Orientalism*, New York: Vintage Books.

Said, Edward W. (1993), *Culture and Imperialism*, London: Vintage Books.

Santos, Boaventura de Sousa (1995), *Toward a New Common Sense: Law, Science and Politics in Paradigmatic Transition*, London and New York: Routledge.

Sarwar, Ghulam (1989), *Education Reform Act 1988: What Can Muslims Do?* London: Muslim Educational Trust.

Sayyid, Bobby (1994), 'Sign O' Times: Kaffirs and Infidels Fighting the Ninth Crusade', in Ernest Laclau (ed.), *The Making of Political Identities*, London and New York: Verso, 1994.

Shah, Prakesh (1994), 'Legal Pluralism – British Law and Possibilities with Muslim Ethnic Minorities', in Christopher McCrudden and Gerald Chambers (eds), *Individual Rights and the Law in Britain*, Oxford: Clarendon Press.

Shahid, W.A.R. and P.S. van Koingsveld (1991), *Integration of Islam and Hinduism in Western Europe*, Kok Pharos Publishing House.

Solomos, John and John Wrench (1993), *Racism and Migration in Western Europe*, Oxford: Berg Publishers.

Tamimi, al- Azzam (1996), *'Nahwa Muntalaqat Insaniyya li al-Ta'amul ma' al-Mujtama' al-Gharbi ...' Al-Mujtama'*, **26**, (1182), 2–8 January, p. 44.

Vertovic, Steven (1993), *Annotated Bibliography of Academic Publications Regarding Islam and Muslims in the United Kingdom, 1985–1992*, Bibliographies in Ethnic Relations **11**, Coventry: Centre for Research in Ethnic Relations, University of Warwick.

Vertovec, Steven (1996), 'Multiculturalism, Culturalism and Public Incorporation', in *Ethnic and Racial Studies*, **19**, Jan., 49–69.

Wright, Patrick (1985), *Living in An Old Country: The National Past in Contemporary Britain*, London: Verso.

CASES CITED

Choudhury v. *U.K.*, ECHR Decision of 5 March 1991.

Nyazi v. *Rymans Ltd.*, E.A.T., 10 May 1988, unreported.

R. v. *Chief Metropolitan Stipendiary Magistrate ex parte Choudhury* (1990).

R. v. *Lemon* 1 All ER 989 (1979).

R. v. *Horseferry Road Metropolitan Magistrate ex parte Siadatan* 3 WLR 1006, QBD (1990).

12 The Construction of the Other in the European Human Rights Enterprise: A Narrative about Democracy, Human Rights, the Rule of Law and My Neighbour Uncle Blaze

Krisztina Morvai

The Council of Europe's statutory principles are pluralist democracy, respect for human rights and the rule of law. Its members recognize the principles of the rule of law and the enjoyment by all persons within their jurisdiction of human rights and fundamental freedoms. (Article 3 of the Statute of the Council of Europe)

Number of individual applications introduced in 1994: 9968. Number of applications registered: 2944. Decisions taken: 2372. Applications declared admissible: 582. (Survey of activities and statistics, 1994, European Commission of Human Rights)

A

We did not live in a democracy since Hungary had but one political party, the Communist Party, and elections were mere formalities. We did not study Human Rights because Human Rights was a bourgeois concept. We

experienced the Law of Rule as opposed to the Rule of Law. We knew that in Europe, in the Real one, there was democracy, human rights and the rule of law.

My family had a neighbour, Uncle Blaze. I had admired him ever since I was a small child. Uncle Blaze was tall, good-looking, well-dressed, self-confident and always cheerful. He had lived in France for fifteen years before returning to Hungary. One day my mother announced to the family: 'You know, the thing about Uncle Blaze is, that he is a real *European*.' When I was older, whenever I saw Uncle Blaze in the neighborhood I immediately thought about democracy, human rights and the rule of law.

Communism collapsed. It was a revelation. We had free elections with several parties. Law students began to memorize statutes more enthusiastically, knowing that now the Law was really the Law, nothing but the Law. Moreover, it was now really Our own Law. Judges applied the Law *objectively* and they began to refer to the Rule of Law in their decisions.

We decided to work on joining Europe. When I went to check the map, my mother told me to simply look at Uncle Blaze instead. We ratified the European Convention on Human Rights because human rights was no longer a bourgeois concept.

I saw Uncle Blaze at the newstand one day and proudly told him that I got a job at the Council of Europe, an organization which spends £137 million a year for the promotion of democracy, human rights and the rule of law. I was sure he knew that the European Commission and Court of Human Rights were the most successful human rights organizations in the world. Individuals can bring applications against their governments, who must pay large sums to those whose human rights were violated. In interpreting the Convention, these two organs define the meaning of human rights in Europe. Ultimately, they define *Europe*. I was to be tasked with corresponding with those applicants and with drafting decision and reports for the Commission. Uncle Blaze was cheerful, as always. However I thought that his smile was somehow more mysterious than normally.

B

When I arrived at the Council of Europe in Strasbourg I was very impressed. Everybody looked and behaved just like Uncle Blaze. Nice suits, self-confidence, good perfumes, cheerfulness. In the restaurant everyone ate salmon and salads, all the time. My mother was right, Europeans are different.

The buildings looked nice, no wonder they keep building new ones every year. The walls were covered with tasteful posters, black and white letters announcing the Europe-wide 'All Different – All Equal' campaign against racism. The Council of Europe has more than a thousand employees. One day I saw a Black man in the corridor. He did not sport a suit and tie, and I was disappointed to find him changing lightbulbs in the restaurant. The other two non-white people I saw working at the organization were washing dishes in the restaurant. They were (equally) Grade C-technical personnel.

Secretaries inhabited Grade B, while lawyers and the other international civil servants were esconced in Grade A. People qualified for different car number plates on the basis of their grades: from B4 up to A4 the plates were green with white numbers, and from A4 up the letters became orange and a CD plate was added. B3 and below had normal number plates and lower Cs used the bus. In the new Human Rights Building, Grade B employees' offices overlooked the dark backyard; the Grade A offices faced the hills and river. Because I was A2 I had two windows. My superior was A4, with four windows.

On the first working day my superior at the Secretariat of the Commission, the head of our Unit of four lawyers and two assistants, explained my duties. In the first few months, I was expected to work solely on correspondence with applicants. The initial instruction took about ten minutes. I received a copy of the Convention (the Law) and I learned to fill-in all kinds of forms. My superior told me something like this: 'Here are your files and here is the collection of form letters. We respond to the very first submission with a PO type form letter. The PO is a brief description of the proceedings and a copy of the Convention. You should not deal with the merits of the complaint before the applicant responds to the PO, except where the case is really serious and substantive. I mean, one that's written by a good lawyer. If the applicant comes back after the PO you should look for grounds of inadmissibility. Review the Convention and you will know what they are. You will prepare a brief summary of the case and choose the suitable form letter. Submit these to me. I will make the necessary corrections and return them to you. After preparing the final version of the letter, submit it to me again for signature.'

During the first weeks I was sitting in an office with a desk, files of some current applications, a word processor and a copy of the Convention. Just the Law and me. An ideal site for pursuing the Rule of Law.

As I began to work on the cases, I realized that most applications were submitted by poor, uneducated and really desperate people. Their letters were mostly handwritten and the applicants were not represented by lawyers. The first problem I faced followed from the fact that these submissions were not model legal briefs, or even homework done for legal writing assignments, but long, detailed testimonies of suffering, pain or 'just' allegations of injustice. The long description of facts is typically not followed by reference to a particular provision of the Convention, or where there is such a reference, it is hardly 'accurate'. In other words, people often tell their stories without translating them into the language of the Law, or if they do, the translation does not appear faithful to those who speak the Law. For example, many applicants characterize their suffering as 'degrading and inhuman treatment' under Art. 3 of the Convention just because they are treated inhumanely by bureaucrats, judges, husbands or neighbours. If they spoke the Law they would know that there is nothing unLawful in the fact that, for many people, life is a degrading experience and the world is a pretty inhuman place to live in.

Since no one had told me about the real role of the Secretariat in the proceedings, I was happy to discover it for myself. I first needed to make legal sense of the applications, to translate them from Life-language to Law-language as faithfully as I could. I also needed to ask the applicant for further information or documents where necessary, inform applicants, with reference to the case-law, of their lack of prospects where the case really was hopeless, and do whatever was needed to put the proceedings in motion.

C

In my Old No-Europe, the collapsed one, there was no separation of powers because it was seen as a bourgeois concept. In this Europe, the Real one, there is. To me, that should imply that cases should be decided by the actual decision-making body, the Commission, as opposed to the bureaucracy behind it. Those ideas turned out to be the second major step in my pain-in-the-neck-trouble-maker career at our Eurocracy.

After all those lectures I had heard from Western visiting professors after the democratic transition at home, I am totally obsessed with the idea of the Rule of Law. But what is the Law, and where is it in the context of Europe's human rights Law? According to the statistics, two out of three applications never pass the stage of the initial correspondence. These cases are 'introduced' but not 'registered', in other words, they are never seen by the Commission itself. Whether the applicants 'come back' after the so-called warning letters largely depends on what we bureaucrats write in those letters.

In my experience, European civil servants with an annual salary of approximately 100 000 US dollars (tax-free) tend to have little empathy with people who dare to submit an application to the haven of European human rights without the services of a lawyer. Moreover, they tend not to understand why these people are not more educated, coherent or intelligent. Lack of education, lack of style and lack of means make most applicants the Other. Even a rich criminal is less of the Other than a poor applicant with any kind of complaint. The lawyer of the rich criminal (or sometimes the criminal himself) provides coherent submissions, straightforward legal analysis. He is stylish and easy to handle. He and we speak the same language. The whole thing is smooth and elegant. Sort of *European*. The bureaucracy constructs a legal issue of him and a procedural efficiency issue of the Other.

The discretionary power of the civil service – the Eurocracy – is almost completely unrestricted at the initial stage of human rights proceedings. Who is in and who is out depends largely on the values of the individual lawyer who first gets the case, or more precisely, on the values of his or her superior who supervises the work until the newcomer proves that she or he is reliable in not trying to change the status quo. In other words, until the European civil servant is proven to be *European* enough.

An old woman from a village, with difficult handwriting, describes in detail how she has been hurt and harassed by her neighbour for many years. Finally, the neighbour destroyed the fence adjoining their properties and moved it two metres into her land. She went to court, without a lawyer. She claimed that the judge never wanted to listen to her or her witnesses. The neighbour's lawyer talked incessantly in all proceedings before the domestic courts. She lost her case. I wrote a brief summary for my superior, arguing that the dispute involved a property rights issue combined with due process complaints, and suggesting that I should request the necessary court documents and register the case.

My superior instructed me to send a P8 form letter, stating that 'no public authority can be held responsible for the alleged violation'. Fearing that I would be exposed as ignorant of the Law, I nonetheless risked the question, 'Is this not state action?' My superior was not looking as European as he did five minutes earlier. He was angry. 'We do not need much theory here, Krisztina. We have to do the Law and we have enough work with that.' I sent the P8 form letter to the applicant. She never came back. A pity she missed her classes on state action at Harvard Law School and therefore did not know how to argue against the P8.

The applicant is a seven-year-old-child, represented by her working-class parents. She received mandatory vaccination as a baby and remained physically disabled for life. The domestic court found the State liable and ordered a small monthly alimony. Before the domestic courts the family claimed a right to a wheelchair-accessible car arguing that, as public transport in Budapest was inaccessible to the disabled, the child would otherwise be confined to her home. The appellate court dismissed the claim, stating that, according to Hungarian case-law, an injured party can never be placed in a better position following the injury than she was prior to the event. Given that the family did not own a car prior to the tragic vaccination, they could not qualify for one now. The final judgement explicitly stated that there was no further appeal against the decision. The applicant's family did not have a lawyer at that stage of the proceedings but they did some research and found that, in fact, there was a further remedy by recourse to the Supreme Court. They filed the application for review of the appellate court decision. The Supreme Court did not register it, informing them that such an application had to be brought by a lawyer. By the time the family received this reply and reintroduced their application through a lawyer, the time limitation on appeals had expired. And since they had therefore not complied with domestic procedural requirements, their case was not, I was told, acceptable under the Convention either. 'Are principles and policies not part of European human rights law?' I asked my superior. 'You are on your probation period. If you prefer to be an activist, you are still free to go home,' he replied.

D

August is extremely hot and humid in Strasbourg. There is no air conditioning in the brand new Human Rights Building. How come?, I asked an A4. 'There is democracy here,' he answered. 'We had to vote on whether or not we wanted air conditioning in the new building.' 'I see,' I replied on my way towards fully understanding the concept of democracy. Whatever the reason, however, I begin to feel that the place is totally un-cool.

After a few months my Head of Unit informed me that I was the most irresponsible person he had ever worked with at the Organization, that he had given up on supervising me, and that I would be placed in another Unit. Moreover, he told me, 'You better pull up your socks, Krisztina, otherwise you will be in trouble.'

We never had any discussions on principles, policies or cases at our Unit meetings. However we made important decisions on new guidelines on filling in The Forms. On one occasion my Head of Unit announced some news on a different subject. She said, 'At the Heads of Unit meeting we agreed upon some standards regarding the evaluation of those in their probation period.' Everybody remained silent so she moved on and continued talking about The Forms. In the end she asked if we had any questions. I asked her to tell me something about the evaluation. 'An important expectation is *loyalty*,' she said looking deeply into my eyes. 'Loyalty to whom?' I asked naively. 'Loyalty to the Organization,' she said very seriously. Even though I did not know how exactly one could be loyal to a publically accountable institution, I knew that I *was* in trouble.

E

Another woman submits that she is unemployed, has two kids and her divorced husband has not paid child support for two years. They are cold, hungry and desperate. She asks for some help but does not refer to the Law. Article 5 of Protocol 7 of the Convention states that

> Spouses shall enjoy equality of rights and responsibilities of a private law character between them, and in relations with their children, as to marriage, during marriage and in the event of dissolution. This article shall not prevent States from taking such measures as are necessary in the interests of the children.

My superior instructs me to write a letter saying that 'her submissions about their social problems do not appear to raise any issues under the Convention'.

I recall a lecture by one of the many Western professors who came to Eastern Europe as advisors after the transition. He kept saying 'In a Rule of Law system you have to ...', 'the Rule of Law requires ...' etc. Young practising lawyers and academics from all over the region were listening and taking notes carefully. After a while a Romanian woman raised her hand, kind of fearfully. 'Excuse me, Professor, could you please tell me what you mean by the Rule of Law?' she asked. Some people were laughing, others looked embarrassed. A strong and serious young man from the audience replied, 'Don't worry, professor, I shall explain it to her during the break. Just carry on with what you wanted to say.' Two years later, sitting in my office in the Real Europe, I wish I had not gone to the cafeteria in that break.

Dozens of applications arrive each week, from poor people, from disabled people, from battered wives ...

If you look at the published decisions of the European Commission and Court of Human Rights you do not see these people. You learn that there are some problems in Europe: civil proceedings are too lengthy, journalists cannot always say what they want, the due process rights of white collar defendants are often not fully observed.

But on the whole, Europe is in good shape. It looks nice, smells nice, feels nice and it is cheerful. Just like Uncle Blaze.

Index

For Product Safety Concerns and Information please contact our EU representative GPSR@taylorandfrancis.com
Taylor & Francis Verlag GmbH, Kaufingerstraße 24, 80331 München, Germany

www.ingramcontent.com/pod-product-compliance
Lightning Source LLC
LaVergne TN
LVHW010621300926
849162LV00001B/24
9780367001452